D0567141

Navigating the New Retail Landscape

'This very clearly-written book will be of immense value to retailers facing the huge changes taking place in the retail landscape today and into the future. It identifies the driving elements of retail transformation from a truly international perspective covering most retail formats across the world.

The authors then address the practical issues facing retail leaders and offer guidance on how to realign their retail business with the newly engaged customer and technological developments, which characterise this new challenging landscape.'

Dr Christopher Knee
Assistant General Manager
International Association of Department Stores

'Perplexed by the extent and pace of changing customer behaviour and expectations? This book buries the notion of a single roadmap to success, instead it describes the key attributes retailers must adopt in order to build a sustainable business model.'

Michael Flood
Strategic Customer Analysis, John Lewis, UK

Navigating the New Retail Landscape

A Guide for Business Leaders

Alan Treadgold and Jonathan Reynolds

OXFORD
UNIVERSITY PRESS

OXFORD
UNIVERSITY PRESS

Great Clarendon Street, Oxford, OX2 6DP,
United Kingdom

Oxford University Press is a department of the University of Oxford.
It furthers the University's objective of excellence in research, scholarship,
and education by publishing worldwide. Oxford is a registered trade mark of
Oxford University Press in the UK and in certain other countries

First Edition published in 2016
Impression: 1

Published in the United States of America by Oxford University Press
198 Madison Avenue, New York, NY 10016, United States of America

British Library Cataloguing in Publication Data
Data available

Library of Congress Control Number: 2016933338

ISBN 978–0–19–874575–4

Printed in Great Britain by
Clays Ltd, St Ives plc

Acknowledgements

In one sense this book began around twenty-five years ago when we first started working together. Our early interests then in themes of change in global retail landscapes and the transformative role of technology on retailing and retail enterprises find expression in this book, albeit in ways we could never have anticipated a quarter of a century ago. In another sense it began around ten years ago when, independently and in very different roles and geographies, we were researching, discussing, presenting, and refining several of the themes in this book. In a more formal sense it began around two years ago when we committed to writing this book. Along this trajectory, both short and long, many, many people have—often without their knowing it—helped to frame, reframe, and finesse the themes in our book through their exposure to and feedback on earlier versions of them in executive education sessions, workshops, conference presentations, and discussions. We thank them all.

Several of our friends and colleagues of long standing have helped greatly to bring this book to fruition by both their enthusiasm for our initial idea and their support along the way, especially in diligently reviewing earlier drafts and fearlessly suggesting how we could make them better. In this regard we are particularly indebted to Simon Brodie, Robert Clark, Alan Giles, and Elizabeth Howard. Many executives in retail businesses have been instrumental in the development of our thinking through their willingness to share with us their perspectives and experiences. We are grateful to them all. (This is not the place to discuss again what it means to be a retail business any more. Chapter 5 tries to address that particular tautological conundrum.)

We are grateful to Oxford University Press for their enthusiasm to publish our book and for their friendly professionalism and support to us in doing so. We are especially indebted to our editors at OUP, David Musson and Clare Kennedy. Despite all the help and guidance we have received from so many, it seems unlikely that some inaccuracies and misrepresentations will not have crept unobserved into our work. We ask forgiveness and, as ever, the fault is ours alone.

ADT & JR

March 2016

Contents

Contents

List of Figures

List of Tables

List of Cases

List of Cases

Introduction

A central defining proposition frames the rationale for and the content of this book: namely that the retail industry globally is in the early stages of a transformation that will be more profound and far-reaching than any which has gone before.

A bold assertion? Certainly. Over the last 200 years or more, the retail industry globally has experienced a series of changes which have transformed the sector or large parts of it: the earliest formalization of retailing from market-based to store-based, the transformation of grocery stores from served to self-service environments, the rise of integrated shopping malls (often in locations away from traditional town and city centres), and the application of technology within retail enterprises and across supply chains to manage their operations. All of these changes have had transformative impacts on the retail sector. But none of these developments changed the fundamental character of the retailing sector or challenged the essential nature of what it means to be a retail enterprise. At the end of these phases of change, retailing was still a store-based activity (only the nature of the stores had changed); retailing was still conducted by retail enterprises (only the nature of the enterprises had changed), and geography still constrained choice (shoppers still needed to visit stores).

Today we are standing on the edge of an entirely new landscape of retailing. What is so very different and so disruptive is that the very fundamentals of what it means to be a retailer and what the act of retailing is are being challenged and changed totally. No longer is it a prerequisite to have stores in order to be in the business of retailing. No longer are shoppers constrained by geography and their choice set limited only to those physical stores which they can access locally. Neither is it automatic that a traditional retail enterprise is the only—or even the most effective—type of enterprise to fulfil the needs of shoppers, as other enterprises such as consumer goods, logistics, and payment companies move to establish direct relationships with shoppers. Nor does transformative disruption stop here. Entirely new kinds of enterprises are engaging directly with shoppers. These range from search engine firms to social media networks; from price comparison websites to online market-places; and from mobile phone enterprises to software engineers. In so doing they disintermediate others—including traditional retail enterprises.

The new landscape of retailing is being created by the combined effects of a series of powerful forces for change. At the epicentre is the impact of technology in the hands of shoppers. It is, above all else, reliable high-speed internet access, increasingly available on mobile devices, that is changing profoundly and irreversibly the relationship between shoppers and retailers, how shoppers choose to shop, and the choice sets to which they have access. This alone would be enough to transform the landscape for retailers. But other important forces of change are at work also. Concomitant with the huge growth in shoppers' access to technology is the global growth of a new consuming class with a great appetite to embrace those new technologies. Meet the Young Millennials: they are entering their high-spending years and they have never known a world without reliable high-speed internet access. They do not behave like previous generations of shoppers and they do not think of shopping as a store-centric or even a store-mostly activity. Digital is not a late addition to their lives—digital *is* their lives. The rise of the Millennials as a shopping group ('tribe' might be a better descriptor) would of itself be suffi-cient to precipitate far-reaching change to the retail industry, but there is still more change taking place. The modernization, rising affluence, and rapid urbanization of the major economies of the Far East—most prominently, but by no means exclusively, China and India—are transforming the landscape for retailing and retailers. These economies are very obviously not developing along the same trajectories that have been experienced in the now mature markets of Western Europe and North America. Rather, they are leapfrogging entire phases of development to become—at great speed—amongst the most sophisticated, complex, and creative retail environments on the planet. Today it is no longer justifiable to regard the mature markets of the West as the epicentre of innovation and new retailing techniques.

Technology transforming shoppers' lives, Millennials with entirely different lifestyles and expectations, the rise of consumer power in the major econ-omies of the Far East, the rapid emergence to prominence in retailing of enterprises with entirely different approaches to engaging the shopper: any one of these phenomena by itself would have the power to transform the landscape for retailing and retailers in much of the world and in many categories. It is their coincidence and the ever-accelerating pace of their combined impacts that justifies our assertion—and the starting point for this book—that we are in the early years of nothing less than a transformation of the retail industry globally. But it goes further even than this. In the new landscape of retailing, new business models and new ways of engaging the shopper are being created, often at great speed and with great reach. New era retailers created in (and out of) the internet age tend often to view large networks of stores established over decades, even a century or more, as an irrelevant legacy of an age that no longer exists. 'We're a bunch of tech guys that saw an opportunity to reinvent retailing' is the mantra for many. Let us be in no doubt: traditional retailers are not only competing with each other—they are now competing against entirely different enterprises with entirely different business models. These are the themes we explore in Part 1 of our book.

The new landscape of retailing is rich in opportunities to engage with new shopper audiences in new ways and to participate in new geographic markets. But it is also a challenging and an unforgiving landscape. Shoppers may very well be better informed about products than the enterprises from which they are making purchases, and choice—both of what to buy and from whom—is close to limitless. New entrants with new business models challenge traditional retailers. The old protections afforded to retailers by being better informed than shoppers and only competing against other retailers within the same catchment have been swept aside. Enterprises are gaining customer relevance, influence, and scale very quickly while others are losing it even more quickly.

The conventions of earlier eras of the capabilities and attributes that retail enterprises and the leaders of those enterprises need if they are to achieve enduring success must now be revisited. In a world where shopping is no longer synonymous with physical shops, what is the role of and the future for store networks? What enterprise and personal skills need strengthening in a 'digital first' world rather than a 'store only' world? And, crucially, how do enterprises and their leaders transition a business from where it is today to where it needs to be in the near-term future? This is an especially elusive goal in a world where the future is so uncertain—how can it be anything other when some of the technologies which may significantly shape the future of retailing have yet to be fully developed?—and where there is no single, clearly signposted pathway of how to get from where you are today to where you need to be tomorrow.

For many (probably most) retail enterprises this does not imply 'steady as she goes' leadership where the existing business merely needs to be tweaked and refined a little. This is an era of discontinuous change where the core principles of how the enterprise has worked—perhaps for 100 years or more—need to be revisited, challenged, and, very likely, changed in fundamental ways. This need to contemplate and probably initiate fundamental change is not just to address the new set of challenges that the enterprise faces but also to realize the new opportunities that are being created in the new landscape of retailing. Neither are these challenges confined to traditional, established retail enterprises alone. The 'new to retail' technology-enabled enterprises are reaching a level of establishment, scale, and maturity such that they too have their own transitional challenges if they are to move from where they are today to where they need to be in the near-term future. For such enterprises the issue is especially around addressing the 'profitless growth' challenge where sustained acceptable profits prove frustratingly elusive despite sales, reach, and scale increasing sharply. These are the themes we explore in Part 2.

The aims then of this book are two-fold. First, to assist the reader in navigating the complex changes which are profoundly and irreversibly reshaping the landscapes in which retail enterprises (new or traditional) are operating (Part 1). Secondly, to offer guidance on the skills and capabilities that retail enterprises and the leaders of those enterprises will require if they are to be successful in these much changed landscapes (Part 2). We have profiled numerous retail enterprises—some established, some new—to illustrate our themes. But this is not a book about merely showcasing examples of retail 'best practice' or 'retail innovation'. Such is the pace of change in this industry that 'best practice' dates fast and a medium as traditional as a book is not the best place to showcase the newest and the most innovative. Look online for that.

The new landscape of retail can look challenging, intensely competitive— even bewildering. It is all of these things. But it is in periods of discontinuous change that opportunities are also at their greatest. We are of the view that the opportunities are at least as compelling as the challenges. Welcome to the new landscape of retail.

Part 1
Navigating the New Retail Landscape

Part 1 of this book explores the new landscape of retailing, its nature and characteristics, and the forces of change which are reshaping the retail industry and challenging long-established conventions of what it means to be in the business of retailing and to engage with shoppers. Profound changes in shoppers' expectations, choices, and engagement options are central features of the new landscape of retailing and comprise the subject of Chapter 1. Technology has already transformed the landscape for shopper engagement and yet it is likely that, when we look back over the current era of retailing, we will appear today to have been only in the foothills of change driven by technology in the hands of shoppers. As shoppers have ever-more access to ever-more choices of how they shop, which enterprises they engage with and how their demands are fulfilled, so they become less passive and more participative in the shopping process. No longer do established retailers hold the balance of power now that shoppers have ever-greater access to information and alternatives. Yet this is also an environment rich in opportunities for thoughtful enterprises to engage effectively with highly networked and informed shoppers. These themes are discussed in Chapter 1.

Chapter 2 focuses explicitly on the transformational impacts of technology both in the hands of shoppers and within retail enterprises themselves. There are, we believe, very compelling opportunities for businesses to develop much closer and more personal relationships with shoppers through the use of technology in customer-facing roles to enhance efficiency, experience, and engagement for the shopper. However, the challenges for enterprises of actually realizing all of the potential benefits from technology, especially in the form of highly nuanced shopper information, are considerable.

One of the central challenges for established retail enterprises in the new retail landscape is how to keep physical stores at least relevant and, moreover, desired in environments where ever more shoppers have the option to fulfil all of their shopping needs without using physical stores at all. Retail enterprise leaders will have to be prepared to take a radical view of their store networks and the configuration and roles of stores in those networks. Very considerable change seems inevitable for many. This will have further impacts on the built environments of urban areas as well as on the role and configuration of purpose-built shopping centres. These themes are discussed in Chapter 3.

Today, technology in particular is transforming the scale, ambition, nature, and geography of international expansion. This is the central proposition of Chapter 4. Historically, retail enterprises have in general (albeit with numerous high-profile exceptions) been slow and reluctant to expand their presence internationally, certainly by comparison with many of the major branded goods businesses that supply to the retail sector. This is no longer the case. We are in the early stages of a new and much more dynamic era in the true globalization (as distinct from internationalization) of the retail industry. Clearly, this is a double-edged sword. On the one hand, enterprises have more opportunities to engage with more shoppers globally. But on the other, they are themselves subject to far more intense competition from more diverse enterprises and locations than has ever been the case. Entire sectors of retailing and country markets are being transformed globally and in ways and at speeds which would not have been possible in previous times.

Retailing is no longer the sole preserve of established retail enterprises. There is a sense in which everyone can be a retailer today: technology companies, banks, logistics firms, product suppliers, and even private individuals. Chapter 5 discusses the emergence of entirely new business models enabled, inevitably, by technology and which challenge long-established notions of what it means to be a retail enterprise. The business models for established retail enterprises are being reshaped by the need to make heavy investments in areas such as logistics and IT that have historically been regarded as support functions rather than as integral to the sustained competitive advantage and success of the enterprise. Moreover, established retailers are competing with aggressive and effective enterprises such as internet-enabled platform providers with entirely different business models. As well as a competition between philosophies of what it means to be a retailer, this is a competition between different business models.

Such is the scale, pace, and disruptive nature of change that it can feel overwhelmingly difficult to understand, let alone to anticipate, plan, and manage its impacts on an enterprise. Chapter 6, the final chapter in Part 1, offers an organizing framework for locating the major drivers of change in the new landscape of retailing, according to the extent to which change is an opportunity or a threat; the level of immediacy of change; its anticipated impact on the enterprise; and the level of certainty or uncertainty that the change represents.

1

The New Landscape for Customer Engagement

Customer Centricity in the New Retail Landscape

The best retailers always pride themselves on their so-called 'customer centricity'. Yet for many retail enterprises, in the modern era of large networks of permanent physical stores, the reality of their operations has often been rather different. For many retail enterprises the way to quickly build scale and profitability has, in fact, been by taking a heavily process driven 'one size fits all' approach. The defining features of such enterprises is that store sizes and layouts, the merchandise within them, and the service experience delivered to the shopper is overwhelmingly the same irrespective of store location or the subtleties of shoppers' different needs and expectations. Mass retailers especially would talk of 'conforming' stores—each one conforming to a common footprint and product assortment. Most mass retailers have built their businesses by adopting this approach. In reality, almost all of the sector leaders in almost all countries have built scale by managing to the principles of conformity and operational efficiency to a far greater extent than they have been built around the principle of customer centricity. Where a trade-off has had to be made between the scale benefits of conformity and the customer benefits of customization, most mass retailers have chosen the former over the latter. While such an approach is aligned to the core needs of many, it can hardly be said to be precisely tailored to the very specific needs of the individual shopper. In this respect, mass retail is not so very different from the early days of mass production of consumer products—the drive for scale, operational efficiency, and ease of management exceeds the desire or the ability to personalize. Indeed, it can reasonably be argued that in a previous era developing highly personalized approaches to production and distribution was very often inimical to the desire to build scale and efficiency.

Today, the retail industry globally stands on the cusp of a new and very different era in customer engagement. Many leaders of retail enterprises are inclined to believe that they have already seen in the last five to ten years change in consumer landscapes on an unprecedented scale. And they would be right. But, even so, this is only the foothills of a transformation which will reframe the shopper engagement landscape over the next decade and beyond. It will be global, it will be driven if not by all shoppers then by many, and it will very definitely impact all retail enterprises and indeed all businesses that engage, or aspire to engage, with shoppers.

Technology change tends often to be identified as the single most important driver of change in consumer landscapes. Terry Leahy, the highly respected former CEO of Tesco, talks of the internet as having 'given people more power than ever before to organise, to protest, to revolt'.[1] While the centrality of technology change is undeniable, it is not the only decisive change that is reshaping consumer landscapes. What makes the current era of transformation in the customer engagement landscape so profound is that it is being driven by a uniquely powerful combination of drivers of change which are themselves enabled and accelerated by the disruptive effects of technology. It is a landscape of change sufficiently profound that all enterprises need to reconsider what being customer centric means, what shopping and consumption even are any more, and what the role of a retail business is in this new landscape.

The Era of the Actively Engaged Shopper

Figure 1.1 presents a generalized description of the way in which shoppers' engagement with retailers and their participation in the shopping process can be considered. We distinguish four main types of shoppers according to the level of involvement they have in the shopping process and the level of engagement they have with the retailer from which they are making a purchase:

1. **Unengaged Shoppers.** These are shoppers with little if any interest in the shopping process and no deep engagement with the retailers they use. This is not to say that they are not active shoppers. Indeed, they are often very active, in particular because they are very price driven and move frequently between retailers and brands according to their view of who is delivering the strongest value. Clearly, such shoppers are—and

---

[1] T. Leahy, *Management in Ten Words* (London: Random House, 2013), 294. but see also e.g. R. Lewis and M. Dart, *The New Rules of Retail: Competing in the World's Toughest Marketplace* (New York: Macmillan, 2014).

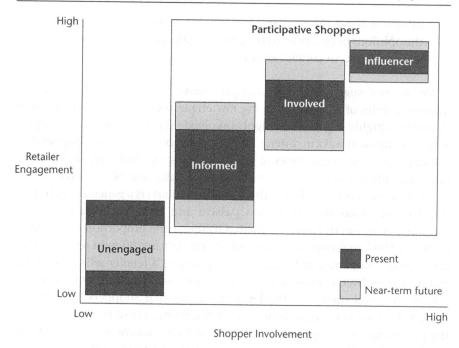

Figure 1.1 Generalized schema of shopper types
Source: Authors.

will remain—numerically very important for many retailers in many categories. Whether they are profitable to the retailer is a different question, however, given their typically very high levels of price sensitivity.

2. **Informed Shoppers.** Informed shoppers have moderate levels of involvement in the shopping process and in the retailers they use. They are engaged enough to want to equip themselves with information about the products they are planning to purchase. This might be motivated by necessity in the case of price-driven value-orientated shoppers or because they are style conscious and fashion aware in other higher involvement categories, such as apparel and home furnishings.

3. **Involved Shoppers.** Involved shoppers are fully engaged in the shopping process and in the businesses from which they purchase. Involved shoppers actively seek to find out all they can about the products that interest them, the alternative choices they have, and the attributes of the retailers they use. They are not content to rely solely on information sent to them. They are motivated to search out the information they feel they need in order to make fully informed choices.

4. **Influencers.** Influencers are opinion-shapers. They are highly informed and highly involved in the shopping process as well as highly

informed about the retailers they use. Influencers are active in shaping the opinions of others by sharing their experiences online amongst often wide networks of contact groups.

We are not suggesting that shoppers move inevitably and inexorably through a series of stages from being low engagement and low involvement shoppers to highly engaged and highly involved shoppers. Moreover, shoppers behave in different ways in different product categories. The same shopper that is highly involved in categories of great interest to her/him may, at the same time, have little involvement (and influence) in categories of low interest.

What we are suggesting is that there is in most markets a general direction of travel for shoppers to become less passive and more participative in the shopping processes that interest them. Of course, the proportion of shoppers in each of the four groups we define will vary widely for different retailers. This is influenced in particular by the type of products a retailer sells (where the distinction between high involvement and low involvement products remains a useful one), and the level of affinity that shoppers have to the retailer. Our general proposition is that for many, possibly most, retailers the proportion of shoppers who are content to be passive purchasers of the retailer's offer will diminish substantially in the near-term future.

By contrast, we define three levels of progressively greater participation—Informed, Involved, and Influencer—all of which we expect to increase as the proportion of Unengaged shoppers declines. For many retailers the Informed and Involved shopper groups will be the 'new normal' that defines the expectations of the majority of shoppers. These two groups expect full access to all of the information that they need to make fully informed choices. They may well be sceptical of information from conventional marketing sources and, for the Involved group especially, they are motivated to actively search for the information they feel they need. For many retailers, the relatively small proportion of Influencers will likely be a disproportionately important group to focus on given their importance in shaping the opinions of others.

These three groups of actively engaged shoppers—but, in particular, the numerically small but highly important Influencer group—will exert a tremendously important influence on the type of offer and experience they expect from the retailers with which they wish to engage. Their expectations of the product offer, service experience, engagement experience, and brand experience across all touchpoints will be raised as their awareness of alternative offers and different competitor benchmarks continues to be both broadened and raised. So too will their expectations of the standards—environmental, ethical, social, community, supplier relationships—to which they expect retailers to conform. All of this will force retailers to reappraise in fundamental ways the offers they deliver and the DNA of their enterprises. For many, radical change will be needed. These themes are discussed throughout this book.

Also being reframed are the value expectations of the Participative Shoppers. As their expectations of the offer and the enterprise rise so, for many (very probably most), the price they are willing to pay in order to secure that offer from that retailer is falling. Persistent downward pressure on prices is already for most retailers a defining, structural feature of the new retail landscape. This is a consequence especially of shoppers being both better informed than they have ever been in the past and having access to far more alternative sources of supply than they have ever had before. (The cyclical effects of recession give added impetus to shoppers' focus on low price and compelling value but, while it may not seem so at the time, the structural drivers of this change are far more important than relatively short-term cyclical effects.) Both dimensions are related and are a consequence of the enabling effects of the internet. These themes are discussed further throughout this book. But it is important to be clear at the outset that the structural reframing of shoppers' value expectations and persistent downward pressure on price points do not mean that all categories and all retail sectors will inevitably migrate to low price value propositions. Certainly some will and all enterprises in the business of retailing—established or new—will have to engineer into their enterprises cost structures and competencies which allow them to deliver on the very much more demanding expectations of their Participative Shoppers. But they will need also to understand to a fine level of insight what the points of competitive advantage are that justify a price positioning which is not the lowest in the market. We believe that there are very considerable opportunities in this regard. We discuss what they are throughout this book.

Participative Engagement

We are at the start of the era of the actively engaged shopper. If the twentieth century was the century of mass consumption, then the twenty-first century already looks likely to be defined as the era of participative engagement.

A defining feature of the rapidly transforming landscape for retailers is that consumers now expect to be at the centre of a retailer's world. In the previous era of mass consumption, retail enterprises were able to organize and operate their businesses in an essentially linear fashion with the shopper regarded—sometimes explicitly but more often implicitly—as a passive purchaser at the end of a process which pushed product down a supply chain. However much they would recoil against being characterized in this way, this has been the reality for many. Today, this is no longer an appropriate way for retailers either to conceive of or to organize their enterprises. As Hugh Raeburn, Chief Information Officer at Reiss, a leading UK-based fashion apparel

11

retailer, observed: '20 or 30 years ago it was us saying to them, "This is how you shop with us". Now it's the other way round. We are being led by the customer.'[2]

At its most elemental, being 'led by the customer' means giving customers the ability to purchase what they want, when they want it, where they want it, and at a price they are willing to pay. Many leaders of retail enterprises will doubtless say that this is what they have been doing for their entire career and throughout the entire history of the businesses they lead. But was it ever really accurate to call an enterprise customer centric and built around the needs of the shopper when stores were closed more hours than they were open, when product knowledge resided overwhelmingly with the retailer not the shopper, and when the shopper had few, if any, realistic choices of where else to fulfil their needs other than from stores in the catchment areas in which they lived or worked? Today, for technology-enabled shoppers (we will discuss technology and information divides in Chapter 2), shopping is a 100 per cent transparent and 100 per cent 'always on' activity. At an execution level the challenges of organizing a retail enterprise around this beguilingly straightforward vision of customer centricity are profound. The nature of these challenges and ways to address them are discussed in Part 2 of this book.

PARTICIPATIVE ENGAGEMENT AND THE INFORMATION ASYMMETRY CHALLENGE

The actively engaged shopper is a highly informed shopper. As Niemeier et al. presciently observed, 'new technologies have put an end to the information asymmetry between retailers and consumers. In short, customers have been empowered at the expense of swaths of retailers.'[3] This is a powerful proposition. When retailers held the balance of power or at least the balance of influence in value chains they did so in large part because they were very substantially better informed than the customers to whom they sold: better informed about from where products had been sourced, the conditions in which they had been produced, their specification, the price at which they had been purchased, and the profit margin that they sought to achieve. In the era of the actively engaged and informed shopper this is no longer the case. It is far safer for retailers today to assume that shoppers have perfect knowledge than that they have insufficient knowledge to make fully informed choices of both the products they wish to purchase and from whom. If, in fact, they do

[2] Drapers, *Retail Market Report* (2014). <http://k3retail.com/assets/resources/Drapers_Retail_Market_Report_full_April14.pdf>, 11.

[3] S. Niemeier et al., *Reshaping Retail: Why Technology is Transforming the Industry and How to Win in the New Consumer Driven World* (Hoboken, NJ: John Wiley & Sons, 2013).

not presently have perfect knowledge in globally transparent marketplaces, it is prudent for enterprise management to assume that they very soon will.

Engaged shoppers are demonstrably concerned with the behaviours of enterprises across their value chains, in their relationships with suppliers, their environmental, social, and community involvement practices. Research undertaken by Nielsen in 2014 suggested that 55 per cent of consumers worldwide were willing to pay extra for products and services from companies committed to positive social and environmental impact—an increase of 10 percentage points from 2011.[4] In environments defined by high levels of concern amongst shoppers for the practices of enterprises and with the ability to easily search for reassurance on these practices or else to uncover poor performance, it is in the interests of retail enterprises to make it easy for shoppers to find out what they want to know, not to try to hide unpleasant truths—an increasingly futile objective in the internet era. As Doug Stephens has observed, 'It doesn't seem to matter how deep brands bury the truth, there's someone in the world with the time, bandwidth and determination to dig it up and tell the world.'[5] This can be uncomfortable: not only do retail enterprises need to have clear codes of conduct, they need also to be confident that they are being adhered to. But it can also offer interesting opportunities for retail enterprises to differentiate themselves on the basis of their transparency and commitment. One enterprise doing this very explicitly is the US clothing retailer, Everlane (everlane.com), with their 'Radical transparency' platform: 'Know your factories. Know your costs. Always ask why.'[6] As the company says, 'We believe customers have the right to know what their products cost to make. At Everlane we reveal our true costs, and then we show you our markup.' Levis works in conjunction with International Finance Corporation (IFC), part of the World Bank Group, to embed its values into its suppliers by aligning their financial rewards with the extent to which they adhere to Levis' sustainability objectives. In this case, IFC's interest rate on loans to suppliers is based on the supplier's rating against Levis' evaluation criteria for labour, health, social, and environmental performance: the better the performance, the lower is IFC's interest rate on their loan.[7]

Actively engaged shoppers are also being more vocal and more active in exposing practices that do not meet their expectations by, for example, organizing boycotts of retailers and brands perceived by the activist shopper not to

[4] Nielsen Company, *Doing Well by Doing Good: Corporate Global Responsibility Report* (June 2014). <http://www.nielsen.com/content/dam/nielsenglobal/apac/docs/reports/2014/Nielsen-Global-Corporate-Social-Responsibility-Report-June-2014.pdf>.
[5] D. Stephens, *The Retail Revival: Reimagining Business for the New Age of Consumerism* (Chichester: John Wiley & Sons, 2013).
[6] <https://www.everlane.com/about>.
[7] Olaf Schmidt, 'Retailers' Obligation to the World: The New Sustainability Agenda', World Retail Congress, Rome, Sept. 2015.

be conforming to the standards they expect (see, for example, <http://www.ethicalconsumer.org/boycotts/boycottslist.aspx>).

PARTICIPATIVE ENGAGEMENT AND THE UBIQUITOUS ALTERNATIVES CHALLENGE

The second defining feature of the era of the actively engaged shopper is that, as well as having access to almost limitless information, shoppers increasingly also have access to almost limitless alternatives. In the old retail, barriers to switching between retailers and brands were insurmountably high for many. Geography especially was a powerful restrictor of choice. A shopper in one location had no real possibility of choosing to make purchases in another location where they felt the alternatives to be better—if they were even aware of those alternatives. Of course, it is true that better transport links opened up greater choice and that the early pioneers of catalogue selling (notably Sears, Montgomery Ward, and Hammacher Schlemmer in the US and Universal Stores, La Redoute, and 3 Suisses in Europe) offered shoppers far more choice than was available in their own neighbourhoods.

Today the very notion of choice being constrained by geography is nonsensical for many shoppers. In the very near-term future it will likely be nonsensical for most. Furthermore, the irrelevance of geography is a global phenomenon because it is driven by increasingly ubiquitous mobile technologies in the hands of shoppers everywhere, by the ability of retail and distribution businesses to fulfil orders internationally and by the accelerating awareness (enabled by access to information) of shoppers globally about brands and propositions in other locations that they may very well never actually set foot in. This is not to say, however, that there are no impediments to the creation of a globally connected, barrier-free retail marketplace. Indeed, in some locations—particularly emerging markets—barriers of access to information and to the means of fulfilment remain high and may well stay so for some time to come. We discuss this theme in Chapter 2.

Active shoppers are not just activist shoppers. Active engagement extends also to some shoppers wanting to be involved in the selection and even the development of products themselves. Already there are myriad examples globally of shoppers becoming involved in the product design process and then committing to purchase the products they have played a role in creating. This moves shopping well away from the passive purchase of mass-produced products and into the active co-creation of products. One example amongst many is Quirky (www.quirky.com). Quirky is a New York-based crowdsourcing web-enabled group of design-orientated individuals. Quirky is the enabling platform that allows participants (1.1 million in mid-2015) to design products (280,000 initiated by mid-2015), select product ideas submitted by others, and, ultimately, have those products produced and appearing in retailers' businesses. However, the fact that Quirky filed for Chapter 11 bankruptcy in September 2015 with net liabilities of around US$80 million[8] points to the difficulty of commercializing innovation in new product development, whether it is crowdsourced or otherwise. Despite these undoubted challenges, we expect shopper participation in product development to accelerate in the near-term future. Furthermore, it seems likely that many categories will be impacted by this trend. Consider, for example, that there already exist enterprises such as Local Motors in the US, which is both crowdsourcing and co-creating new vehicles for subsequent micro-manufacture in the automotive sector. As they say, 'We make the coolest machines together' (http://localmotors.com).

It is not difficult to conceive also that shoppers' desire to participate in product design and development could extend into the production of products themselves. Rapid advances in 3D printing (also known as additive manufacturing) and the lowering of price points for such printers makes it possible to reconceive some purchases as taking the form of purchasing the software template to allow manufacturing of a product at home rather than a physical product provided by a retail enterprise. The potential for 3D printing by individuals to be a highly disruptive force of change in the retail sector should not be under-estimated. As *The Economist* noted as early as 2011, 'Three-dimensional printing...may have as profound an impact on the world as the coming of the factory did...it is impossible to foresee the long-term impact of 3D printing. But the technology is coming, and it is likely to disrupt every field it touches.'[9] Given that the International Space Station is trialing 3D printing of the tools needed to carry out on-craft maintenance ('which will be critical on longer journeys to Mars'[10]), the idea of 3D printing at home does not seem at all remote, either literally or figuratively.

It is, though, the rise and rise of social media that is doing most to transform the engagement landscape and the shopping experience from one of passive acceptance to participative engagement. One of the key defining features of the new landscape for retailers is the much changed media environment in which they now operate. At a headline level it is clear that for many shoppers and retailers, traditional mass media are far less important for communicating with shoppers. This is not to say that mass media have no role to play now and in the future. Far from it. But businesses will need to be very clear on what that role is: to entertain and inform and reach broadly rather than to drive

[8] <http://www.wsj.com/articles/invention-startup-quirky-files-for-bankruptcy-1442938458>.
[9] *The Economist*, 'Print me a Stradivarius', 10 Feb. 2011. <http://www.economist.com/node/18114327>.
[10] Niki Werkheiser, space station 3D printer program manager at NASA's Marshall Space Flight Center in Huntsville, quoted in <http://www.nasa.gov/mission_pages/station/research/news/3Dratchet_wrench>.

immediate change in purchase intentions. By contrast, social media is highly participative and increasingly influential in informing shoppers' purchase intentions as well as in shaping their views of retailers and their offers. Jerry Black, Chief Digital Officer with AEON Group (Japan's second largest retailer), echoes the views of many when he says, 'we cannot control social media but we want to be part of the conversation'.[11] The youth fashion market is a case in point. In this category it is already perfectly usual for shoppers to share amongst their social networks an item of clothing that they are interested in and then use feedback from friends to decide whether or not to make that purchase. Post-purchase it is equally usual for the shopper to share the purchase they have made so that their friends can either approve or disapprove and themselves have their subsequent purchase intentions informed.

There are several points to be made about the impact that social media is having on the engagement landscape for retailers:

1. Some of the most influential opinion shapers amongst Millennial shoppers especially are people who may be largely unknown in the traditional mass media. The huge global audiences of the most influential 'vloggers' (video bloggers) are a case in point. In beauty, fashion and lifestyle categories, UK-based Zoe Sugg—best known by her online alter ego Zoella—is one such example. Zoella (born in 1990 and right in the middle of the Millennials cohort) was virtually unknown in the mainstream media until around mid-2013, yet her main YouTube channel has over 10.2 million subscribers,[12] 4.4 million followers on Twitter, and over 7.5 million on Instagram. (When she entered the arcane world of print media, her debut novel, *Girl Online*, established a new record for highest ever first week sales in the UK.)

2. The growing reach and influence of social media points to the reality that many shoppers are more trusting of and more influenced by their friends and their personal contact networks than they are by the messages created by businesses and disseminated in traditional mass media. According to Nielsen, 84 per cent of global consumers would rather trust recommendations from friends and family than any forms of advertising.[13]

3. It is not just friends and peer groups on social media that are influencing attitudes and shopping behaviours. Complete strangers offering advice and views online either in direct response to queries or indirectly by depositing online endorsements and reviews are entirely commonplace already and very often far more influential to far more shoppers than traditional reviews from known 'experts'.

---

[11] Jerry Black in panel discussion, World Retail Congress, Rome, 8 Sept. 2015.

[12] <https://www.youtube.com/user/zoella280390>.

[13] Nielsen Company, *Global Trust in Advertising*, 2013. <http://www.slideshare.net/iabmexico/global-trust-in-advertising-report-nielsen-2013>.

4. Social media moves the point of influence much closer to the point of purchase. It is perfectly usual for shoppers to use social media to solicit views on their purchase intentions when they are in store or online and at the point of making a purchase. Retailers need to accept this reality and equip their businesses to facilitate shoppers' desires to behave in this way.

5. High and still growing use of social media highlights the enthusiasm of many shoppers now to be actively engaged in the shopping process. For younger shoppers in particular, this is an absolutely established and integral part of how they shop. For example, Instagram (which has a preference amongst 18–29 year-olds and the visual nature of which has a natural affinity with shopping activity) has seen such strong growth in usage over the past few years that it is now larger than Twitter. Moreover, Instagram users are significantly more likely to engage with brands than are users of either Facebook or Twitter.[14]

Case 1.1 GROUP BUYING AND THE RISE OF SHOPPER POWER

Tuángòu is a phenomenon in China. Tuángòu translates as something like 'team buying' and probably originated in its current form in Guangzhou in around 2006 (the precise origins are obscure). Shoppers organize themselves into groups to buy a particular item or service. Once there are sufficient members interested in making a purchase, the group team leader approaches vendors to bid for the sale and the lowest price secures the sale. As well as making purchases online, the group members will go to a vendor's store, warehouse, or office, which is often where they meet in person for the first time. The scenes can be dramatic when a tuángòu group mobs a store for their purchases. Vendors get volume, shoppers get discounts. Shoppers also get the security of buying in volume from a vendor they may be unfamiliar with so that any post-purchase issues—warranties, for example—are more likely to be honoured. Naturally, in a country with as many internet users as China (around 640 million and counting[15]) the internet has hugely extended the scope of tuángòu from localized groups of friends to much larger, geographically spread groups of strangers. And tuángòu groups organize themselves to buy pretty well anything. Thousands of intermediary websites have emerged which, for a fee (25 per cent to 50 per cent of the discount secured is usual) will organize the tuángòu group, including negotiating with possible vendors.

The *China Daily* newspaper talks of tuángòu as 'a form of e-commerce with unique Chinese characteristics'.[16] But more structured versions of the same idea—leveraging buying scale and connecting shoppers directly with vendors—have emerged in many countries in almost all categories of shopper spending. Groupon, begun in Chicago in late 2008, is arguably the pioneer. For non-believers, Groupon is a prime example of the profitless growth malaise of high-growth tech start-ups. While Groupon revenues grew

(continued)

---

[14] V. Goel, 'It's Official: Instagram is Bigger than Twitter', *New York Times*, 10 Dec. 2014. <http://bits.blogs.nytimes.com/2014/12/10/its-official-instagram-is-bigger-than-twitter/?_r=1>.

[15] <http://www.internetlivestats.com/internet-users-by-country>.

[16] <http://www.chinadaily.com.cn/life/2010-08/05/content_11101045.htm>.

Case 1.1 Continued

---

ten-fold in four years to around US$3.2 billion in 2014 and losses have narrowed, the plain hard fact is that Groupon has never reported a significant annual operating profit.[17] Sucharita Mulpuru, a Forrester Research analyst said pithily in late 2011, 'Groupon is a disaster'.

What Groupon and others like them are doing is, in essence, corporatizing a consumer movement—the essential heart of the tuángòu proposition. There are a number of useful learnings to be extracted from these experiences:

- The internet massively changes the scale of what is possible amongst shoppers seeking to leverage their purchasing power.

- Structured and unstructured groups that consolidate shoppers' buying scale and power have the potential to deliver very substantial volumes to existing retailers but also to bypass retailers entirely and engage directly with other suppliers. The stakes are very high in the new retail landscape: on the one hand very large sales gains are possible but, on the other, so too is the risk of being disintermediated (i.e. bypassed) entirely.

- This points to one of the realities of the new retail landscape: established retailers cannot assume that they will be the default enterprise from which shoppers want to make their purchases.

- The new landscape of retailing has seen the emergence of a plethora of different business models, many of which start from a fundamentally different philosophy and set of capabilities than do traditional retailers. Yet as scale and customer reach increase, the business of actually delivering profits to stakeholders can prove highly elusive.

Personalized Engagement

As well as participative engagement, personalized engagement is a defining feature of the new consumer landscape. The actively engaged shopper expects to be engaged in a highly personalized way.

The rise of the actively engaged shopper and the need for retailers to engage with shoppers in ways which are both participative and personalized is as rooted in fundamental demographics as it is in the nuances of shopper psychographics. This might seem on first glance to be a somewhat blunt and unsophisticated interpretation, but there can be no doubt that it is the teens and young adults of today who are in the vanguard of changing how retailers will need to engage with their shoppers. Precisely when they were born and what label should be attached to them is the subject of almost constant debate amongst demographers and social scientists. It is sufficient here to say that for many retailers the most influential shoppers in the new era of retailing are those who are currently between around 15 and 20 years old. The margins are

---

[17] <http://files.shareholder.com/downloads/AMDA-E2NTR/240239925x0x824897/96A29ED7-0479-409A-970F-1439D7556C1C/2014_Annual_Report_FINAL.PDF>.

somewhat hazy. In some countries they may be a little younger, in others a little older. They are towards the younger age range of the Millennials 'tribe' and they are the children of Generation X-ers. In many important behavioural respects they are not at all like the age cohorts that have gone before them. From a retail perspective, what makes this group so important and influential is, first, that they are entering their high-spending years; secondly, that their behaviours strongly influence and are strongly influenced by other members of their 'tribe', and, thirdly, that the behaviours they exhibit are quickly becoming evident also amongst other, older age groups.

The single most important defining feature of what we choose to call the 'Young Millennials' is that the ways in which they perceive the act of shopping and the ways in which they want retailers to engage with them is not a reframing of their old behaviours in light of the enabling impacts of technology. Rather, technology-enabled retailing is the only world they have ever known. They have never lived in a world without high-speed internet access, without social media platforms, without 3G and 4G mobile devices, without Amazon, Alibaba, and eBay. For these shoppers, technology is not oppressive, it is liberating; it is not to be feared, it is to be embraced. Remotely engaging with friends online that they have never met physically does not replace or undermine their 'real world'—it *is* their real world. The Young Millennials force far-sighted retailers to re-examine the very fundamentals of their business because for Young Millennials shopping is very definitely not synonymous with physical stores. As Christopher Bailey, CEO and Chief Creative Officer at Burberry, has observed, 'Most of us are very digital in our daily lives now...To the younger generation who are coming into adulthood now, this is all they know.'[18] Neither is shopping synonymous with retail businesses, and especially not with old, mature retail businesses of long standing. Their willingness to engage with businesses is not driven by the reassurance of longevity or even familiarity; it is driven by those they feel understand them best and engage with them most effectively—and that means in personalized and participative ways.

Until recently the personalization efforts of retail enterprises, where they existed at all, were largely confined to attempts to tailor product assortments and promotional offers to clusters of shoppers of varying degrees of aggregation. The work of pioneers of personalized customer engagement, perhaps most notably dunnhumby in the UK, are rightly acknowledged and admired. This approach takes retail enterprises somewhat closer to where their shoppers are increasingly expecting them to be, which is to say with communication, promotional offers, and product assortments tailored to the level of the single

---

[18] J. Cartner-Morley, 'Burberry Designs Flagship London Shop to Resemble its Website', *Guardian*, 12 Sept. 2012. <http://www.theguardian.com/fashion/2012/sep/12/burberry-london-shop-website>.

individual. But as Robin Terrell, Chief Customer Officer of Tesco, the owner of dunnhumby (at least at the time of writing) says, 'I do think we are entering an age of mass personalisation but it needs much more work, it is not there yet.'[19] If the ideal of truly personalized shopper communication seems a long way off, then consider that some of the most important work presently taking place in medical research involves creating medicines tailored to perform most effectively to the level of an individual person's unique DNA structure. Given that every cell in a human body contains DNA and an 'average' human has around 37 trillion cells, the challenges of creating individually personalized medicines are readily apparent. The analogy with the retail industry is apposite. True customer centricity is quickly coming to mean products, offers, and communication precisely targeted to specific individuals and not just to clusters of assumed similar shoppers.

Many of the efforts of retail enterprises to personalize their engagement with shoppers have so far been driven largely by analysing and interpreting historic sales data of shoppers within their own enterprise. The limitations of this approach are obvious: the retailer's only source of insight is a historic view of sales by a shopper transacted within their own business. What a retail business really needs to know is what purchases that shopper has made in other enterprises; what purchases they might have been persuaded to make with more engaging or relevant communication activity, and what purchases they actually made elsewhere. This much more insightful and holistic view of a shopper's behaviour and desires cannot be obtained by a single source of historic sales data. Truly personalized shopper communication is far more than a till receipt at the checkout alerting the shopper to promotions based on the contents of their current shopping basket. The ability to see, analyse, combine, and—crucially—act on meaningful shopper insights from a range of sources is the critical enabler of truly personalized engagement with the shopper.

Pizza Hut is one example of a business that has made impressive progress in the area of personalizing communications in their operations in Asia. Pizza Hut established 'The Social Hive' to track what people are saying online about their food service brands. These insights are delivered to the business in the form of a weekly dashboard of online brand tracking metrics, which are then used, along with sales and personal data, to create over 17,000 'micro segments' of shopper types to which specific promotional messages are sent. As Pankaj Batra, Chief Marketing Officer for Pizza Hut in Asia, says, 'The biggest challenge is learning how to act on the data...Marketers today have to think

---

[19] *Retail Week*, 'Analysis: Tesco's Robin Terrell on the Retailer's Multichannel Future', 22 Sept. 2014. <http://www.retail-week.com/companies/tesco/analysis-tescos-robin-terrell-on-the-retailers-multichannel-future/5064430.article>.

of themselves as journalists. We don't own the content. We have to go out and find it.'[20]

Humanizing Engagement

As retailing becomes ever more digital and conducted online without human interaction, many shoppers will attach much greater value to interactions which, while lacking a human element, are nevertheless very humanized. Tim Kobe, founder and head of Eight Inc design (responsible for most Apple stores globally), illustrates this thought with a beautiful example of a vending machine designed by Eight Inc and of which there are now many thousands across Japan. One of the main challenges in operating vending machines in Japan is the high number of power outages when earthquakes happen—which is often. Vending machines usually have their own power supply to allow them to continue to operate during such occasions. Eight Inc designed for Acure a vending machine which sells soft drinks. During a power outage, when the machine is still using its back-up supply after an hour, the machine shows a message saying: 'If you want a drink, take one.' As Tim Kobe explains, 'It's about building personal, human engagement into the device and making a human connection.'[21] It is this small type of thoughtful humanization which goes such a long way to creating 'irrational loyalty'—a depth of engagement between a shopper and a brand that is quite out of proportion to the rational benefit that the brand is delivering to the shopper. This anthropomorphizing of devices seems to us likely to be a growing theme as device makers address themselves to the paradox of consumers feeling a greater sense of alienation in their ever more globally connected worlds. LG, for example, introduced in late 2014 its family of, initially, four AKA phones, each of which has a distinct look, personality, and user experience. (If you need to know, Eggy falls in love easily; Wooky always speaks in slang; Soul likes music and beer, but never to excess; and YoYo is so called because her weight fluctuates but she enjoys style too.[22])

In the online world, Rakuten—the biggest e-commerce platform in Japan and one of the largest B2B2C platforms globally[23]—organizes itself on the principle of humanizing its online business. As Masatada Kobayashi, co-founder of Rakuten Inc and CEO of Rakuten Asia, says, 'We Asians have been valuing human connection for over 1,000 years...Humanizing the

---

[20] Pankaj Batra, speaking at Asia Pacific Retail Congress, Singapore, Mar. 2015.
[21] Tim Kobe, speaking at Asia Pacific Retail Congress, Singapore, Mar. 2015.
[22] <http://www.cnet.com/uk/products/lg-aka>.
[23] Fiscal 2014 revenue of US$4.9 billion. Source: FY2014 Fourth Quarter and Full Year Consolidated Financial Results, 12 Feb. 2015, Rakuten Inc. <http://global.rakuten.com/corp/investors/documents/pdf/14Q4PPT_E.pdf>.

online shopping experience is essential to breaking down the barriers between sellers and customers.'[24] In Rakuten's world this desire to humanize expresses itself in every one of its online sellers being allocated an e-commerce consultant, of which there are over 1,000 in the business. Rakuten also hosts an annual expo in major cities around the world that over 5,000 merchants attend. A Store of the Year award ceremony takes place annually and the number one merchant in each category is invited to participate in a global study tour. All of these initiatives are conducted with the objective of humanizing relationships between vendors and the approximately 106 million shoppers globally that use Rakuten. (Impressive also was Rakuten's decision in 2010 to change the language of its company from Japanese to English—a decision that required over 8,000 employees to learn English, many of them from scratch.)

New Shoppers: New Purchase Journeys

Retail enterprises (and others, notably FMCG businesses) have often tended to conceive the process of engaging shoppers in terms of a purchase journey which begins with creating awareness and ends with the shopper making a purchase, while passing in sequence through a number of discrete stages in between. Indeed, so predictable was the so-called 'path to purchase' considered to be that marketers frequently portrayed the stages leading towards an inevitable purchase in the form of a 'marketing funnel' where, in concept, prospective shoppers poured into the top and actual buyers came out of the bottom. (Figure 1.2 shows one of many such marketing funnels. They are all much the same). Such a conception of shoppers as behaving in entirely predictable ways, following a linear path that leads to an entirely inevitable purchase is more than a little demeaning to the notion of shoppers as sentient free thinking beings. That it is also a totally inappropriate way of characterizing how shoppers actually behave in the new landscape of retail merits rather more thought and consideration.

Thoughtful marketers, in retail enterprises and elsewhere, are alert already to the notion that there is today no such thing as *the* path to purchase—if indeed there ever truly was. Nuances of shopper behaviour do, of course, vary very widely according to the type of shopper, the product category, and the location of both the shopper and the products or service they wish to

---

[24] Masatada Kobayashi, speaking at Asia Pacific Retail Congress, Singapore, Mar. 2015.

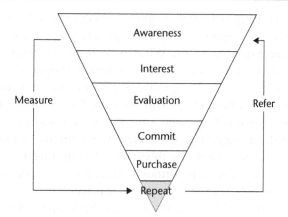

Figure 1.2 Generic marketing funnel
Source: Authors.

purchase. There are nevertheless a number of points that can usefully be made about shopper behaviour in the new retail landscape:

(i) The notion of a path to purchase is outdated and unhelpful. Shoppers do not engage with retail businesses (or any others) in linear pathways that follow predictable steps and outcomes.

(ii) As well as being non-linear, shopper behaviour is also highly fragmented. The 'always on' shopper is not, in fact, constantly searching to make purchases and wishing to be engaged with marketing messages of the same intensity all of the time.

(iii) Shopper decision-making is being influenced by a far wider set of stimuli and media than has ever been the case before. This fragmentation and proliferation of media and 'points of influence' will only continue to increase.

(iv) Retailers very often do not own the media and sources of information that most influence shoppers. Indeed, it is increasingly evident that many shoppers are much less trusting of marketing messages placed in bought media than they are in the free advice and information given by people in their social networks.

(v) Shoppers are moving constantly online and offline in their search for information, in where they ultimately wish to make a purchase, and in how they want that purchase to be fulfilled.

(vi) Engagement does not end when a purchase has been made. As well as being very active users of social media to inform a purchase decision, many shoppers are also actively using social media to share the purchase experience with their networks once a purchase has been made.

23

In the new landscape of retail, shoppers expect to be able to engage with a retailer on their own terms, not in a way prescribed by the retailer and into which they are expected to fit. What this means in practice is that the permutation of combinations of ways in which shoppers wish to receive information, search for products, make purchases, and have those purchases fulfilled is almost limitless. Or, as Tim Allinson, former UK Logistics Director of Dixons (now Dixons Carphone, one of the UK's leading consumer electronics retailers), has suggested, 'Customers now want to order from anywhere at any time and they want the flexibility of collecting the product from different places, be it the store, through click-and-collect, delivered to home or office, or to drop-boxes placed in strategic places.'[25]

Returning to the highly influential Young Millennials, it is important to recognize that their behaviours as they enter their high-spending years seem certain to be very different from those that have gone before. There are two reasons in particular for this. First, for the Young Millennials tribe shopping is not a store-centric activity with an online component tacked on. Because technology is at the centre of their worlds and always has been, the default setting of the Young Millennials is much more likely to be that shopping is an online activity that might or might not have a store-based component. It is already the case that retail enterprises—especially established ones with a significant store presence—need to address themselves to the reality that stores only or even mostly will likely *not* be the preferred way that many Young Millennials will want to engage with them. We discuss in Chapter 7 possibilities for keeping stores relevant to shoppers in their omnichannel worlds. Secondly, in major urban markets especially, we should not expect younger cohorts of shoppers to behave like their predecessors.

One defining attitude of the Young Millennials is that they do not aspire to, and almost certainly will not have, the same levels of car ownership that have been so defining of the lifestyles and shopping behaviours of previous generations. While the evidence is somewhat mixed, several recent surveys suggest that Young Millennials do not see car ownership as a 'rite of passage' or as important in their lives as owning a smartphone and having high-speed internet access. A 2012 survey in the US, for example, found that 'far more 18- to 34-year-olds than any other age group say socialising online is a substitute for some car trips'.[26] Moreover, as the world continues to urbanize into mega cities, legislators in those environments are actively pursuing policies to make personal car ownership less attractive and alternative mobility solutions

---

[25] *Retail Week*, 'Analysis: Putting the Supply Chain at the Heart of Retail', 11 Apr. 2014. <http://www.retail-week.com/topics/supply-chain/analysis-putting-the-supply-chain-at-the-heart-of-retail/5059292.article>.
[26] KCR survey, quoted in *The Economist*, 'Seeing the Back of the Car', 22 Sept. 2012. <http://www.economist.com/node/21563280>.

based around mass urban transport and car sharing/hiring solutions much more viable. If historically high levels of personal vehicle ownership cannot be assumed to be maintained in the near-term future—and it cannot—then the behaviours of shoppers will change very substantially. In particular, far more emphasis will need to be put on taking the product to the shopper, rather than expecting the shopper to go to a store to transact and collect.

For retail enterprises, the implications of this transformation in the engagement landscape are profound and challenging, but also rich in opportunity. In concept, what needs to be created is a web of engagement points that has each individual customer at the centre of their own engagement universe, able to interact with the retailer in whatever permutation they wish. The organizational and competency implications for a retailer taking this approach are discussed in Chapters 8 and 9. Furthermore, most retailers will need to embrace and live up to a vision of being neutral about where and how a shopper interacts with their business. That is to say, the role of the retailer is to make it as easy and as seamless as possible for the shopper to engage with their enterprise howsoever they wish. This is, of course, an especially challenging proposition for those retail enterprises and leaders whose heritage and focus has historically been entirely or primarily on their physical store networks.

Mature and Emerging Markets

The most important drivers of change in the new landscape of shopper engagement are global in nature. This is especially evident in the attitudes and behaviours of the technology-enabled Young Millennials. For this important tribe there is a strong sense in which shoppers in, say, Shanghai, London, Los Angeles, and Rio de Janeiro are more similar to each other than they are to shoppers in their domestic regional hinterlands of, say, Zhejiang, Norfolk, Arizona, and Minas Gerais respectively. This is much more an urban/non-urban distinction than it is a mature/emerging markets distinction. As Figure 1.3 shows, most Millennials in all of the BRIC economies except Russia feel that they have more in common with their counterparts in other countries than they do with older people in their own countries.

Millennial shoppers in the world's urban hubs are defined more by the characteristics of the tribe they are part of than they are by the heritage and character of the locations in which they happen to reside. Already their familiarity with brands and their consumption of media and entertainment is global and, increasingly, their social networks are too. When Apple launches a new product, Sony a new computer game, or Burberry a new collection, these are global events. The enthusiasm of Young Millennials in particular to

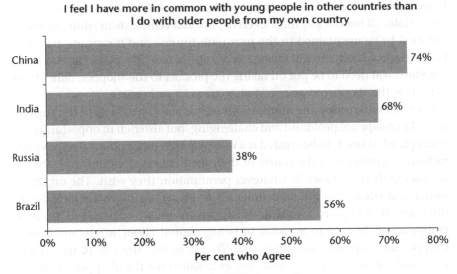

Figure 1.3 Attitudes of Millennials in the BRIC Economies

Source: Sonar/JWT, 2013, Meet the BRIC Millennials. http://www.jwtintelligence.com/wp-content/uploads/2013/09/F_JWT_Meet-the-BRIC-Millennials_09.13.13.pdf.

participate in a wider world and to consume products, media, and stimuli with origins outside their own country, city, or region is enabled by technology and, especially, by the availability of reliable, high-speed internet accessed through mobile devices. While entirely unfettered access to the internet cannot be assumed (depending as it does on prevailing regulatory environments) the devices with which to access the content which is available are increasingly ubiquitous.

The primacy of global forces of change in the shopper engagement environment should not, however, be taken to imply that shoppers and their behaviours are going to converge to a global norm. While we are firmly of the view that the most important drivers of change in shopper attitudes are essentially global in nature, we are equally clear that the ways in which those change drivers manifest themselves in the behaviours of shoppers will play out in very different ways at a local level. Basic needs categories of retail illustrate this more general point. First, what represents a basic grocery offer in, say, Shanghai continues to be very different to a basic grocery offer in, say, Paris. Secondly, how shoppers wish to access their basic grocery needs continues to be influenced in large part by the particular characteristics of their environment as well as by culturally ingrained preferences. So, for example, street and wet markets remain significantly important in major urban centres across Asia despite the plethora of shopping opportunities in modern stores. Thirdly, how shoppers wish to receive advertising communications and the types of messaging they are most receptive to will continue to be influenced heavily, and for many primarily, by local circumstances.

So while we can say with certainty that we are witnessing at a global level a major trend towards shoppers demanding more convenience in their basic needs shopping, the ways in which this dimensionalizes and is delivered will continue to be essentially local in nature. This points once again to the need for retailers to have very finely judged and highly nuanced perspectives on how best to engage with shoppers in different locations. In shopper engagement practices, it is clear that many emerging markets have moved far more quickly than have those in the West to using the internet and mobile internet, especially as a major communication and engagement channel. There has been no need for shoppers and businesses in emerging markets to move from print, to radio, to TV, to internet to engage with shoppers. Rather, many have moved straight to online as the most important engagement channel, thereby missing out a lot of the stages that shopper engagement has moved through in the West.

Case 1.2 ENGAGING THE DIGITAL NATIVES: MILLENNIALS IN CHINA

In the new landscape of retailing and especially the new landscape of consumer engagement, China holds a particular fascination even amongst the other BRIC economies. Change in China is so rapid and the impact of technology so pervasive that the behaviours of the Millennials in particular are very different to those which have gone before. As well as being fascinating in their own right, they might also offer something of a window into the types of changes we might expect to see in Western markets in the near-term future—perhaps the next five to ten years. Looking to China for insight into future behaviours in the West might seem strange to those unfamiliar with the country. Welcome to the new landscape of retail.

Of China's approximately 1.4 billion population, 688 million are internet users (50 per cent penetration), 619 million are mobile internet users (44 per cent), and 482 million are active social media users (34 per cent).[27] For context, the total population of the European Union member states is 503 million[28] and the US around 323 million.[29] Mobile is without question the key platform for engaging digital natives in China. In 2016, the global average of mobile internet users to total internet users was 27 per cent, whereas in China the comparable figure was 90 per cent.[30] Mobile devices are a body extension for many—20 per cent of Chinese people who have one check their mobile phone 100 times or more a day and 23 per cent say that they 'feel panic' when their mobile is not at hand.[31] On average in China, people spend more than three hours a day

(continued)

---

[27] China Internet Network Information Centre, *37th Statistical Survey on Internet Development in China* (2016). <http://www.cnnic.cn/hlwfzyj/hlwxzbg/hlwtjbg/201601/P020160122444930951954.pdf>.
[28] <http://europa.eu/about-eu/facts-figures/living/index_en.htm>.
[29] <http://www.census.gov/popclock>.
[30] <http://wearesocial.com/uk/special-reports/digital-in-2016>.
[31] <199it.com>. Mobile Internet Usage in China 2014.

Case 1.2 Continued

Figure 1.4 Smartphone soup bowl
Source: www.misosoupdesign.com.

on mobile devices. In 2016, mobile commerce is expected to account for over half of all online purchases in China for the first time.[32] WeChat (developed by Tencent and launched in January 2011) is the dominant mobile messaging platform. Growth has been remarkable. As of October 2015, WeChat had around 650 million active users, of which 100 million are outside China. WeChat users skew around two-thirds male, one-third female and three-quarters of users are 20 to 30 years old. 34 per cent of users say that they go onto WeChat as their first act in the morning, 24 per cent say that their purchase decisions are influenced by their friends on WeChat, and 12.5 per cent make a purchase via WeChat. Over 70 per cent of Chinese consumers have five or more MCommerce apps on their smartphone.[33]

If it took 60 seconds to read the above data points, then during that time WeChat acquired 366 new users, youku had over 200,000 video games played, and Baidu.com had almost 800,000 page visits.

The blitz of numbers is always impressive in China—how can they not be in a country of 1.4 billion people? But it is the nuances of the ways in which consumer behaviour is being so totally transformed by the combined effects of a new digital landscape and an outward-looking, highly connected shopper that makes the changes taking place in shopper, retail, and indeed general society so remarkable. As Evan Osnos put it in his excellent book, *Age of Ambition*, 'I was accustomed to hearing the story of China's metamorphosis told in vast, sweeping strokes involving one-sixth of humanity and

---

[32] Vijay Vaitheeswaran, 'Consumers on the Move', *The World in 2016*. {London: The Economist, 2015), 116.
[33] <http://expandedramblings.com/index.php/wechat-statistics/>.

great pivots of politics and economics. But, up close, the deepest changes were intimate and perceptual, buried in daily rhythms in ways that were easy to overlook.'[34]

The reason for throwing a lot of data into this discussion is so as to make a number of points:

1. There is no sense in which the Digital Natives in China should be regarded as any less sophisticated, connected, or technology-enabled than their counterparts in Western Europe and the USA. This serves to reaffirm the point we have made before that digital tribes transcend national boundaries—their behaviours are more similar to those of their counterparts internationally than they are to older generations in the same country.

2. In China as elsewhere, the only way to effectively engage with the Digital Natives of the Millennial generation is on their terms—and that means with digital, and mobile specifically, at the heart of the engagement strategy.

3. It is no longer helpful to think of North America and Western Europe as developed markets and the rest of the world as emerging. China—especially in the Tier 1 cities but increasingly outside them also—is already a highly evolved retail and consumer environment.

Conclusion

The most important feature defining the new landscape of retailing is the radically changed landscape of shopper engagement in the internet age. In previous eras, many—perhaps most—retail enterprises built scale and influence by emphasizing the consistency of their offers and, implicitly or explicitly, the assumed similarities of the shoppers they sought to engage. It is surely open to question whether many retailers could be said to be truly customer centric or whether they were, in reality, driven more by a desire to achieve operational efficiency than true customer centricity. Today, shoppers are too well informed, too well aware of their alternatives, and too able to access those alternatives for them to be treated as mass cohorts of, in some senses, 'conforming shoppers'. The more effective participative and personalized dimensions of engagement with shoppers define the new landscape. While this started with technically literate Millennials and, especially, the younger part of that tribe, it has very quickly become mainstream and defines the way that the great majority of shoppers expect now to be engaged. Indeed, any shopper with reliable internet access and a smartphone expects to be at the centre of a retailer's world and treated as such.

As a result, the suite of engagement possibilities for retailers with their shoppers is very much more complex. Purchase journeys cannot be conceived of as linear, sequential, largely passive, and wholly predictable. The influences

[34] E. Osnos, *Age of Ambition: Chasing Fortune, Truth and Faith in the New China* (New York: Vintage, 2015).

on shopper choice are far wider today than they have ever been in previous eras of retailing; and only some of them are controlled, or even influenced, by the retailer. Furthermore, shoppers have the ability and often the desire to organize themselves into groups to leverage their purchasing power—either with the assistance of retailers or by usurping the traditional role of the retail enterprise as a fulfilment intermediary. It is also the case that the ways in which shoppers expect to be able to fulfil their needs and desires is far more complex and multi-dimensional than it has ever been in the past: 'deliver to wherever is most convenient for me, not to where it is easiest for you' is a new mantra of mainstream retailing. It is not the role of the retailer to force the shopper into a single fulfilment method. Rather, today it is the role of the retailer to provide a range of engagement and fulfilment options from which the shopper can create their own purchase journeys.

The challenges for retailers—be they long-established or new to the sector—in these very changed shopper engagement landscapes are considerable. These are discussed in Part 2 of this book. Suffice to say here that for a retail enterprise and the leadership group of that enterprise they are especially around introducing into the enterprise more cost, more complexity, and more risk of under-delivery to the shopper. But be in no doubt either that the opportunities are enormous for those that can create truly shopper-centric enterprises that are genuinely equipped to engage with shoppers in the ways in which they now wish to be engaged.

2

The Transformational Role of Technology

Technology: The Heart of the New Retail

It is not hyperbole to suggest, as we do, that technology is at the heart of the transformation of shopping behaviour and of retail industry change. The nature of technological change throughout societies, in the hands of shoppers and within retail enterprises themselves, is so pervasive in its scope, so fast in its adoption, and so profound in its impacts that we believe the global retail landscape to be in the early stages of a transformation more important and far-reaching than any which has taken place before. But caution and subtlety are needed in any useful discussion of the nature and impacts of technological change. Technology investments work for the economy and the enterprises within it in two ways. They either allow firms to do existing things better, leading to improvements in efficiency or in the existing customer experience; or they permit them to do wholly new and better things, leading to improvements in the ability of enterprises to meet customers' evolving needs through, for example, more effective engagement. Technology can also lead to social—as well as economic—transformation, by changing the scale, style, and ways in which individuals, groups, and, indeed, whole societies behave.

The effects of technology on people and enterprises are therefore like currents in an ocean—while it is possible to chart a general direction of movement, it is at least equally important to understand the subtleties of the eddies and the smaller currents that create less predictable turbulence and backwash, especially when they oppose the general direction of travel. Impacts and consequences can be uncertain and unpredictable. Herein lies the rub. Whilst the impact of economic transformation through technology is not always wholly predictable, the social consequences of its adoption hardly ever are. We only have to think of all the short-sighted predictions of technology adoption from earlier eras. For example, the Chairman of Western Union's famous response to Alexander Graham Bell's patent application for the telephone that: 'There is nothing in this patent whatever, nor is there anything in the scheme itself, except as a toy.'[1] Or more recently, Steve Ballmer, then CEO of Microsoft, and his assertion in 2007 that, 'there's no chance that the iPhone is going to get any significant market share'.[2] This chapter is as concerned with the unexpected eddies as it is with the main transformational currents of change. That said, we should begin with the main current of change.

The Transformational Role of Online

It is the internet that is, of course, at the heart of the transformation of the retail landscape globally. Notions of both space and time are changed, compressed, and distorted in the digital age. In the London Victoria & Albert Museum's stellar 2015 retrospective of Alexander McQueen's extraordinary contribution to fashion and couture, the introduction to his last complete collection—Spring/Summer 2010—spoke of the influence on the collection of McQueen's perspective of nature being supplanted by technology 'and the extreme space-time compressions produced by the digital age'.[3] Extreme space-time compressions are a defining feature of the digital age in retailing also. Because of the internet, retailing is no longer synonymous with physical stores. Highly localized demand by individual consumers can increasingly be met by supply at a truly boundary-less global scale as consumer trends move close to instantaneously across globally connected networks of people. Global e-commerce sales will likely exceed US$1 trillion in 2016, a 30 per cent growth rate from 2014 and equivalent to a 7.2 per cent penetration of total sales.[4]

Lack of access to a retailer's stores is now no barrier to the ability of a shopper to engage with that retailer or to the ability of that retailer to make their proposition available in areas where they have no physical presence. The

---

[1] *The Electrical World* (1898), vol. 31, p. 9. Quoted in P. Lapsley, 'The Greatest "Bad Business Decision" Quotation That Never Was', The History of the Phone Phreaking Blog, 8 Jan. 2011, <http://blog.historyofphonephreaking.org/2011/01/the-greatest-bad-business-decision-quotation-that-never-was.html>.

[2] <http://usatoday30.usatoday.com/money/companies/management/2007-04-29-ballmer-ceo-forum-usat_N.htm>.

[3] Victoria & Albert Museum, London, 'Alexander McQueen: Savage Beauty', 14 Mar.–2 Aug. 2015.

[4] P. Marceaux, 'Global E-Commerce Value to Breach US$1.0 Trillion in 2016', *Euromonitor In Focus*, 5 Feb. 2015.

Table 2.1 Online retail sales category breakdown for selected countries, 2013

Region	Country	Consumer electronics & appliances	Apparel	Media, toys & games	Food and drink	Furniture & homeware	Beauty & personal care	Home improvement & homecare	Other
World	World	25%	19%	12%	5%	4%	3%	2%	30%
North America	US	21%	18%	13%	3%	4%	2%	1%	39%
Asia	China	52%	27%	3%	1%	1%	6%	0%	10%
	Japan	21%	18%	13%	12%	6%	6%	2%	22%
	South Korea	13%	12%	6%	3%	2%	3%	1%	59%
Western Europe	France	22%	16%	13%	11%	2%	4%	1%	31%
	Germany	27%	32%	6%	2%	7%	2%	2%	11%
	UK	10%	18%	20%	14%	4%	2%	2%	30%
Latin America	Argentina	31%	3%	4%	15%	2%	2%	1%	42%
	Brazil	50%	6%	10%	3%	2%	4%	1%	23%
	Chile	28%	1%	1%	9%	1%	2%	3%	54%
Eastern Europe	Russia	31%	21%	10%	3%	7%	3%	9%	16%
	Slovakia	35%	13%	3%	3%	1%	1%	0%	43%
	Turkey	22%	2%	9%	1%	3%	2%	2%	60%
Middle East	UAE	83%	2%	3%	0%	0%	0%	0%	12%

© A. T. Kearney, Inc., 2013.

Note: Other includes healthcare products, tobacco products, pet food and pet care products, tissue and hygiene products, prescription drugs, sports equipment, watches, sunglasses, handbags, jewellery, antiques, souvenirs, collectibles, bicycles, candles, vases, picture frames, and pictures. Sales of services, subscriptions, travel & tourism, and tickets are excluded.

Source: <https://www.atkearney.com/documents/10192/3609951/Online+Retail+Is+Front+and+Center+in+the+Quest+for+Growth.pdf/f6693929-b2d6-459e-afaa-3a892adbf33e>.

internet is transforming the geography of retailing. We consider the real estate consequences of this in Chapter 3. Table 2.1 shows the approximate proportion of sales transacted online by retail subsector, both globally and by selected countries. Several subsectors have, of course, already migrated almost totally online in some geographical markets, notably books, music, travel services, and, increasingly, financial services also. It has, at least with the benefit of hindsight, been largely unsurprising that low-involvement, low-risk categories have migrated online very quickly—convenience to the shopper and, at least in principle, relative ease of fulfilment for the retailer being powerful drivers of this migration. What has perhaps been somewhat more surprising is the appetite that many shoppers have also to purchase expensive, high engagement products online, often without recourse to visiting a physical store at all during the search process. Furthermore, looking solely at sales transacted online very substantially underplays the importance of the internet across the total purchase journey, the amount of sales influenced through browsing or research online being substantially in excess of actual non-store sales levels. Consultants Deloitte estimate that, in the US alone, digitally influenced in-store consumption already exceeds US$1.7 trillion, compared to US$300 billion in e-commerce sales.[5] In many categories, the initial search for product information, price comparisons, and checking availability starts online even when the purchase itself continues to take place in store.

We feel certain that we are today only in the early stages of the transformation of the retail landscape through the impact of online. We anticipate a sharp acceleration in the near-term future in the impact that online has on retail due to the interaction of two powerful forces of change: technology and shopper demand.

For many shoppers, online is already their preferred way to engage with retailers. Within this, mobile devices are fast emerging as the preferred way to engage online: 44 per cent of global consumers had planned to shop or make a purchase online using a mobile device in the first half of 2015. In Middle East/Africa, this was as high as 55 per cent and in Asia-Pacific 52 per cent.[6] In 2015 in the UK online shopping sales using mobile devices exceeded for the first time a third of all internet shopping sales. A seemingly relentless wave of innovation has driven down price points while simultaneously improving the functionality of mobile devices and interfaces. Technology research firm IDC suggests that the average price of a smartphone globally will fall from US$297 in 2014 to US$241 in 2018. In emerging markets, such as India, prices are forecast to fall from US$135 to US$102 over the same period, as component prices drop and competition increases.[7] It is already clear in India that smartphones will be the dominant device through which shoppers access e-commerce. Kulin Lalbhai, Executive Director of Arvind Retail Group, echoes the views of many when he says that, 'We [in India] will be a mobile-first market. Unlike the West, we have very little legacy so we can build our networks for an omni-channel world.'[8] In mid-2015, Flipkart—the largest e-commerce operator in India—announced that it would shut down its e-commerce website by September 2015 and migrate totally to a smartphone app. This followed the successful experience of Myntra doing the same thing with its fashion e-commerce business. (Myntra is owned by Flipkart.) When it announced its decision, Flipkart said that around 70 per cent of its sales already came from its app against just 6 per cent twelve

[5] Deloitte, 'Navigating the New Digital Divide: Capitalizing on Digital Influence in Retail', 2015. <http://www2.deloitte.com/content/dam/Deloitte/us/Documents/consumer-business/us-cb-navigating-the-new-digital-divide-v2-051315.pdf>.

[6] Nielsen, 'E-Commerce: Evolution or Revolution in the Fast-Moving Consumer Goods World?', 2014. <http://ir.nielsen.com/files/doc_financials/nielsen-global-e-commerce-report-august-2014.pdf>.

[7] IDC, 'Worldwide Smartphone Growth Forecast to Slow from a Boil to a Simmer as Prices Drop and Markets Mature, According to IDC', 1 Dec. 2014, <http://www.idc.com/getdoc.jsp?containerId=prUS25282214>.

[8] Kulin Lalbhai, speaking at World Retail Congress, Rome, Sept. 2015.

months earlier.[9] The rationale for app-only transactional e-commerce centres largely around the ability to keep the shopper within the provider's own ecosystem rather than be part of the open web ecosystem and, as such, the recipient of competitor communications and offers, enabled by cookies. The app-only approach also makes sense in the context of a country where smartphone penetration is expected to increase from around 150 million devices in 2015 to 500 million in 2020.[10] This is a further demonstration of the ways in which the presently emerging markets globally are likely to follow development pathways which are very different in both direction and speed from those of Western Europe and North America. In explaining their move, Flipkart's Chief Product Officer, Punit Soni, said, 'India is gradually transitioning from a mobile first to a mobile only country.'[11]

Longer term, far more intuitive interfaces and devices are emerging which seem likely to give further impetus to online shopping. These may well include forms of wearable technology such as headsets and watches. But we might also expect that in the next wave of innovation the notion of devices at all as a means to access the internet will be replaced by currently more unusual interfaces, including haptic (i.e. touch-based) technologies such as the ARC Pendant.[12] Immersive technologies such as Microsoft's HoloLens or Oculus Rift may well also start to acquire retail capabilities as developers move increasingly away from the screen as the principal interface. The role of automated proxies—whether in the form of drones, personal robotics, or self-driving cars—can also be envisaged in retail-related roles.

As we discussed in Chapter 1, it should not be assumed that there is a 'mature' and an 'emerging' market model of the take-up and use of online amongst shoppers, with the former running ahead of the latter. Rather, the internet is borderless and is changing shopping behaviours globally. According to research by Nielsen the propensity to buy online in Asia Pacific markets is already on average higher than in Western Europe and North America for every category of retailing except one (videos, DVDs, and games).

The enabling architectures of device penetration and broadband access (Figures 2.1 and 2.2 respectively) are, in general, currently lower in emerging than in mature markets but are growing more quickly.

---

[9] <http://timesofindia.indiatimes.com/tech/tech-news/Why-e-commerce-giants-are-shutting-websites/articleshow/47999914.cms>.

[10] <http://www.ft.com/cms/s/0/b8deaa7c-2549-11e5-9c4e-a775d2b173ca.html#axzz3hwgyNDef>.

[11] Quoted in <http://articles.economictimes.indiatimes.com/2015-07-07/news/64178320_1_e-commerce-major-flipkart-myntra-mobile-app>.

[12] <http://www.arcwearables.com>.

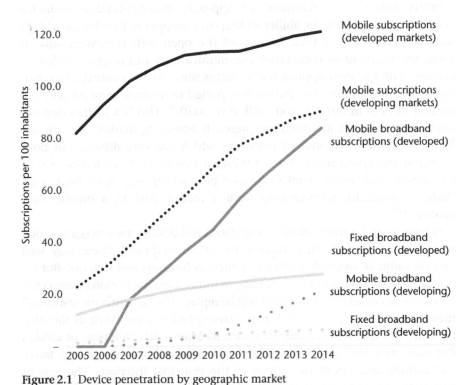

140.0

120.0

Mobile subscriptions
(developed markets)

100.0

Mobile subscriptions
(developing markets)

Subscriptions per 100 inhabitants

80.0

Mobile broadband
subscriptions (developed)

60.0

40.0

Fixed broadband
subscriptions (developed)

Mobile broadband
subscriptions (developing)

20.0

Fixed broadband
subscriptions (developing)

2005 2006 2007 2008 2009 2010 2011 2012 2013 2014

Figure 2.1 Device penetration by geographic market

Note: Device/subscription penetration per 100 inhabitants.

Source: International Telecommunications Union, 2015. http://www.itu.int/en/ITU-D/Statistics/
Documents/statistics/2014/ITU_Key_2005-2014_ICT_data.xls.

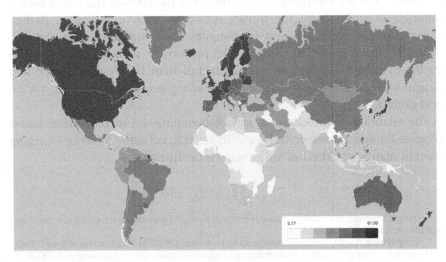

Figure 2.2 Broadband access by geographic market, 2013

Note: Broadband subscriptions per hundred people. Fixed (wired) broadband subscriptions refers to
subscriptions to high-speed access to the public internet (a TCP/IP connection), at downstream
speeds equal to, or greater than, 256 kbit/s.

Source: World Bank, http://data.worldbank.org/indicator/IT.NET.BBND.P2/countries/1W?display=map.

The New Retail and the Digital Divide

The world's citizens are divided into those who are information rich and those who are not.[13] In August 2013, Mark Zuckerberg published a white paper in which he explored the question 'Is connectivity a human right?'[14] Unsurprisingly, he believes that it is. And he is not alone. As early as 2010, four out of five adults surveyed in twenty-six markets agreed that internet access is a fundamental human right.[15] Indeed, in Finland and France, such rights are already enshrined in regulation. Historically, the world's population has tended to be defined according to two divides: first, those who live in mature versus emerging markets and, secondly, those who live in urban versus rural areas. Today, there is a third divide which may well prove to be more important than either of these geographically defined distinctions—those with digital access and those without.

In mid-2015, just 3.1 billion or 40 per cent of the world's population had internet access.[16] This means that fully 4.4 billion people in the world did not. A high proportion of the world's population that is not online is, in fact, in the high-growth, digitally energized BRIC economies (in Brazil 97 million people are not online, Russia 55 million, India 1 billion, China 736 million), and most of the rest are in emerging economies, especially those in Africa and SE Asia.[17] Moreover, the global rate of growth of internet adoption has slowed in the last decade, from a three-year compound annual growth rate of 15.1 per cent from 2005 to 2008 to 10.4 per cent from 2009 to 2013.[18]

There is, of course, a strong correlation between that proportion of the population that already has internet access and those with sufficient disposable income to be able to and to want to engage with modern retailing formats, brands, products, and services. But this does not mean that the approximately 60 per cent of the world's population that presently does not have internet access is unimportant. This is not true from the broad perspective of their economic and social importance, but neither is it true from the much narrower perspective of their significance to the retail sector. While the

---

[13] J. Feather, *The Information Society* (4th edn). London: Facet Publishing, 2004.

[14] <https://fbcdn-dragon-a.akamaihd.net/hphotos-ak-ash3/851575_228794233937224_51579300_n.pdf>.

[15] BBC World Service, 'Four in Five Regard Internet Access as a Fundamental Right: Global Poll', 2010, Press Release, <http://news.bbc.co.uk/1/shared/bsp/hi/pdfs/08_03_10_BBC_internet_poll.pdf>.

[16] For an oddly addictive view of internet usage, go to <http://www.internetlivestats.com>.

[17] <http://www.washingtonpost.com/blogs/wonkblog/wp/2014/10/02/4-4-billion-people-around-the-world-still-dont-have-internet-heres-where-they-live>.

[18] <http://www.mckinsey.com/insights/high_tech_telecoms_internet/offline_and_falling_behind_barriers_to_internet_adoption>.

approximately 4.4 billion people presently without internet access have far less purchasing power than the 3.1 billion who do, their importance should not be under-estimated: 4.4 billion people are far too numerous to ignore. Many of these people will likely enter the digital world long before they have local access to modern retail formats (if they ever will) and long before they have access to the paraphernalia of mature economies—notably personal mobility, vehicle ownership, home fridges, and so on—that has done so much to support the development of modern retailing in all of its physical forms (if they ever do). It may prove to be the case that those people who will in future enter the digital world, especially in the emerging markets, will be still more enthusiastic to use digital to access their retail needs, especially in the relative absence of a physical option. Indeed, retailers themselves are becoming change agents in this regard: research shows that content and service creation online can substantially accelerate internet adoption rates and even encourage economic and social change.[19]

Barriers inhibiting more widespread internet access are numerous, but cost and economics are at their heart. Most obvious is the cost of smartphone devices themselves and of data plans to access richer online content in particular. However, there is a considerable economic challenge also given that the 'internet poor' are disproportionately educationally and income poor also and are concentrated in expensive to access rural areas. Clearly, the continuing urbanization of populations will add 'natural' momentum to more people crossing the digital rubicon as they move from rural to urban areas. Others aspire to give far more impetus to the process. Mark Zuckerberg is one. Facebook's August 2013 White Paper said, 'We believe it's possible to sustainably provide free access to basic internet services in a way that enables everyone with a phone to get on the internet and join the knowledge economy.'[20] So was born internet.org—'a Facebook-led initiative bringing together technology leaders, non-profits and local communities to connect the two thirds of the world that doesn't have Internet access'.[21] The heart of the not uncontroversial internet.org idea is to provide a very basic, free internet service which accesses a limited number of websites of basic functionality and, therefore, with low data and cost to deliver requirements. In this way, people without expensive smartphones, broadband service, and the ability to pay for high-cost data plans are able for the first time to access the internet, at least in a very basic way. The commercial opportunity for Facebook and its commercial partners in internet.org (all of which are

---

[19] V. B. Viard and N. Economides, "The Effect of Content on Global Internet Adoption and the Global "Digital Divide"', *Management Science*, 61(3) (2015), 665–86.
[20] <https://fbcdn-dragon-a.akamaihd.net/hphotos-ak-ash3/851575_228794233937224_51579300_n.pdf>.
[21] <https://internet.org/about?locale=en_GB>.

technology companies) is to migrate free users of the internet into paying users as their circumstances allow.

Criticism of this initiative has been widespread and centres largely around the notion that Facebook decides which websites people can access and, as such, destroys the notion of 'net neutrality'. There are also concerns over the privacy that users have, given the very basic nature of the sites they can access and their attendant low security. Rather than provide a free stepping stone to the full, rich world of the internet, its detractors say that internet.org is, in fact, creating a two-tier internet where the information and cash poor are 'ghetto-ized' and compelled to enter a walled garden from which it will be hard to escape. In early 2015, sixty-seven digital rights groups signed an open letter to Zuckerberg setting out their concerns.[22]

The debate between the proponents and the sceptics of the internet.org initiative is mostly one of philosophy and perspective—where one side's vision of vaunting altruistic inclusiveness is the other side's scepticism that the vision is, in fact, one of narrow commercial self-interest by globally aggressive tech companies. (On one day in 2015—1 August—*The Times* newspaper in London (and presumably many others elsewhere) ran two stories. The first was Facebook's announcement that it would begin prototyping a solar-powered drone to be used to provide internet coverage to remote areas of the world. This was said by Facebook to represent an important next step in achieving Facebook's vision to 'connect everybody in the world'.[23] The second story reported on Google's announcement that Sri Lanka had become the first country to sign up to its Project Loon initiative whereby high altitude balloons are used to deliver internet access to remote regions.[24]) Whichever side of the debate one sits, what is surely not in doubt is that, while the rate of growth of global internet penetration has slowed, the near-term future will see more people experience an impact on their lives as they migrate into an internet-enabled world. Retailing will not be the first or the most important activity that will be changed by their new digital lives. But further momentum will be added to the notion that for a growing proportion of people in a growing number of locations, retailing is an internet-enabled, very possibly an internet-led activity, that takes place in a world where access to digitally enabled possibilities matters far more than old world notions of physical proximity and geography.

---

[22] <http://www.bbc.co.uk/news/technology-32795270>.

[23] Jay Parikh, a vice president of Facebook. Quoted in *The Times*, 'Facebook Unveils Drone to Get the World Online', 1 Aug. 2015, 14.

[24] J. Dean, 'Balloons Beam Internet to Rural Sri Lanka', *The Times*, 1 Aug. 2015, 34.

Not Channels—Engagement Webs

As the (anonymous) CEO of a UK specialty retailer recently observed: 'The purpose of a retailer today is quite different from what it was. We need to come up with a different terminology to encompass modern retail.'[25] Many retailers and commentators default to the language of retailing as an omni-channel activity. Originally attributed to market research company IDC and probably first coined in 2010, the term omni-channel has taken on a universal appeal.[26] To us, this is not an altogether helpful term to characterize the way in which retailers need to address the task of how best to engage with shoppers. The problem is less with the 'omni' and more with the 'channel'. As long as retailing is described as a channel-based activity it gives the impression of a series of discrete, separate channels converging on the shopper and also a sense that the channels of engagement are essentially linear and directed from the retailer to the shopper. This is unhelpful for several reasons. First, purchase journeys for many (possibly most) products and many (probably most) shoppers are most definitely not linear. Secondly, there is a tendency for this view of retailing to become excessively channel centric and insufficiently shopper centric. Third, and perhaps of most importance, the primary objective of the retailer is too often taken to be to optimize integration of activity across multiple channels, rather than to optimize engagement with the customer. Channel integration should not be seen as the ultimate objective of an omni-channel retail business. Rather it is a necessary prerequisite for achieving the real objective, which is to deliver the optimal experience to the shopper, howsoever that is defined (and which is, of course, specific to individual enterprises as well as to individual shoppers).

Rather than defining retailing as an omni-channel activity it is, we suggest, more helpful to think of effective retailing in the new landscape as taking the form of an 'engagement web' with the shopper at the centre. This is not a semantic point. To us it is important to conceive of the role of the retailer in the new landscape as being to create a web of engagement possibilities comprising multiple touchpoints, some virtual some physical, but always with the shopper at the centre of the engagement web and, therefore, at the centre of the retailer's world.

---

[25] Kurt Salmon. 2014. *Retail 2014: The Definitive Report on the State of the Retail Industry, from the Leaders in UK Retail*, Retail Week special report, 2014. <http://www.business.mmu.ac.uk/crpcc/files/retail-2014_retail-week.pdf>.

[26] I. Ortis et al., 'Unified Retailing—Breaking Multichannel Barriers, Global Retail Insights Executive Brief', IDC, 2010.

Application Areas of Customer-Facing Technology

From the shopper's perspective, there are three main territories in which technology can be applied by retailers to improve the shopping process:

- efficiency enhancement
- experience enhancement
- engagement enhancement

Technology for Enhanced Efficiency

Many of a shopper's purchases are frequent, repetitive, predictable, and essentially rather dull at least in their eyes. This is true especially in what are usually called basic needs categories. While grocery buying tends often to dominate in discussions of basic needs shopping, large parts of other categories such as health & beauty and clothing essentials have similar properties of being repetitive, low-involvement, and low-risk categories. Moreover, within retail categories that might be thought of as broadly experiential and discretionary in nature, there are nevertheless many products that also have the attribute of being low-risk, low-engagement, and very familiar. Home improvement and sporting goods retailing are two cases in point where some parts of the product assortment are unfamiliar and high touch (such as buying new tennis shoes or door handles), while other parts are not (such as buying new tennis balls or screws).

In the low-engagement, low-risk part of the retail marketplace the primary opportunity to apply technology to the shoppers' benefit is to improve the efficiency of the shopping process. It is well understood (and was noted in Chapter 1) that for many shoppers a desire for greater convenience is a major driver of their behaviours and their enthusiasm to engage with one retail business rather than another. Within physical stores, technology has an increasingly important role to play in smoothing out the pain points in the purchase process. Obtaining correct price information, product information, and processing the products purchased are all often 'pain points' for the shopper where technology can play a facilitating role. There are myriad examples of retailers with well-developed applications in all of these areas. While developing the usability and commercial cases for such investments is critical to avoid the development of solutions in search of problems, sometimes the need for experimentation should properly win out.

PRICE INFORMATION
Electronic shelf-edge labelling has been trialled for a number of years but has never quite embedded itself in companies' in-store setups—largely because of

upfront costs—other than in France where more than 60 per cent of shelf-edge labels amongst grocery retailers are digital, driven predominantly by legislative pressure.[27] Technology is evolving from RFID (radio frequency ID) to NFC (near field communications). Carrefour's Villeneuve-la-Garenne hypermarket opened in 2014 outfitted with 55,000 NFC-powered shelf-edge labels.[28] In principle, the technology can provide customers with accurate prices while eliminating the costly manual pricing process. Tesco once estimated that it changed between 5 and 10 million labels manually every week.[29] Dynamic pricing using such technologies allows retailers to respond in a much more agile way to price competition. In the back office, products like profitero.com can provide online competitor pricing data.

PRODUCT AND SERVICE INFORMATION

The proliferation of digital display and information screens in stores has been extensive. This takes a wide range of forms. For example, conventional small screen displays are being used to demonstrate the latest offers and information at point of sale or at shelf edge (e.g. Nike has installed motion-sensitive screens in its larger stores). At a further level of sophistication, large format high-resolution displays are being employed to show complementary content to the shopper's intended purchase. For example, apparel retailer Burberry uses RFID to trigger catwalk footage of some products when they are taken near to a screen or into a fitting room.

PROCESSING PRODUCTS PURCHASED

Technology also assists through offering efficiency improvements in purchasing products. This can range from straightforward 'queue-busting' technology, designed to more efficiently allocate queuing shoppers to the next available pay point; to countdowns for those awaiting product pickup for click and collect; to self-check out (SCO) applications of varying degrees of sophistication (although such technologies are not without their detractors: see the case example towards the end of this chapter). Contactless payment systems for small purchases are also becoming increasingly common. Some 2.9 billion smart payment cards will be issued globally in 2016, of which some 43 per cent will be contactless, driven by growth in Asia and Europe,[30]

---

[27] <http://www.retail-week.com/technology/analysis-is-dynamic-pricing-about-to-take-off-in-retail/5054635.article>.

[28] <http://www.nfcworld.com/2014/04/09/328650/carrefour-equips-new-digital-hypermarket-nfc>.

[29] <https://www.tescoplc.com/talkingshop/index.asp?blogid=164>.

[30] <http://www.eurosmart.com/facts-figures.html>.

while in mid-2015, the UK Government suggested that it may make the provision of contactless payment facilities compulsory in all retail outlets by 2020.[31]

Case 2.1 APPLE PAY AND THE RISE OF PAYMENT PROVIDERS

Apple's Apple Pay service seems certain to give considerable additional momentum to moves to contactless payment. Apple Pay uses near-field communication technology in-store to allow shoppers to make payments by holding their Apple device (iPhone 6 and Watch at the time of writing) close to a device reader. The system also works with online retailers. Apple Pay launched in the US initially in October 2014 and the UK was Apple's first international market for the service (July 2015). In the US Apple Pay registered more than 1 million credit cards in its first three days of launch and started with an initial 220,000 shops accepting payment, including Macy's, Bloomingdales, Walgreens, Subway, and McDonalds.[32]

While some US retailers, most notably Walmart, said that they would not support Apple Pay, what Apple Pay needs in order to work is not the agreement of host retailers in a formal partnership, but simply the presence of NFC terminals in their stores. Walmart, Best Buy, 7-Eleven, and many other retailers in the US are part of a group that created MCX (the Merchant Customer Exchange) in mid-2012. The purpose of MCX is to create a retailer-owned and developed payment system—called CurrentC—that allows shoppers to make payments using a smartphone app and a digital wallet and, crucially from the MCX participants' point of view, offers a payment system which bypasses the interchange fees paid to banks. At launch in the US (scheduled for early 2016 at the time of writing) CurrentC will only support the use of QR codes rather than NFC. There have been suggestions that some retail members of the MCX group have disabled their NFC readers in store in order to be able to deploy CurrentC as their mobile payment platform and not Apple Pay and other NFC-enabled products (notably Google Wallet and Android Pay). Best Buy, an MCX member, said initially that it would not support Apple Pay, but six months later in April 2015, it announced that it would.[33] Best Buy's decision followed that of Meijer, a regionally important grocery retailer and MCX member, which said at the end of 2014 that it too would not disable its in-store NFC service in order that it could accept Apple Pay.[34]

There are several reasons why Apple Pay could prove to be very significant. This is the world's most valued brand extending its reach into another part of its customers' lives—in this case the provision of payment services. Apple Pay has the potential to disintermediate still further the relationship between the retailer and their shoppers. Arguably for the first time, a payment provider sits in the foreground of the relationship with the

(continued)

---

[31] <http://www.dailymail.co.uk/news/article-3213659/Shop-told-offer-tap-Contactless-payment-points-compulsory-shop-five-years.html>.

[32] <http://www.forbes.com/sites/markrogowsky/2014/10/20/apple-pay-is-here-and-its-going-to-be-great-why-the-skeptics-have-it-wrong/2>.

[33] <http://arstechnica.com/apple/2015/04/best-buy-will-acce/pt-apple-pay-despite-allegiance-to-currentc-and-mcx>.

[34] <http://www.theverge.com/2014/10/30/7132059/meijer-breaks-with-other-currentc-retailers-to-accept-mobile-payments>.

Case 2.1 Continued

---

shopper, not in the background supporting the ability of retailers to deliver to their shoppers. It will also likely either accelerate the development of alternative payment providers or else itself become the dominant provider. This raises the critical question: who has the strongest relationship with the shopper—a technology company that is also the world's most valuable brand or the product brands the shopper is purchasing or the retailer from which they are making those purchases? In the old landscape of retailing, the default view was that the retailer commands the relationship with the customer. In the new landscape of retailing, no retailer should assume that they will automatically occupy this position. Highly disruptive participants in the shopper engagement landscape are no less confident that they have a still stronger claim. Apple's claim to 'own' the shopper relationship may prove to be stronger than most.

While these applications of technology are helpful and relevant for many shoppers, in the new era of retail they should be considered to be essentially low order, even hygiene, applications of technology sitting at the low end of a spectrum of applications that extend from those which address pain points to those which change shoppers' expectations of what is possible. Consider grocery retailing as a case in point. Without doubt customer-facing technology has an important role to play in easing the shopper through the store. But far more exciting for the shopper and defining for the retailer are those technologies which truly change expectations of what is possible in the category. The very rapid growth of online retailing in grocery in many countries, but especially the UK, points to a truth that for many shoppers the ultimate expression of convenience is not to have to go into the store at all. Rather, convenience is having the products they wish to purchase assembled on their behalf and then delivered on their behalf, or made available for collection. Less than ten years ago this would have been considered a high order technology application that changed category expectations. Today it is a hygiene factor for any grocery retailer—certainly in the UK—that aspires to an industry competitive proposition. This points to another defining theme in the application of customer-facing technology: what was once unique, differentiating, and a source of competitive advantage very quickly becomes the norm and simply a part of doing business and delivering an industry competitive and shopper relevant offer. Retailers need constantly to innovate in their applications of technology, even for those that are relatively low order functional applications. The necessity of and capabilities needed to drive effective innovation is a theme we explore in Chapter 9.

The next wave of technology in the hands of consumers set to transform the possibilities for retailers to deliver greater convenience looks set to be one consequence of what is collectively being called 'the Internet of Things'

(IoT). This is the notion of 'dumb' devices being turned into internet-enabled 'smart' devices connected both to each other and to wider networks. As the research group Mintel has observed, 'Google's Android is no longer just a smartphone operating system; it's the backbone of a rising class of synced-up home appliances such as refrigerators, ovens and even watches.'[35] So it becomes possible for a fridge to communicate that it is, for example, low on milk and to automatically reorder more milk from the retailer without any intervention by the shopper. For example, GE's Chill Hub fridge runs an open development platform for developers who have already launched milk jug and water pitcher sensors, butter softeners, a quick drink chill device, and a food scale.[36]

For some categories there is obvious potential to remove the shopper from the purchase process entirely if they so wish. Amazon's launch in 2015 of its Dash button to Amazon Prime members, as a 'simple way of re-ordering the important things you run low on' presages an age of automatic reordering. Amazon already has plans for this with its Dash Replenishment Service which it aims to become an integral part of household appliances.[37] This came closer to fruition in late 2015 when more than a dozen leading domestic appliance makers, including General Electric and Samsung, announced that they planned to incorporate Amazon's Dash Replenishment Service into numerous of their devices.[38] Related to this is Amazon's patent application in late 2013 for 'anticipatory' shipping, the idea being that Amazon uses purchasing history data together with product searches, wish lists and shopping cart content movements, to anticipate what shoppers are likely to buy. This can be used to reduce order fulfilment times by shipping products from an Amazon fulfilment centre to a local shipping hub in anticipation of a purchase being made in the very near future. As the patent application says, 'speculative shipping of packages may enable more sophisticated and timely management of inventory items, for example by allowing packages to begin flowing towards potential customers in advance of actual orders'.[39] One scenario in Amazon's patent application is that products are 'speculatively

[35] Richard Cope, quoted in Z. Wood, 'Dixons and Carphone Warehouse Look to Exploit Internet of Things', *Guardian*, 9 May 2014. <http://www.theguardian.com/business/2014/may/09/dixons-carphone-warehouse-merger-internet-of-things>.

[36] <https://firstbuild.com/mylescaley/chillhub>.

[37] I. Crouch, O'The Horror of Amazon's New Dash Button', *The New Yorker*, 2 Apr. 2015. <http://www.newyorker.com/culture/culture-desk/the-horror-of-Amazons-new-dash-button>. N. Olivares-Giles, 'Amazon's Dash Button is Not a Hoax, it's Phase One', *Wall Street Journal*, 31 Mar. 2015. <http://blogs.wsj.com/personal-technology/2015/03/31/Amazons-dash-button-is-not-a-hoax-its-phase-one>.

[38] <http://www.businesswire.com/news/home/20151001005915/en/Amazon-Dash-Replenishment-Service-Adds-Device-Partners#.VhPay6_luP8>.

[39] <http://techcrunch.com/2014/01/18/Amazon-pre-ships>.

shipped' to local destinations and might remain in near-continuous transit until the customer is ready to make a purchase.[40] In concept, this is more akin to the way in which utility providers use algorithms to anticipate demand and manage a constant flow of, say, electricity or water, to the customer than it is to the conventional view of logistics in retailing as being the provision of a single product at a single point in time *after* an order has been placed.

Clearly, there are important implications in this automation of retailing which go to the very heart of what retailing is, what retail enterprises do, and what type of enterprises are in the business of retail. It is, for example, entirely possible to envisage basic needs retailing in particular as transformed from a customer-purchased store-based activity to an automated logistics driven activity with no shopper interaction and for retail enterprises as we currently understand them to either evolve into, or be replaced by, logistics and fulfilment enterprises. We discuss these themes in Part 2.

Technology for Enhanced Experiences

For many retailers there are also rich opportunities to use technology to enhance, perhaps transform, the shopping experience. While basic needs retailing is, as we suggest, defined especially by many shoppers' desire for what might be termed 'ultimate convenience', the higher touch, more discretionary parts of the retail market are by contrast coming increasingly to be defined by shoppers expecting richer, more interesting experiences. In a physical store setting, this proposition can be simply stated: if the in-store experience is no more engaging than the online experience there is little reason for visiting the store at all (beyond social engagement and perhaps loyalty which is certainly important for many and discussed in Chapter 8).

There are a number of ways in which technology can be applied in-store to deliver enhanced experiences. These are set out in Table 2.2. Web-enabled kiosks which broaden product choice beyond that which can be presented in-store and tablet screens that display more information than a sales associate has to hand already feel, as we have suggested, somewhat run of the mill—which is not to understate their usefulness to many shoppers. But what we feel sure will come to define the new landscape of retail in high touch store and shopping environments are those possibilities for technology to be applied in ways which are truly inspiring, immersive, and transformative.

---

[40] <http://techcrunch.com/2014/01/18/Amazon-pre-ships>.

Table 2.2 Online buying Intentions in the second half of 2014

Category	Asia-Pacific	Europe	Middle East & Africa	Latin America	North America
Clothing, accessories & shoes	57%	34%	26%	28%	42%
Electronic equipment	41%	25%	26%	29%	30%
Tours & hotel reservations	53%	33%	35%	32%	43%
Airline tickets & reservations	59%	34%	39%	36%	43%
Mobile phone	44%	22%	28%	27%	22%
Events tickets	50%	33%	28%	31%	35%
Computer hardware	36%	23%	25%	20%	29%
Hardcopy books	50%	30%	22%	24%	31%
Computers software	33%	19%	27%	18%	27%
e-Books	43%	22%	29%	23%	35%
Sporting goods	42%	19%	20%	19%	21%
Music (not downloaded)	33%	19%	21%	19%	30%
Videos, DVDs and games	32%	21%	23%	21%	33%
Cosmetics	43%	21%	19%	20%	21%
Personal care	43%	17%	18%	14%	16%
Groceries	41%	14%	15%	11%	14%
Toys & dolls	40%	16%	18%	17%	24%
Car, motorcycle & accessories	20%	13%	16%	11%	15%
Pet-related products	26%	15%	14%	11%	19%
Baby supplies	29%	12%	16%	11%	12%
Flowers	21%	11%	16%	10%	21%
Alcoholic drinks	25%	9%	11%	8%	10%

© The Nielsen Company, 2014.

Source: The Nielsen Company, E-commerce: Evolution or Revolution in the Fast-Moving Consumer Goods World, 2014. <http://ir.nielsen.com/files/doc_financials/Nielsen-Global-E-commerce-Report-August-2014.pdf>.

This is nothing less than a reconceptualization of the role of physical stores in a connected world. The role of the store, especially in high touch discretionary spend categories, needs to be reframed from stores which are conceived as passive presentations of merchandise to spaces which become immersive and participative showcases. The great merchants and icons of 'high touch' retailing, perhaps department stores especially, have always understood the notion of retailing as theatre. In-store technology offers great potential to reinvent the enduring relevance of this notion for a digital age.

Consider youth fashion as a case in point. This market is as much about feeling part of a community and feeling like an on-trend fashion leader as it is about being persuaded by the style, quality, and value of the actual garment. Topshop, the UK-based icon of affordable youth fashion, has taken this notion and used technology to create far more immersive and participative experiences for shoppers. In some promotions this has taken the form of equipping the winners of its competitions with augmented reality headsets so that they can have the experience in store of being at a fashion show watching catwalk models show off Topshop's latest collection. The proposition at the heart of this idea is to make accessible in virtual form an event, which would otherwise have been inaccessible to the shopper in a physical form and to bring this into the store, or to the individual, as an engaging piece of theatre. H&M, another icon of on-trend, affordable youth fashion, lives in a similar world to Topshop. H&M's exceptional flagship store in New York's Times Square puts the shopper at the centre of a connected experience in 'probably the fashion retailer's most digitally enabled branch'.[41] Shoppers can go to the Runway on the mezzanine level and strike poses and have photos and video clips made. These then appear on small screens around the store, on runway.hm.com, and can be shared on social media. But most special of all, if staff think you look good enough the video is put on a huge screen overlooking Times Square with a message sent to the shopper's phone telling them when they will be appearing. Narcissistic? Very possibly. But this is also a compelling example of how technology can be applied in ways that bring a far more heightened experience to the shopper and connects the retailer's physical world with the shopper's digital life (Table 2.3).

Table 2.3 Territories where technology can be applied for enhanced experiences

Strategic Objective	Example technologies
Providing product/price information	Shelf-edge labelling In-store information screens Information kiosks Holographic displays
Enabling range extensions	Kiosks Virtual shelves/product displays
Enhancing overall customer experience	Virtual catwalks 3D headsets Smart hangers
Personalizing customer experience	iBeacon/Near Field Communication Augmented reality/virtual mirrors Personal viewing devices Additive manufacturing (3D printing)
Gaining customer insight	Eyetracking Big data Neurometrics (measuring brain electrical activity)

[41] <http://www.retail-week.com/stores/store-gallery-hm-runway-times-square-new-york/5058457. article>.

Technology for Enhanced Engagement

The distinction between experiences and engagement is not, we readily acknowledge, altogether clear and precise. Deeper engagement could be thought of as one consequence of delivering an enhanced experience: but here the focus is on the individual and the delivery of a personalized, involved experience. The ways in which we choose to define engagement is in terms of shoppers' engagement with the product, with the retailer, and with other people in their networks. In the new retail landscape, technology will increasingly and rapidly transform the ways in which many, very possibly most, shoppers engage with all three.

We have discussed already (Chapter 1) the notion of shoppers being able to participate in product design, personalization, and even product development. For retailers it is important to facilitate high levels of engagement with products in ways that enable and promote the notion of shopping as a personalized and participative activity. Augmented reality technologies, such as virtual mirrors in fashion outlets and 3D headsets in gaming rooms, offer interesting possibilities in this regard. In the online space, the challenge for many will be to create experiences that bring to life in a highly engaging way both the product offer and the story of the brand in ways that do not assume that the shopper will be able to or will even want to visit a store to gain the full experience.

In physical spaces, near field communication (NFC) and equivalent technologies offer the means by which retailers can engage more personally with shoppers. Whilst NFC requires active intervention by the shopper, Bluetooth low energy (BLE) devices such as Apple's iBeacons and Shopkick's Shopbeacon, can 'push' marketing and information messages to shoppers in store, directing them to other parts of the store and alerting them to special events and promotions. For marketers this creates opportunities to move the point of influence closer to the point of purchase when shoppers' propensity to switch brands or be influenced by a promotion is often at its most heightened. Moreover, the messaging should be contextually relevant to the shopper. In Shopkick's model, shoppers earn 'kicks' when they engage with a product in a store by, for example, scanning a barcode, or just entering a store rather than necessarily making a purchase—although that is rewarded with more 'kicks'. The Shopkick app has already captured shoppers' product preferences. 'Kicks' can then be exchanged for gift certificates. (In early 2016, the Shopkick app was being used by around 19 million shoppers in the US.[42]) NFC/BLE look like appealing enhancements to well-established and often very effective in-store marketing activities, especially of the major FMCG brands with the significant added benefit that detailed information is being captured about the shopper and the effectiveness of the communication.

---

[42] <https://www.shopkick.com/about>.

Facilitating the desire of shoppers to engage with their social networks during the purchase process is fast emerging as mandatory for many, perhaps most, retailers. Stores need to be equipped with the enabling technology to make this possible for the shopper. This can take interestingly quirky forms that enhance the brand's reputation and profile and simultaneously deliver a more engaging shopping experience. For example, the clothing retailer C&A has in some of its stores in Brazil been using so-called 'smart hangers' (whether a hanger could ever be considered smart is perhaps a moot point) that show in a digital display how many 'likes' that product received on C&A's Facebook page. The shopper, presumably according to their mindset, is then influenced to purchase a product with many 'likes' or not to purchase it if they prefer not to follow the crowd.

It is important to appreciate that customer-facing technology must be configured in store in ways which enhance the desired experience without overwhelming it. For some retailers and some categories, such as consumer electronics, there is a sense in which the technology *is* the experience. But for many others, technology that is customer facing should nevertheless live more comfortably in the background so that the shopper is aware that they are having a more interesting and immersive experience without being particularly aware of quite how that has been enabled. Here again, individual retailers will need to form their own judgements on what is most appropriate for their audiences and their desired brand positioning and customer experience. Whatever the precise resolution of these considerations, the guiding principle must always be to see the customer as being at the centre of the picture and to organize everything around a deep and detailed understanding of his or her needs and expectations.

Case 2.2 SHOES OF PREY: SHOPPER CO-CREATION AND THE NEW RETAIL

Shoes of Prey is a women's shoe retailer founded in Sydney in 2009 (www.sho esofprey.com). Its first store, a concession in the iconic David Jones department store in central Sydney, won the World Retail Awards small store of the year design award in 2013. But this should not lead to the conclusion that Shoes of Prey is a conventional store-based footwear retailer. The fact that the business was founded by three former Google executives hints at something rather different. As co-founder Jodie Fox explains it, 'I was solving a problem of my own. I'd always liked shoes, but I never loved them because I couldn't find exactly what I was looking for . . . When I was travelling, in the same way that you find someone who will make a custom suit for you, I found someone with whom I could commission shoe designs. My shoe collection became really exciting, and my girlfriends asked me where I was getting my footwear. When I explained, they asked me to create shoes for them too. Concurrently, my two business partners Michael and Mike were at Google and they became really excited about the opportunities in online retail. We all came together and Shoes of Prey was born.'[43]

Shoes of Prey allows shoppers online to design their own shoes using a 3D design tool. Shoppers select from a range of twelve shoe shapes and 170 fabrics. The design is then made by hand. The process takes around six weeks and shoes are shipped worldwide free of charge. Prices range from around £120 to £220 per pair. If a shopper is, for any reason, not happy with their pair of shoes, they have 365 days to return them (unworn) and a new pair will be made free of charge.

Shoes of Prey is a very appealing illustration of the possibilities in the new retail landscape: make the product creation process participative with the shopper; deliver to the shopper a unique product for much the same price as a standard product; leverage online technology to quickly build global scale; and deliver across both digital and physical touchpoints. Jodie Fox would like to take Shoes of Prey in still more radical directions, especially by harnessing the possibilities of 3D printing at home. In late 2015, she suggested that 'My dream of the future is manufacturing in the home. But for the moment it's manufacturing on demand.'[44]

In late 2014, Shoes of Prey announced a partnership with Nordstrom whereby Shoes of Prey design studios will be located in an initial six Nordstrom department stores across the US. Given the heritage of Nordstrom as initially a footwear retailer, this seems entirely fitting (pun irresistible) as well as an excellent example of the possibilities for the best of the 'new world' retailers to collaborate with the best of the established ones.

While we feel confident in presenting these generalized trends in the application of customer-facing technology, it is important to recognize also the presence of additional and somewhat counter-trends—the eddies in the main currents that we alluded to earlier. Two such trends, both enabled by technology, seem likely to be especially important to many shoppers and for many retailers.

HUMANISING THE ENGAGEMENT EXPERIENCE

As technology becomes ever more embedded into people's lives so, for many, the yearning for greater human interaction increases too. This is one area especially where store-based retailers can win over online retailing. It may seem somewhat paradoxical to suggest that technology can have an important role to play in enabling more human engagement but we believe this to be so. This is not the world of automated vending machines delivering a human message or robots performing human tasks such as collecting the groceries. Rather, this takes the form of truly human interactions such as, for example, tablet devices that equip store staff with the knowledge they need to have a more informed and engaged conversation with shoppers. This can also be characterized as a necessary investment that store-based retailers especially

---

[43] <https://www.shoesofprey.com/content/media-release>.
[44] Jodie Fox speaking at World Retail Congress, Rome, Sept. 2015.

will need to make if they are to counteract the growing information asymmetry between frontline staff and ever more knowledgeable shoppers—an asymmetry which is, of course, the reverse of the historic position.

ADDRESSING THE CHOICE PARADOX

For many years, it has been assumed that large product assortments have always benefited shoppers. This is not necessarily so. The choice paradox is the proposition that more choice can, in fact, lead to dissatisfaction due to the difficulty of making 'good' decisions of what to choose. Therefore, almost infinite choice in an internet-enabled world could lead to almost infinite unhappiness or, at least, to never feeling totally satisfied with the choices one has made. The notion of the choice paradox was popularized by Barry Schwartz in 2004[45] but was identified by behavioural psychologists many years earlier.[46] It might be noted that, since Schwartz addressed the paradox in 2004, choice of products available to many shoppers in many categories has increased exponentially. By the end of 2015, Amazon in the US stocked over 385 million items in thirty-five departments, for example.[47]

There are interesting possibilities for businesses to help shoppers to navigate through the almost limitless choices available to them. In a sense, all retailers are curators, and hence also editors, of the products they range. But the smart application of technology and, especially, the ability to usefully interrogate and act on shopper derived data (as we discuss later in this chapter), holds out the possibility of taking the role of retailer as curator much further by making product recommendations based on detailed profiling of individual shoppers. In this way, product is not push marketed onto reluctant shoppers, rather content is carefully tailored and targeted to shoppers thought likely to appreciate the guidance offered. This is a subtle, but very important distinction. It should also be recognized, however, that this curatorial role does not necessarily automatically reside with retailers.

There exist already many examples of online businesses positioning themselves explicitly as choice curators of various kinds, sometimes building upon crowdsourced insight, sometimes upon behavioural targeting. Examples of such businesses include:

- *Spring*. The consumer chooses brands to follow on their mobile, or explores brands by category. Orders are placed through the site rather than through the brand directly (www.shopspring.com).

---

[45] B. Schwartz, *The Paradox of Choice: Why More is Less* (New York: Harper Perennial, 2004).

[46] See e.g. R. Dhar, 'Consumer Preference for a No-Choice Option', *Journal of Consumer Research*, 24 (Sept. 1997), 215–31.

[47] <https://sellerengine.com/how-many-products-does-amazon-sell-amazon-marketplace-stats/>.

- *Wanelo* (Want, Need, Love), launched in 2012, offers a choice of 350,000 'stores' that consumers can elect to follow in a personalized feed (http://wanelo.com).

- *Threadless.* Founded in 2000, Threadless is an online community of artists creating mostly clothing designs and e-commerce platform. 1,000 designs are submitted weekly to a public vote, from which ten designs are selected for printing on clothing and other products (www.threadless.com).

- *The Hunt.* Consumers post a photo of an item that they're looking for, along with specific requirements such as budget and size. The Hunt community of over 3.5 million users suggests products that meet the criteria (www.thehunt.com).

The role of an enterprise as curator of edited assortments for shoppers is leading to a blurring of content information and commerce. The fashion category is a case in point where traditional media properties such as *Grazia* have launched their own e-commerce enterprises.[48] Given that *Grazia* is read by around 17 million people in twenty-three countries, the possibilities for it to shape fashion trends and then, through graziashop.com, fulfil the demand it creates is obvious, although the fulfilment challenges should never be under-estimated. Conceptually similar is the initiative of the fashion magazine *Marie Claire* to establish a *Marie Claire* branded e-commerce beauty products retail business using the UK Ocado's subsidiary, Speciality Stores, as their fulfilment partner.[49] In the reverse direction, Net-a-Porter, the high-growth luxury fashion internet retailer that began in London in 2000, launched its own magazine, *Porter*, in early 2014. This is a premium luxury magazine (US $9.99 at the newsstand. *Vogue* is US$5.99), which is discreetly shoppable in the sense that readers can use the app to take a photo of a printed page which will then call up the shopping programme—both Net-a-Porter itself and other brands' sites where they are not stocked by Net-a-Porter. *Porter* was distributed to an initial sixty countries and as a digital edition also.[50] In a much less elevated part of the fashion market ASOS also has its own magazine. Launched in 2006, the ten print editions a year reach around 525,000 people a month, and the magazine is free to UK shoppers who have joined ASOS Premiere. A further 2.3 million view the web edition each month.[51]

Quite where the balance lies between technology to deliver more convenience, more experience, or more engagement will depend on the objectives of individual businesses. We can, however, offer some general guidance. For

[48] <http://www.shopsafe.co.uk/news/grazia-debuts-ownbrand-online-shop/11219>.
[49] <http://internetretailing.net/2015/02/marie-claire-to-launch-ecommerce-website-in-partnership-with-ocado>.
[50] <http://www.wsj.com/articles/SB10001424052702303442704579362900001314062>.
[51] <http://www.nrs.co.uk/latest-results/titles-at-a-glance/quick-view/>.

those categories that are defined principally as basic needs, the customer facing technology investments of retailers should focus mostly on delivering much greater convenience. By contrast, for high involvement purchases, the focus should be on dialing up engagement and experience. But importantly, retailers aspiring to deliver much more immersive experiences to shoppers must nevertheless deliver to a base standard of convenience and see this as a hygiene factor not to be overlooked.

Technology and the Retail Enterprise

The scale and complexity of the technology transformation challenge can be daunting for many retail firms and particularly for retail enterprise leaders. Research by OXIRM (Oxford Institute of Retail Management) at the University of Oxford's Saïd Business School has suggested that an important perceived barrier to the effective commercialization of technology is the lack of technical literacy at senior management level.[52] This is particularly the case in store-based businesses where senior managers are focused on the operational legacy of running such businesses. 'They have secretaries and drivers; they don't even know how to use Google Maps' said one respondent in the research. Even for the experts, understanding the consequences of investment in technology in such a fast-moving environment can be problematic. Speaking at the US NRF (National Retail Federation) 'Big Show' in 2015, Michelle Garvey, CIO of Ann Taylor and Loft, observed: 'I used to say, "Don't bring me a solution that is looking for a problem", but digital is moving so fast that it now makes sense to have some funds in reserve that can be used for testing approaches that would appear to provide value.'[53] But is identifying genuinely transformational technologies therefore just a matter of timing or luck? The introduction of the iPad tablet in 2010 was certainly accompanied by excitement from Apple's so-called 'fanbois' (fanboi: 'someone who is unusually attracted or devoted to a particular technology or tech company'[54]), but puzzlement from journalists and commentators at the time: precisely what was the iPad *for*? By 2015, whilst over 1 billion tablets were in use worldwide, with Apple commanding just over a quarter of 2014 shipments, growth rates are forecast to slow dramatically, largely because of the luxury nature of the tablet and preferences for cheaper smartphones and so-called phablets (somewhere between a phone and a tablet) in emerging markets. Moreover, many

---

[52] Oxford Institute of Retail Management, *Productivity and Skills in Retailing*, Report for Skillsmart Retail, 2010.
[53] Quoted in: <http://www.digitalsignagetoday.com/articles/drinking-from-a-digital-signage-firehose-at-retails-big-show>.
[54] <http://www.techopedia.com/definition/28754/fanboi>.

commentators are still unconvinced of the need for a 'third device' even in mature markets. Said one: 'the iPad risks permanently becoming the least practical way for people to traverse their digital lives'.[55]

Transformational technologies in retailing are nothing new. Taking a historical perspective usually provides some useful context and one only has to look back to the nineteenth century to see developments in

- refrigeration systems, both in store and at home, dramatically affecting the nature of grocery retailing,
- information systems such as pneumatic tube transport permitting centralized payments and information flows, and
- transportation systems, ranging from in-store implementation of elevators and escalators—which permitted much easier access to multi-storey premises—to the revolution in personal transportation with over 1 billion motor vehicles now in use worldwide.[56]

European research in the early 1990s suggested that most retailers were conservative in their approach to technology, being adapters rather than innovators, using technology to support existing operations and to raise rudimentary barriers to entry for competitors.[57] For many, successful R&D did not involve long-term R&D, or extensive capital commitments, but provided a tangible, and often rapid, financial benefit. The three exceptions to this general picture were named as Tesco, Carrefour, and Metro who, the research suggested, used technology to achieve integration or broader strategic goals. And yet by the beginning of the twenty-first century, only two retail technologies really stood out over the previous twenty-five years as having been widely embraced by retailers: the barcode and the point-of-sale terminal.

Today, these kinds of incremental approaches are not of themselves sufficient, but the scale and complexity of transformational IT projects sit poorly within businesses which may have both relatively constrained capital available for investment and a shortage of appropriate talent to deliver the projects. Even though the global retail sector was estimated to have spent over US \$175bn on IT in 2015, existing retail enterprises continue to face the challenge of overcoming the burden of their legacy systems.[58] The average life of store

[55] K. Vanhemert, 'Nobody Knows What an iPad is Good for Anymore', *Wired*, 27 Jan. 2015. <http://www.wired.com/2015/01/nobody-knows-ipad-good-anymore>.

[56] <http://www.greencarreports.com/news/1093560_1-2-billion-vehicles-on-worlds-roads-now-2-billion-by-2035-report>.

[57] S. L. Burt and J. A. Dawson, '*The Impact of New Technology and New Payment Systems on Commercial Distribution in the European Community*. DGXXIII, Series Studies, Commerce and Distribution 17, Brussels: Commission of the European Communities, 1991.

[58] Gartner,.'Forecast: Enterprise IT Spending for the Retail Market, Worldwide, 2013–2019, 1Q15 Update', 5 May 2015. <https://www.gartner.com/doc/3045523/forecast-enterprise-it-spending-retail>.

systems is around ten years, and of e-commerce systems around five years. One US retailer told us that: 'ageing technology investment and ageing stores are the primary limitations to productivity [improvements].' Moreover, heavy spend on technology architecture without commensurate change in the enterprise can often serve only to introduce further cost rather than enhanced efficiency and effectiveness. As Luis Reis, Chief Corporate Center Officer of the Portuguese retailer Sonae, wryly observed, 'If you add new technology to an old organization, you get a costly old organization.'[59]

To overcome these obstacles requires ingenuity and imagination—as well as capital. IT research and advisory firm Gartner has proposed that we should think increasingly of 'bimodal' technology investments: in the forms of *traditional* and *agile* IT. The former focuses on security, process efficiency, and 'keeping the show on the road'. The latter involves experimentation, prototyping, and non-sequential development.[60] Up to 30 per cent of technology spending already happens outside the IT departments of firms. (IT services supplier Wipro says 40 per cent of its retail business is now done with people other than the CIO, notably with e-commerce and marketing divisions.[61]) It is this spending which is more likely to be agile in character.

What makes the arena of customer-facing technology so challenging for many retailers is the absolute certainty that many initiatives will fail to deliver on the expectations businesses have for them, either because the technology does not work as anticipated or because it does not, in fact, meaningfully enhance the shoppers' experience in ways that they value—or indeed both. Case study 2.3 on self-checkout (SCO) technology illustrates some of the unforeseen consequences of a technology which was ostensibly designed to address shoppers' frustrations with queuing—but which in practice serves to deliver different frustrations. Furthermore, it is equally certain that something better/quicker/smarter/cheaper will come along in a further wave of (often unanticipated) innovation. As the Head of Information for one of the UK's largest multi-channel retailers said (anonymously—perhaps unsurprisingly), 'You have to get used to not knowing what the end game is going to be.' It is far more important for retail business leaders to have a clear view of the role that they want technology to play in enhancing the customer experience than it is to have clarity on the precise pieces of technology that are going to enable the desired experience. We return to this theme in Chapters 9 and 10 in the context of the needs of retail enterprises and the attributes of their leaders respectively.

---

[59] Luis Reis, speaking at World Retail Congress, Rome, Sept. 2015.
[60] <http://www.gartner.com/it-glossary/bimodal>.
[61] <http://www.retailtechnology.co.uk/news/5483/survey:-retail-it-spend-is-dropping>.

Case 2.3 'UNEXPECTED ITEM IN BAGGING AREA'

When businesses make unreasonable assumptions about the inevitability of benefits arising from a new technology, so-called 'technological determinism' can kick in. The growth of technology-based self-service (TBSS) or self-checkout (SCO) in stores has been promoted as being beneficial for both customers and retailers, but has also led to criticism that the main reasons behind implementation has focused on the cost savings available to retailers, through the removal of serviced checkouts, rather than improvements to the customer experience. SCO is a good illustration of the complex and evolving inter-relationship between technology and customer engagement. Those supporting SCO argue: 'SCO is a proven solution for increasing positive customer service metrics by reducing queues at checkout, trimming labor costs and delivering a strong ROI that pays for the technology in 12–18 months.'[62]

SCO adoption has increased internationally, but is by no means widespread, being concentrated in the US and Europe. It is estimated that there were over 190,000 SCO machines in service around the world at the beginning of 2014. To put this into context, although the SCO base is forecast to increase to 325,000 by 2018, numbers of SCOs shipped in 2013 comprised less than 2 per cent of electronic point-of-sale shipments.[63] Nevertheless, some businesses are making major investments: Walmart introduced 10,000 SCO units in the US in 2014, for example.

Customers' early experiences of SCO were varied. First-generation technology (NCR's first SCO prototype was developed in 1997) was often assembled from off the shelf components rather than being specifically designed and manufactured around ergonomic and customer journey principles. Interfaces were inelegant, pre-recorded messages hectored customers and worked on the principle that they were not to be trusted. The misadventures of SCO machines and the unhappy experiences of customers became not just an urban folk myth and the subject of stand-up comedy, but also of survey research: '8 percent of people asked thought self-service checkouts were a nightmare. 46 percent said that items wouldn't scan properly. 13 percent complained about having to do all the work, and 12 percent said they always had to get help.'[64]

Machines originally designed more around banking principles are now more carefully embedded in retail environments and reportedly generate fewer weighing, scanning, and other exceptions that need to be resolved. More importantly, the extent to which SCO should completely replace, or should be supplemented with supervisory or other employee support, has become a more complex judgement. Originally, supervisors were put in place to smooth the checkout process for customers. Interventions would seek to correct both user and system errors and staff required a degree of technical skill to understand and correct failures. Newer technology is now generally more reliable and provides lower failure rates and a reduced need for supervisor intervention. Supermarket companies continue to talk of the real improvements in productivity that can result. However, more recent work suggests that efficiency benefits cannot simply be taken for granted. To realize them may actually require additionally skilled human capital, rather than simply replacing the previous interaction between employees and customers: 'offering interaction with an employee as a fall-back option offsets the negative

(continued)

---

[62] Bruce Kopp, Selfservice World.com, 2010.
[63] <http://www.rbrlondon.com/retai>.   [64] Fatcheese.com survey, May 2010.

Case 2.3 Continued

---

consequences of forced use [of self checkouts]'.[65] One US retailer commented: 'If you put a brand new cashier on self-checkout that isn't experienced, it'll be a much worse [customer] experience because . . . it's all about errors.'[66]

An often-neglected aspect of this judgement is different customer attitudes to technology. There is a substantial body of academic literature on the nature and extent of technology acceptance by different customer groups.[67] Suffice to say that: 'Life's aggressive pessimists . . . are enraged before they even begin and so begin to fling things onto the scanner with wild abandon, almost glorying in the fact that they will soon bring the process to a standstill, simply because they have expected of the computer more than it is capable of giving.'[68] The UK retail trades union, USDAW, commented: 'In our latest survey, self-service checkouts were cited for the first time as a cause of abuse.'[69] Certainly, the very poor experience of Tesco with its Fresh & Easy business in the US (now exited) was in part a consequence of its decision to equip stores with SCO only and not give customers—used to having their purchases not just scanned by a staff member but their bags packed also, remember—any choice.

Managing such interactions requires strong emotional intelligence and social skills of staff, at least as much as it does technical capabilities. As a result of these considerations some retailers, including UK grocery retailer Morrisons, have elected to reduce their reliance on SCOs. Indeed, Morrisons reintroduced 1,000 staffed express checkouts in 2015, thereby rebalancing the checkout options for the shopper, and—perhaps more importantly—their staff interaction choices.

A further area of complexity for retailers lies in judging which horse to back amongst competing technologies and applications, in fields where standards have yet to be agreed and which appear to be changing rapidly in ways that could positively enhance the customer's experience—but where those customers' preferences are presently unclear. 'Poor calibration' describes the lack of understanding or appreciation of the link between the attributes of a new product or service and the benefits of it on behalf of the customer. Payment systems are a classic example of this. In the UK, whilst cash accounted for just over half of all payments in 2014, people under 35 years of age comprised over half of the 2.3 million who rarely used cash.[70] There has been a proliferation of

[65] M. J. Reinders et al., 'Consequences of Forcing Consumers to Use Technology-Based Self-Service', *Journal of Service Research*, 11(2) (Nov. 2008), 107–23.

[66] Quoted in Oxford Institute of Retail Management, *Productivity and Skills in Retailing*. Report for Skillsmart, the Retail Sector Skills Council, 2010.

[67] K. Gelbrich and B. Sattler, 'Anxiety, Crowding, and Time Pressure in Public Self-Service Technology Acceptance', *Journal of Services Marketing*, 28(1) (2014), 82–94.

[68] L. Mangan, 'The Self-Service Till's Divisive Powers', *Guardian*, 23 Aug. 2010. <http://www.theguardian.com/commentisfree/2010/aug/23/self-service-tills-divisive-powers>.

[69] John Hannett, USDAW, quoted in A. Jamieson et al., 'Self-Service Checkouts "Have Not Cut Supermarket Queues"', *Daily Telegraph*, 21 Aug. 2010. <http://www.telegraph.co.uk/finance/newsbysector/retailandconsumer/7957800/Self-service-checkouts-have-not-cut-supermarket-queues.html>.

[70] Payments Council, 'UK Cash & Cash Machines 2015'. <http://www.cashservices.org.uk/sites/default/files/cash_cash_machines_summary_-_may_15.pdf>.

service providers meaning that retailers have had to go beyond the banks in thinking about how to address payment issues. For example, BitPay, the largest payment processor, claims that over 60,000 merchants worldwide are now accepting the bitcoin online payment system.[71]

Poor calibration might also describe those commentators who have pointed in particular to the apparently inexorable growth of mobile payment systems and their attractiveness to customers.[72] Yet no single mobile payment market exists and the proportion of mobile phone subscribers using mobile payment at all was estimated to be just 7 per cent of the user base in 2013, and to be growing more slowly than expected.[73] The majority of these were using older technologies such as text messaging. Amongst consumers, ease of use, value for money, and trust remain the three most important facilitating factors in the adoption—or not—of mobile payment technology. Oversight and regulation of mobile payments remains fragmented and complex, where it exists at all. In part, this is because of the development of isolated initiatives to suit particular markets—for example, in emerging markets such as the Philippines and Kenya, where the so-called 'unbanked' have few formal, institutionalized payment mechanisms available to them. Steps are being taken in some parts of the world to harmonize electronic payment regulation (such as the European Union's Single European Payments Area[74]).

Retailers too have their own challenges in dealing with poor cross-business awareness of different payment options and, for those businesses active in a range of markets, understanding the often very different consumer attitudes towards payment methods in those markets. This is not just a matter of distinctions between emerging and mature markets. In Germany, for example, very traditional attitudes to the use of credit by comparison with other Western European markets can be traced back to deeply ingrained beliefs about the avoidance of debt within large parts of the population. These attitudes are changing, but only slowly.[75] Data protection is also a highly politicized question in Germany. This has affected the amounts spent online by German consumers, who have tended to rely on giro cards, charge cards, or cash transactions at the door to pay for online goods. The share of cash in exchanges by volumes exceeded 80 per cent in Germany compared to 46 per

[71] <https://bitpay.com/about>.

[72] M. Isaac, 'U.S. Mobile Payments Market to Boom by 2019, Research Firm Says', 17 Nov. 2014. <http://bits.blogs.nytimes.com/2014/11/17/u-s-mobile-payments-market-to-boom-by-2019-research-firm-says>.

[73] Gartner, 'Gartner Says Worldwide Mobile Payment Transaction Value to Surpass $235 Billion in 2013', 4 June 2013. <http://www.gartner.com/newsroom/id/2504915>.

[74] <http://ec.europa.eu/finance/payments/sepa/index_en.htm>.

[75] T. Fairless, 'Germans Warm to Credit Cards—Slowly', *Wall Street Journal*, 17 Oct. 2012. <http://blogs.wsj.com/eurocrisis/2012/10/17/germans-warm-to-credit-cards-slowly>.

cent in the US in 2011–12, with only one-third of German consumers owning a credit card, although the usage of such cards has increased over the past five years.[76] This has had a direct effect on the amount spent online by German consumers, despite ingenious attempts by online retailers to avoid the need for credit card payments, by allowing consumers to use bank transfer or direct debit mechanisms. Amazon even trialled so-called 'carrier payments' in Germany with Telefónica Deutschland during 2015, through which shoppers could charge their purchases to their monthly phone bill. Whilst online payment systems are making progress, retailers must be mindful of the cultural factors that can significantly inhibit the adoption rates of new technologies by consumers.

Ubiquitous Retail Intelligence?

Gaining insight into consumers' attitudes, intentions, and behaviours has also increasingly become a matter of technology, although sometimes the rhetoric can outweigh the reality. Chapter 1 discussed the extent to which consumers themselves are much better informed about the buying choices available to them, thanks to greater transparency in product, pricing, and review information and the growth of social networks, which have encouraged consumer-to-consumer interactions and electronic word of mouth. But this is not a one-way-street. The availability of new sources of data on consumer behaviour can at least in principle be correspondingly helpful to retailers, provided that we can escape the big data rhetoric to which the retail sector, like many others, has been exposed.

Major retail enterprises are not new to large datasets. For many years, Walmart had one of the biggest commercial datasets in existence in the form of its Retail Link decision support system and associated database, launched in 1991. Aimed at providing suppliers with access to sales and inventory data, it was already 1.5 petabytes[77] in size by 2004—and today contains some 64 sextillion data points (a million raised to the power of 6, or 6.4e+22). The latest version can provide insights that are less than an hour old.[78]

[76] J. Bagnall et al., *Consumer Cash Usage: A Cross-Country Comparison with Payment Diary Survey Data*. Federal Reserve Bank of Boston Working Papers, 14-4, 2014. <http://www.bostonfed.org/economic/wp/wp2014/wp1404.pdf>.

[77] One petabyte is sufficient to store the DNA of the entire population of the US three times over and, at the time, Walmart's systems stored six times as much data online as did the Library of Congress. <http://www.computerweekly.com/feature/What-does-a-petabyte-look-like>.

[78] S. Cwinn, 'The Scoop on Retail Link 2.0', 2014. <https://www.linkedin.com/pulse/20140915154156-17222406-the-scoop-on-retail-link-2-0>.

For many, however, big data offer the possibility of obtaining real insight into retail business problems—ranging from customer insight and merchandising through to operations and supply chain. Often defined to be differentiated from more traditional datasets (no matter how big) in terms of the 'three V's'—to describe the sheer *volume, velocity,* and *variety* of data being collected or analysed—the consensus is that big data comprise exceptionally large datasets which are not susceptible to analysis using conventional software tools, or which are inherently too complex to easily reveal patterns, trends, and associations. Data on consumer behaviour and attitudes fall particularly readily into this category of data, given the proliferation of consumer analytics and social media platforms. As an example, Figure 2.3 shows the differences between online sales activity between the US and France over the past three years, derived from the analysis of billions of online sessions. Amongst other insights, the importance of January to retail sales in France and the differences around New Year's Eve with behaviour in the US are both noticeable.

The retail sector has high potential to achieve both efficiency and effectiveness improvements from the meaningful analysis of big data. As early as 2011, the McKinsey Global Institute forecast that a 60 per cent potential increase could be achieved in a typical US retailer's operating margins through the exploitation of big data, largely through annual productivity gains totalling between 0.5 and 1.0 per cent, in areas ranging from pricing optimization to customer micro segmentation.[79] Countering the argument that data had always been part and parcel of the benefits of ICT (Information and Communication Technologies) investment in retailing, McKinsey suggested that it was the capability big data presented to realign decision processes with greater agility—and even in real time—that made the real difference.

Not everyone is convinced that data of this kind are a substitute for personal interaction with customers. Writing in *Harvard Business Review* of UK retailer Tesco's recent fall from grace, MIT academic and innovation expert Michael Schrage argues that 'the harsh numbers suggest that all this data, all this analytics, all the assiduous segmentation, customization and promotion have done little for Tesco's domestic competitiveness . . . How damning; how daunting; how disturbing for any and every serious data-driven enterprise and marketer.'[80] For small- and medium-sized businesses in particular, some commentators have suggested that the resource implications and the complexity and ambiguity inherent in data of this kind may be problematic: 'for most

---

[79] McKinsey Global Institute, 'Big Data: The Next Frontier for Innovation, Competition, and Productivity', 2011. <http://www.mckinsey.com/insights/business_technology/big_data_the_next_frontier_for_innovation>.

[80] M. Schrage, 'Tesco's Downfall Is a Warning to Data-Driven Retailers', *Harvard Business Review*, 28 Oct. 2014. <https://hbr.org/2014/10/tescos-downfall-is-a-warning-to-data-driven-retailers>.

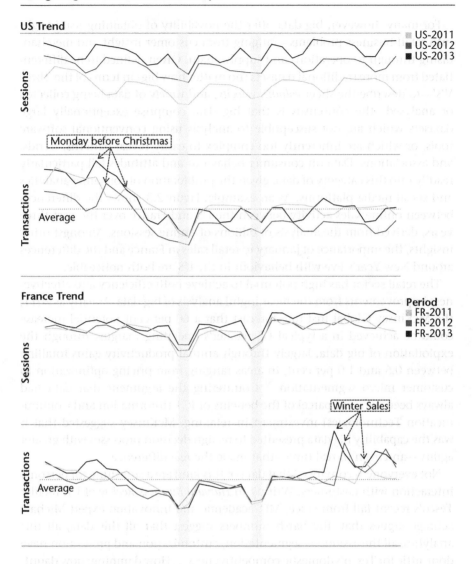

Figure 2.3 Country differences in online retail transactions

Note: Based on billions of transactions reported by authorised Google Analytics users who shared their website data anonymously. All the charts show data from December 11 to January 14 for the three years between 2011–2013, and the two vertical grey areas represent Christmas Day and New Year's Eve. http://analytics.blogspot.co.uk/2014/12/behavior-trends-and-insights.html.

Source: Google Analytics.

SMBs [Small and Medium Businesses], big data is a sham'.[81] Even for larger firms, the need for specialist analytics talent and a mindset amongst leaders that can frame the larger commercial questions to which big data analytics could potentially provide answers means that embracing big data is a challenge. Otherwise the risk is the production of superficially interesting but ultimately uncommercial insights. As renowned UK statistician the late Sir Claus Moser once famously observed, 'if a figure looks interesting, it's probably wrong'.[82] One set of risks with personal data of all kinds, but particularly with somewhat untested datasets with 'big data' characteristics, is that of shopper confidence in data security. Some recent high-profile data breaches involving customer data and household retail brand names, such as the 70 million customers affected by Target's 2013 data breach in the US, create the potential for significantly adverse impacts on confidence and sales.[83] This issue should not be under-estimated and must, of course, be guarded against as assiduously as possible.

Nevertheless, many larger retail enterprises are grappling with the implementation of actionable big data solutions across a variety of business functions. Several clothing retailers in the UK are using such data to improve conversion rates, reduce returns, and to generate high-level insights to inform business strategy, for example.[84] More specific application areas include:

- *Marketing*: There has been significant growth in sentiment analysis of crowdsourced social media content. Application areas range from the tracking of reactions to new store openings, the longer term monitoring of reputation and faster complaints handling. For example, firms such as social data intelligence company TalkWalker track positive and negative sentiment in a range of geographical retail markets.[85]

- *Merchandising and assortment*: Technology based on Bluetooth beacons or wifi-based infrastructure has been deployed to undertake in-store tracking of customers' smartphones and their dwell time, engagement, and interaction with both employees and merchandise, as well as mapping footfall. Analysts RetailNext, for example, integrate a large number of physical

---

[81] C. Porter, 'Big Data and Retail: Saviour or Sham?', *Guardian*, 6 June 2014. <http://www.theguardian.com/technology/2014/jun/06/big-data-and-retail-saviour-or-sham>.

[82] <http://en.wikiquote.org/wiki/Talk:Claus_Moser,_Baron_Moser>.

[83] S. Halzack, 'Target Data Breach Victims Could Get up to $10,000 Each from Court Settlement', *Washington Post*, 19 Mar. 2015. <http://www.washingtonpost.com/news/business/wp/2015/03/19/target-data-breach-victims-could-get-up-10000-each-from-court-settlement>.

[84] Dot.econ/Analysys Mason, *The Commercial Use of Consumer Data*, report for the Competition & Markets Authority, 2015. <https://www.gov.uk/government/uploads/system/uploads/attachment_data/file/435777/The_Commercial_Use_of_Consumer_Data_-_DotEcon_and_Analysys_Mason.pdf>.

[85] I. Ewan, 'It's All about Fashion: Who Wins Our Hearts on Social Media?', Talkwalker blog, 24 June 2015. <http://blog.talkwalker.com/en/its-all-about-fashion-who-wins-our-hearts-on-social-media>.

and digital data sources such as cameras, point of sale systems, and staff scheduling data (http://retailnext.net).[86]

- *Supply chain*: Big data within the supply chain have been used to track, model, and streamline the flow of goods. A predictive analytics technique has been patented by Amazon to precisely direct parcels that have already been broadly dispatched to a potential delivery area based on predicted demand.[87]

Some established retailers are seeking to integrate a number of these application areas within one system. Walmart's newly implemented Retail Link 2.0 offers integration with social media and data from walmart.com, moving from simply learning what customers are buying retrospectively to seeking to predict and analyse what they might want.[88] Others have seen the opportunity to develop new forms of intermediation. For example, in price comparison services, the scraping of price information from websites has led to the growth of a number of price comparison start-ups. Camelcamelcamel, founded in 2011, offers price history charts on Amazon and Best Buy products, with users being able to request alerts on price drops and availability (http://uk. camelcamelcamel.com).

Conclusion

If change in the shopper engagement landscape is at the heart of the new landscape of retailing (as we asserted in Chapter 1), then technology is the critical *enabler* of change in these landscapes. This chapter has discussed the impacts of technology on retailing in two territories: first, shopper-facing technology change and, secondly, technology change within retail enterprises. The two are, of course, strongly connected, and point to a truth that, in the new landscape of retailing, effective retail enterprises and their leaders will have to be far more technologically aware and skilled in quite different ways than they have needed to be in even the recent past. We return to this theme in Chapters 9 and 10.

The possibilities for retail enterprises to employ technology to enhance the shopper experience resolve, we suggest, into three broad territories: those that enhance either efficiency for the shopper, engagement with the shopper, or

---

[86] <http://www.fastcompany.com/3015060/heres-what-brick-and-mortar-stores-see-when-they-track-you>.

[87] <http://blogs.wsj.com/digits/2014/01/17/Amazon-wants-to-ship-your-package-before-you-buy-it>.

[88] Walmart, NYSE:WMT. 20th annual meeting for the investment community, 2013. <http://cdn.corporate.walmart.com/23/31/b2e8bf0b4197a3fedc0f0fa1d01b/analyst-meeting-2013-presentations-leverage-october-15-2013.pdf>.

the shopping experience itself. These are not, of course, mutually exclusive. Indeed, the most far-sighted retailers will be aiming to deliver on several simultaneously. Whilst it is already very old school to suggest that several product categories and many purchase behaviours amongst internet-enabled shoppers have already been transformed by the internet, the scale and reach of technology-enabled shopper change seems to us likely to accelerate very considerably in even the near-term future. The potential for hugely disruptive impacts of technologies such as augmented reality and 3D printing should most certainly not be under-estimated. But this is not a narrative of techno-logical determinism. In mid-2015, 3.1 billion people worldwide had access to the internet, but still 4.4 billion did not. It seems likely that the most import-ant divide between shoppers globally will be between those who have internet access and, therefore, broad information and choice, and those that do not. Furthermore, as technology becomes more embedded into the lives of more shoppers, so the desire for more human engagement appears to accelerate also. The more connected many shoppers become, paradoxically the more disengaged they feel themselves to be. Helpfully addressing this paradox and engaging with shoppers in very human ways is fertile territory for thoughtful retail enterprises.

Within retail enterprises themselves, be they long-established conventional retail businesses or enterprises that are relatively new entrants into the retail sector, the transformative impacts of technology are no less profound than they are in shopper-facing areas. In particular, the possibilities of so-called 'big data' initiatives to find quickly very granular, nuanced, and, above all, action-able insights into shoppers' future needs and their receptivity to different engagement approaches and messages offers considerable opportunity for many. But neither should the challenges be under-estimated. Too often technology-enabled initiatives have unanticipated and adverse consequences for the shopper. Moreover, many retail enterprises face difficult commercial choices around which pieces of their existing technology to retain, upgrade, or replace as they seek to build the enabling architecture to engage effectively with the very changed expectations of shoppers in the new landscape of retailing.

3

The Changing Physical Landscape of Retailing

Transforming Space Needs and Possibilities

The central importance of retailing as an economic activity has historically required the physical presence of retail outlets wherever there is demand from consumers. As national economies have developed, as populations have urbanized, and as consumers' expectations have become more sophisticated, so retail enterprises have sought to operate in the most convenient or appropriate places for shoppers. This has seen retail 'points of presence' established in central urban locations, in dedicated developments out of town, and in locations immediately adjacent to where shoppers live and work. Moreover, common sets of consumer needs have led to the emergence of similar physical formats worldwide, including supermarkets, convenience stores, department stores, specialty retail, and shopping malls of various configurations.

But the continued primacy of physical locations for retailing has now come into question as the ways in which shoppers choose to shop are changing in fundamental ways. Three important drivers of this change are urbanization and the attendant growth of an increasingly demanding and affluent middle class (especially in emerging markets), the impact of technology, and the effects of regulation. As a consequence, pressures are beginning to affect the traditional roles of stores and the requirements for particular formats of stores need to be revisited.

This chapter considers the implications of these changes for the physical landscape of retailing. We address in particular how retailers' space requirements are likely to change; to what extent the role of physical stores needs to be reimagined by retailers; how these roles vary by sector as well as by geography; and what is at risk for a global retail property market, which comprises a substantial proportion of the US$13.6 trillion global property market.[1]

---

[1] K. Sielewicz et al., *Money into Property Global 2014*. Chicago: DTZ, 2014.

Contemporary Drivers of Retailers' Changing Space Requirements

Urbanization

Given the historical importance of retailing as intimately associated with the physical distribution of demand, the extent of urbanization alone is having a transformational effect on the physical characteristics of retail supply. Already, over half the world's population (54 per cent) lives in urban areas, compared to just 30 per cent in 1950. By 2050, the United Nations forecasts that fully two-thirds will be urban. Alongside this startling change are two other significant phenomena with implications for retailing—the sheer scale of that growth and its distribution internationally. When set alongside population growth, the global urban population has increased from 746 million in 1950 to 3.9 billion today and is forecast to increase to 6.4 billion by 2050. Urbanization is already at much higher levels in North America (82 per cent), Latin America (80 per cent), and Europe (73 per cent) than the global average of 54 per cent. In individual countries, such as Belgium (93 per cent) and Japan (91 per cent), the figure is higher still. While urbanization will grow more slowly in the already highly urbanized regions, 90 per cent of future growth is forecast to take place in Asia and Africa, particularly India, China, and Nigeria.[2]

Inevitably, the cities that are home to these urban populations will grow significantly. However, growing urbanization does not automatically imply a simultaneous growth in so-called megacities (i.e. cities with more than 10 million inhabitants). While we may indeed see more of this size of city, demographers forecast that growth will actually be faster in medium-sized cities of between 1 million and 5 million people (Figure 3.1).

Urbanization brings with it greater affluence and a growing middle class.[3] Whilst much attention has been focused on the strong growth of luxury retailing in Asia amongst affluent urban elites, it is the middle class that is more important in driving large-scale retail consumption. There are two reasons for this: first, it is the middle classes that have disposable incomes which they are more likely to spend on durable goods and services to meet their aspirational needs and, secondly, there are simply more of them. By 2030 there is forecast to be more than 3 billion middle-class people in Asia—a close to six-fold increase from the 525 million today. The economist Homi Kharas of the Brookings Institution describes this as a 'crossover from west to east'.[4] As a result of this burgeoning growth, global middle-class consumption is

---

[2] United Nations Department for Economic Affairs, *World Urbanisation Prospects: The 2014 Revision*. <http://esa.un.org/unpd/wup/Highlights/WUP2014-Highlights.pdf>.

[3] The Brookings Institution defines the middle class as earning between US$10 and $100/day.

[4] H. Kharas, *The Emerging Middle Class in Developing Countries*. Washington, DC: Brookings Institution, 2010. <http://www.oecd.org/development/pgd/44798225.pdf>.

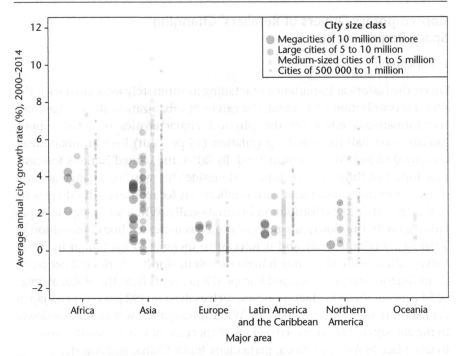

Figure 3.1 The world's fastest growing cities, 2000–14

Source: From United Nations, Department of Economic and Social Affairs, Population Division 2014. World Urbanization Prospects: The 2014 Revision, Highlights (ST/ESA/SER.A/352), © 2014 United Nations. Reprinted with the permission of the United Nations.

projected to increase from US$21 trillion in 2009 to over US$56 trillion in 2030. It is this which, more than anything else, explains why growth in (largely discretionary) non-food retailing has outgrown growth in (largely non-discretionary) grocery retailing in developing markets.[5]

The implications for physical retailing of these accelerating changes will be different in emerging and mature markets. We shall consider the possibilities for each type of market separately.

EMERGING MARKETS

The main focus of retail growth in emerging markets will naturally, but not exclusively, be on cities and other urban areas. Luxury retailers have already discovered this. Consultants McKinsey estimate that the world's top 600 cities will account for 85 per cent of the growth in luxury apparel retailing by 2025, for example.[6] But if they are to build scale, foreign retailers expanding into new markets will need to find ways of growing beyond the so-called 'first tier'

[5] Euromonitor, *Emerging Markets: Overview and Growth in Opportunities in Grocery Channels* (2014).

[6] A. Kim et al., 'The Glittering Power of Cities for Luxury Growth', McKinsey, 2014. <http://www.mckinsey.com/insights/consumer_and_retail/the_glittering_power_of_cities_for_luxury_growth>.

cities in order to secure access to the biggest middle-class urban markets. We might expect to see similar retail real estate developing in the expanding cities of Asia and Africa as we have seen in European and North American cities in the past. (This is the so-called 'convergence' hypothesis in which emerging markets follow the same course of development as the already mature markets.) These include supermarkets, hypermarkets, convenience stores, department stores, and managed shopping centres. To some extent this has already taken place. The early phases of internationalization have already seen attempts by European retailers in particular (most notably Carrefour and Tesco) to grow extensive chains of hypermarkets in South-East Asian markets. Similarly, several of the largest most recent shopping mall developments are to be found in cities in emerging markets. (At the end of 2015 the Mall of Qatar was the largest shopping centre under construction in the world. Due to open in Q3 2016, it will be 5.4 million sq.ft. in size, including 500 shops,[7] at least 25 per cent of which will be first-time brands in Qatar; and 100 food and beverage outlets.)

However, it is by no means clear that the emerging markets will, in fact, follow in the longer term identical or even broadly similar pathways in the development of their physical retailing as those in the West. In fact, we anticipate that it is more likely that they will not, owing in particular to the combined effects of two factors. First, the urban infrastructure in cities in emerging markets is characteristically very different to that of cities in the mature markets. In particular, shopping centres often have a much more important role to play as places for leisure and social engagement owing to the relative absence of other public spaces. Secondly, as we discussed in Chapter 2, the impacts of technology in the hands of shoppers creates very different engagement possibilities for retailers beyond physical stores. It seems likely that these will be at least as, and very possibly still more, disruptive in the emerging markets as they will be in Europe and North America, given the great appetite for shoppers in the emerging markets to quickly embrace new technologies, especially mobile platforms.

Greater urbanization may also bring with it greater emphasis on smaller format, more convenient retailing. This may well be accelerated by the fact that investment in transport infrastructure often lags behind the population growth of large cities in many emerging markets. (GPS maker Tom Tom rated Istanbul, Mexico City, and Rio de Janeiro as the world's three most congested cities in 2014. A commute in Istanbul that should take 30 minutes in fact takes on average twice as long (59 minutes), leading to an extra 125 hours wasted stuck in traffic every year.[8]) Furthermore, car ownership levels

---

[7] <http://www.mallofqatar.com.qa/en/shop.aspx>.
[8] <http://www.tomtom.com/en_gb/trafficindex/#>.

look likely to remain lower per capita than in developed markets in the medium term. Moreover, behavioural changes related to the increasing availability of online shopping alternatives and the congestion caused by such rapid urbanization could constrain growth sooner than has been the case in high-income economies.[9] This may well accelerate the growth of e-commerce long before physical retailing has reached the levels of maturity seen in the mature Western markets. Nigeria is a case in point. Here, the fast-growing online retailer Jumia delivers 'to every corner and address in Nigeria' and encourages shoppers to shop with Jumia because there is 'no traffic, no queues'.[10] (Unfortunately, Tom Tom do not include Nigeria in their study of journey times and congestion but an academic study of traffic congestion in Nigeria noted: 'It is not uncommon for commuters to spend more than two hours en route to work, school, market, hospital etc or back home even when to and fro distance is not much.'[11]) Remember too that, in many emerging markets, a high proportion of their urban populations is young, affluent, and no less information rich and technologically literate than their counterparts in the mature economies.

What of the rural hinterlands in emerging markets? Rural India is a notable example of an environment in which rural consumers are becoming wealthier and more aspirational too. Sixty-nine per cent of India's population is rural. Global information company Nielsen talks about the emergence in India of a new rural 'super consumer' that, 'forms the elite of rural India. A group that has better purchasing power, a propensity to premiumise and the ability to influence the rest of the community.'[12] The real estate consequences of this trend are multi-layered. These consumers still shop locally for low-involvement goods, but—in a culture where 'where you buy something is as important as what you buy'—higher involvement goods (notably consumer durables, electronics, and apparel) are bought from the nearest mall. Nearly every adult (99 per cent) has a scooter and one in five has a car.[13] Retailers and FMCG companies need a good deal of creativity and imagination to successfully introduce new brands to these markets. Consultant Mamta Kapur and colleagues give the example of multi-sector business

[9] OECD/ITF, *ITF Transport Outlook 2015*. Paris: OECD Publishing/ITF, 2015.

[10] <http://www.jumia.com.ng/why-shop-jumia>.

[11] Benjamin O. Uwadiegwu, 'Factors Responsible for Traffic Congestion in Nigeria: A Case Study of Mayor Bus Stop and Coal Camp along Agbani Road in Enugu City, Nigeria', *Journal of Environment and Earth Science*, 3(3) (2013), 71–8.

[12] Nielsen, *The Rise of India's Rural Super Consumer*, 2014. <http://www.nielsen.com/content/dam/corporate/in/docs/reports/2014/nielsen-report-the-rise-of-indias-rural-super-consumer.pdf>.

[13] Nielsen's subset of 'rural super consumers' are drawn four agriculture driven states—Andhra Pradesh, Maharashtra, Gujarat, and Punjab—and covered only opinion leaders or influential villagers belonging to SEC A and B (rural India) and residing in the most agriculturally progressive districts, zones, and villages.

ITC (an Indian conglomerate), and its three-pronged approach to FMCG distribution in rural areas, developed in relation to size of market:

- *10,000–20,000 population:* small-scale sub-distributors carry a smaller range of products oriented around local preferences;
- *5,000–10,000 population:* vans bypass distributors and directly supply local retailers. The retailers use mobile phones to place orders which are delivered up to three times a week;
- *less than 5,000 population:* scooters or three-wheel vehicles deliver to retail kiosks.[14]

MATURE MARKETS

The real estate challenges arising from urbanization and its related effects are very different in mature economies. Here, urbanization is already at high levels and cities already play a major role for retailers. The positive effect of a more affluent middle class has, however, been balanced out—at least partially and often wholly—by the economic shocks that have affected developed economies in particular over the past ten years. Counter-urbanization has also been a feature of some European markets, where households can afford to relocate outside cities for reasons to do with lifestyle choice, although this has reversed in recent years in the UK.[15]

In terms of personal mobility, some developed markets have also witnessed real declines in car usage and ownership. This is true of Japan since 1999 and the UK since 2007 (Figure 3.2). Furthermore, this trend is particularly pronounced amongst young adults, especially males. In part, this may be related to the cyclical impacts of economic downturn and the rising cost of operating a car (as opposed to buying one in the first place). However, as we have discussed already in Chapter 1, there is certainly evidence to suggest that this trend is structural and linked to fundamental changes in attitudes and lifestyles.

In terms of retail real estate, mature market shoppers are generally spoiled for choice. The density of nearly all modern retail formats per household, at least at the national level, is significantly higher in most mature markets than elsewhere. In the US, 79 per cent of the total population lived within a mile of a supermarket in 2014. For the most densely populated areas (comprising 30 per cent of residential areas), this figure was as high as 98 per cent.[16]

---

[14] M. Kapur et al., 'Unlocking the Wealth in Rural Markets', *Harvard Business Review*, 92(6) (June 2014), 113–17.

[15] T. Champion, *People in Cities: The Numbers*. London: Government Office for Science, 2014. <https://www.gov.uk/government/uploads/system/uploads/attachment_data/file/321814/14-802-people-in-cities-numbers.pdf>.

[16] P. Wilde et al., 'Population Density, Poverty, and Food Retail Access in the United States: An Empirical Approach', *International Food and Agribusiness Management Review*, 17(Special Issue A) (2014), 171–86.

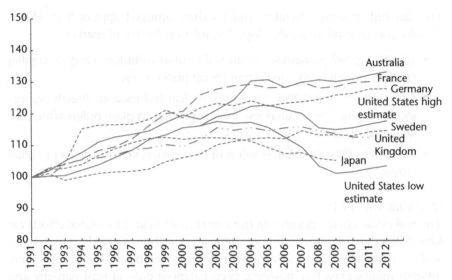

Figure 3.2 Passenger kilometres by private car, selected countries, 1991–2012

Source: OECD. 2015. Passenger-kilometres by private car: 1991 = 100, in ITF Transport Outlook 2015, OECD Publishing, Paris. DOI: http://dx.doi.org/10.1787/9789282107782-graph11-en.

But maturity comes with a price. Mature markets are also characterized by high levels of competition and the legacy effects of large amounts of prior investment. The shopping centre stock in the US is extensive at over 7.4 billion sq.ft. in 2014, or 23.7 sq.ft. per capita. The sector's historic peak development years followed the extensive suburbanization of population. At one point over 140 malls were opening every year. But by their very nature, also, such complex real estate assets take time to bring on stream and can also be slow to adjust to rapid external pressures for change: there is often a substantial lag effect to changes affecting the scale and characteristics of demand. The suburbanization of the US population has slowed very appreciably while, simultaneously, an ageing population has found greater security ageing in the places where they have lived for a long time. Millennials, too, have favoured staying in central town and city locations. Nielsen observed: 'Breaking from previous generations' ideals, this group's "American Dream" is transitioning from the white picket fence in the suburbs to the historic brownstone stoop in the heart of the city.'[17]

More restrictive regulatory constraints are also affecting the size and location of physical development in many mature markets. Many Western European jurisdictions are seeking to protect the viability of existing town and

[17] Nielsen Newswire, 'Millennials Prefer Cities to Suburbs, Subways to Driveways', 4 Mar. 2014. <http://www.nielsen.com/us/en/insights/news/2014/millennials-prefer-cities-to-suburbs-subways-to-driveways.html>.

city centres by redirecting retail investment into these locations and resisting out-of-town growth. However, many traditional town and city centres have complex historic ownership structures, inflexible rental structures, and multiple stakeholder interests, all of which makes rapid change hard to execute.

Technology

Our discussion in Chapters 1 and 2 highlighted how technology is reshaping the ways in which shoppers interact with retail enterprises. Not surprisingly, this is having a direct impact on the physical landscape of the sector as high proportions of shoppers quickly develop a greater appetite to use online in their shopping activity, if not wholly then at least in part. Technology change is putting pressure on the extent, physical location, and configuration of retail real estate, as well as on its performance. At its most extreme, technology is disintermediating the physical retailer altogether because of the effects of product digitization. But in many categories, particularly where the influence of online is strong, retailers are already exploring complementary roles for the store as well as for shopping centres in a larger engagement ecosystem. Furthermore, wholly new kinds of real estate are developing to meet the new needs of shoppers and retailers.

PRODUCT DIGITIZATION

In a number of categories, the transformation of the product itself from physical to digital form has already had profound implications for retail enterprises that have previously sold the tangible versions of products. Recorded music, movies, books, and news media are all cases in point. For example, 46 per cent of the global recording industry's US$15 billion 2014 revenues came from digital sales compared to just 11 per cent in 2005. In three of the world's top ten markets (the US, UK, and Germany), digital channels account for the majority of music revenues.[18] Despite this, revenue growth from digital sales (downloads and subscriptions) has failed to match the decline in physical formats over the past ten years because of the falling price of digital tracks. In consequence, the major retail chains active in the music category have largely exited physical space in developed markets and sales of physical music formats have become increasingly restricted to independent traders. In the UK, for example, there were only just over 400 record and CD specialty stores left trading in 2013.[19] A poignant endorsement of independent record shops can be seen in the movie, *Last Shop Standing*,[20]

---

[18] *IFPI Digital Music Report 2015*. <http://www.ifpi.org/downloads/Digital-Music-Report-2015.pdf>.
[19] According to the Local Data Company <www.localdatacompany.com>.
[20] <http://lastshopstanding.com>.

although a so-called 'vinyl revival' has been a feature of a number of western markets over the past few years.

In categories such as newspapers, where stores have relied on daily visits to exploit cross-selling opportunities, the growth of online news media market share has served to seriously undermine store sales and profitability. The impact of digitization has not yet been as extensive in bookselling as many had anticipated when Kindle, Nook, and other e-readers were widely expected to replace traditional books entirely or nearly entirely. In fact, the number of e-books purchased in the UK increased from one-in-five to one-in-four of all books between 2012 and 2013. However, this relatively modest shift in unit sales masks the greater financial impact of the reader's migration from physical to digital, which has particularly affected commercial fiction titles.[21]

There is every reason to believe that we are today only in the early stages of the digitization of more product categories. We can certainly envisage the process going further in other categories such as clothing and, whilst 3D printing is still some years away from creating palatable food, the erosive effects of product digitization on the extent and nature of store networks is a one-way street, with potentially profound implications in the longer term. We discussed potential impacts of 3D printing on the retail sector in Chapter 2. In the longer term it is entirely possible to conceive that for some retailers a significant proportion of their business will migrate to selling software templates that shoppers then turn into products, rather than the products themselves. With far less inventory and with responsive production, stores can be far smaller. In fact, stores may not be required at all if shoppers are not browsing merchandise, but rather downloading designs: a democratization of production. Further, 3D scanners can permit the increasingly effective reproduction of existing objects. Neither should this be considered fanciful in our view, given the extraordinary transformations that 3D printing is enabling in such areas as medicine, aerospace, and construction. In 2014, a Chinese construction firm printed ten houses in Shanghai in less than a day at a cost of under £3,000 per house using a 3D printer 32 metres long, 10 metres wide, and almost 7 metres high.[22] In Amsterdam, the Dutch architecture practice DUS has built a full-size '3D Print Canal House' as a (very beautiful) exploration into the possibilities of 3D printed buildings.[23] Is it possible to imagine stores and shopping centres being 3D printed at some point in the future as either permanent or semi-permanent 'pop-up' structures? In fact, it's impossible not to.

---

[21] A. Flood, 'Sales of Printed Books Fall by More than £150m in Five Years', *Guardian*, 13 Jan. 2015. <http://www.theguardian.com/books/2015/jan/13/sales-printed-books-fell-150m-five-years>.

[22] <http://www.ft.com/cms/s/2/66684078-e58a-11e3-a7f5-00144feabdc0.html#axzz3Afhb5qOr>.

[23] <http://www.dusarchitects.com/projects.php?categorieid=housing>.

E-COMMERCE AND THE ROLE OF THE PHYSICAL RETAIL STORE

In categories and markets where e-commerce sales have taken channel share, or where non-store platforms play an important role in shoppers' buying decisions, retailers must understand how the physical retail store needs to evolve if it is to remain relevant and valued in a very different competitive context. We say 'evolve', since both consumers and retailers are presently experimenting with new ways of obtaining and delivering retail services even in those markets where non-store sales or influence are furthest advanced. We explore this theme more fully in Chapter 7's discussion of the possibilities for retailers to reimagine the role of the physical store in a digital age.

The critical question is how do shoppers expect to be able to shop? To explore this, OXIRM (Oxford Institute of Retail Management at the University of Oxford's Saïd Business School) undertook research in 2014 with 21,000 shoppers across twenty European national markets with real estate services firm CBRE. The research confirmed that shoppers in all of these geographies are increasingly comfortable, albeit to varying degrees, with juggling a range of channels in the research and buying processes, but that store visits still dominate when they are buying non-food products. Nearly 90 per cent of shoppers reported that they would normally visit a shopping centre as part of making a non-food purchase. However, a significant minority of between 11 and 22 per cent were using tablets and smartphones at all stages in the buying process. Shoppers reported that they already conduct an average of seven 'click and collect' shops a year (rising to nine times a year if their most often visited shopping centre was a large, covered one).[24]

This research also asked shoppers how they expected their shopping behaviours to change in the future. Here, there was greater uncertainty. Nearly one in five (18 per cent) shoppers across all markets anticipated using stores less in the next two years. But while this broad direction of travel was clear, the devil was, as ever, in the detail. For example, there were substantial differences by geography where a broad north-west/south-east divide was evident across the European countries (Figure 3.3). There was also a high proportion of respondents (20 per cent for smart phones users and 24 per cent for tablets) who did not yet know how their mobile devices would be used to support their shopping activity in two years' time, but were confident that they would be used in some way. If shoppers themselves are at present unclear how they will be shopping in the future, it will clearly be difficult for retailers to precisely determine the future shape of their real estate needs. Global retail property agents Lunson Mitchenall note that, 'We have learnt that second guessing

---

[24] CBRE, 'How Consumers Shop 2014'. Research conducted for CBRE by the Oxford Institute of Retail Management.

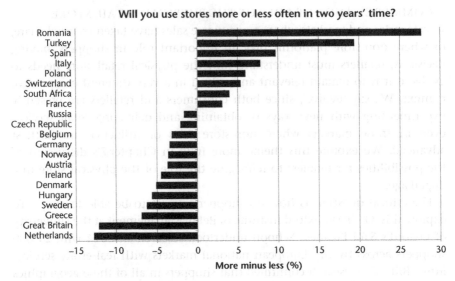

Figure 3.3 Will you use stores more or less often in two years' time?
Source: OXIRM, CBRE, 2014. Question related to non-food stores only.

what retailers will want in the future is a fool's game, as not even they fully understand where technology is taking them.'[25] We explore in Part 2 of this book how retail enterprise leaders can effectively lead their businesses in environments that are characterized by great uncertainty.

This degree of variability and uncertainty does indeed make spelling out the direct consequences of technology on retail real estate more problematic. The kind of responsiveness likely to be required is also a challenge given the inertia inherent in real estate investment and development. What is clear, however, is that in the absence of more customers, retailers must 'cut their cloth to suit' and adapt the ways in which they supply retail services in the context of an increase in channels to market. For many, this may very well mean making substantial reductions to their real estate portfolios: exiting as much as three-quarters of their current store portfolios could be the right solution for some.

Such dramatic restructuring has very considerable implications for those tasked with planning and maintaining the vitality of urban centres where, historically, retailing has often been the dominant land-use element and certainly the most visible. The message for policy-makers in mature retail markets is clear: it should not be assumed that retailers will continue to be the main occupiers of real estate, nor should retail enterprises be relied upon to

[25] Lunson Mitchenall, 'Fit for the Future: How Shopping Centres are Adapting to Change', 1 Sept. 2014. <http://www.lunson-mitchenall.co.uk/fit-for-the-future-how-shopping-centres-are-adapting-to-change>.

provide the vitality and diversity (nor indeed the revenue flows through tax-ation and rental income) that is so essential to the continued viability of urban centres. Other users will have to be encouraged into urban centres to fill the (very sizeable) gaps left by retailers as they 'right size' their portfolios—downwards. This is not, however, to suggest that retailers are not going to be opening any more stores or that no retailers will want to have any presence in central urban areas. Clearly neither is true. But it must be recognized by policy-makers and planners that in the new landscape of retailing the character of urban areas is going to be substantially reshaped in often very challenging ways. The example of Helsinki, Finland, is instructive and illustra-tive of many other urban centres. Jyrki Karjalainen, Director of Real Estate for the S-Group (Finland's largest retailer) comments that: 'The city plans regulat-ing urban development are generally leaning towards more density and urban living, and we also need to comply with them and smaller lots. In the future we'll be seeing more shopping centers that combine retail and apartments.'[26]

An appropriate and extreme response for some retailers is to close the phys-ical chain altogether. Accompanying the closure of Jessops, the UK camera retailer, in 2013 was a sign in one branch's window which read: 'The staff at Jessops would like to thank you for shopping with amazon' (Figure 3.4). There are more thoughtful alternatives also, however. In becoming omni-channel retailers, established retail enterprises with store portfolios must now consider how their stores can support and complement their online offer, or compete with that of others, through the provision of additional services. Such services can be of broadly two kinds: functional and experiential.

FUNCTIONAL SERVICES

Perhaps the most widely explored aspect of the role extension for stores is in relation to the provision of complementary functional services to meet the customer's need for convenience. Most obviously, these have focused upon distribution services. The use of retail real estate as fulfilment points is an obvious opportunity for store-based retailers with excess space. Indeed, in markets such as the US and UK, click-and-collect services have increasingly become the default ordering and fulfilment model. In 2015 there were already 500,000 click-and-collect locations in Europe, an increase of 25 per cent over the previous year[27] (Table 3.1). In-store or non-home collection also has the advantage for the retailer of being cheaper than home delivery since delivery is made to a relatively

---

[26] Quoted in T. Hämäläinen, 'K+S Urbanism: Will Megaretailers Kesko and S-Group Ever Think Outside the Box?', *From Rurban to Urban: Reinventing the Finnish City*, 2015. <http://urbanfinland.com/2015/03/11/will-kesko-and-s-group-ever-think-outside-the-box>.

[27] Deloitte, *Click and Collect Booms in Europe*, 2015. <http://www2.deloitte.com/content/dam/Deloitte/global/Documents/Technology-Media-Telecommunications/gx-tmt-pred15-click-collect-europe.pdf>.

Figure 3.4 Store-based retailers and the online challenge
Source: © ChefJonGay, 2013. https://twitter.com/ChefJonGay/status/291282332986511361/photo/1

Table 3.1 European landscape for click-and-collect services, 2015

Mode	Description	Estimated number
In-store	Includes parking lots.	37,000
Third	In shopping centres or post offices or newsagents; dedicated sites may include changing rooms.	129,000
Lockers	On commuter routes, in post offices or rail stations.	335,000

Source: Predictions made by Deloitte, 2015 in Deloitte, Click and Collect Booms in Europe, <http://www2.deloitte.com/content/dam/Deloitte/global/Documents/Technology-Media-Telecommunications/gx-tmt-pred15-click-collect-europe.pdf>.

smaller number of points from which the shopper then collects their purchase. In France, for example, by the middle of 2015 there were 2,600 drive-through grocery pickup points and shared outlet warehouses.[28]

---

[28] S. Briand, 'Auchan, Carrefour, Leclerc…Comment le drive a explosé en France', Challenges blog, 22 June 2015. <http://www.challenges.fr/entreprise/20150622.CHA7203/auchan-carrefour-leclerc-comment-le-drive-a-explose-en-france.html>.

A number of these services in some markets are managed by third-party organizations. The Collect Plus network in the UK, for example, includes over 5,800 newsagents, convenience stores, supermarkets, and petrol stations, as well as shopping centres. Westfield's London Stratford shopping centre has a Click & Collect concierge service, managed by Collect Plus on behalf of over 240 outlets in the centre, and which offers fitting rooms, an hour's free parking, and free refreshments. 'Click and collect' provides a solution to the reluctance or inability of traditional retailers to carry the additional costs of home delivery and counters the inconvenience to the consumer of staying in to receive a delivery. It may, however, prove to be a transient phase in the development of fulfilment services. The use of geolocation technology and widespread penetration of smartphones may ultimately make 'bring it to me' services far more attractive to the shopper in the longer run. Numerous trials—discussed in Chapter 8—are under way, using different technologies and fulfilment providers to deliver to the shopper orders which have been made online. It seems unlikely that any one model alone will prevail. But what does seem entirely likely is that we will see in the near-term future the development of still more innovative fulfilment options which do not rely upon existing store networks.

EXPERIENTIAL SERVICES

A further response to the impact of technology is for retail stores and shopping centres to accentuate those aspects of their activity that cannot be so easily emulated online. Most importantly, this focuses either on the provision of personalized services or the creation of physical experiential environments or both. Examples are legion. Hobbycraft in the UK provides craft events and training; women's fitness clothing retailer Sweaty Betty offers free fitness classes; and Apple Retail provides educational services ranging from in-store training to summer camps for children. Shopping centre developer Westfield introduced a Fashion Lounge into its London Stratford centre in 2014, where shoppers can book time with a personal stylist in a self-contained suite.

Much attention has been given to the notion of retailing as 'theatre' and stores as places for delivering immersive and entertaining experiences. *The Economist* is right to remind us that 'Shopping is about entertainment as well as acquisition. It allows people to build desires as well as fulfil them—if it did not, no one would ever window-shop. It encompasses exploration and frivolity, not just necessity. It can be immersive, too. While computer screens can bewitch the eye, a good shop has four more senses to ensorcell [bewitch].'[29] In Chapter 7 we present a short case study on the remodelling of Hankyu's department store in Osaka,

---

[29] *The Economist*, 'The Emporium Strikes Back', 13 July 2013.

Japan, which provides a compelling example of the way an established retailer can revitalize what is at heart a very traditional retail format.

NEW KINDS OF RETAIL REAL ESTATE

The third way in which technology affects the space requirements of retailers is by creating demand for new kinds of retail real estate. Three examples illustrate the point:

(1) Argos, the UK catalogue retailer, has long used its real estate in different ways than the rest of the sector, as our case study in Chapter 8 makes clear. The company's transformation plan will see substantial repurposing of the role of property. Three new store formats were launched in 2014/15:

    (i) up to 200 'digital' stores, converted from the original format, in which shoppers' physical/digital interactions can be more easily accommodated;

    (ii) a smaller concession format within the parent company's home improvement stores as well as in selected Sainsbury's supermarkets;

    (iii) A number of even smaller format stores, starting with a collection unit at London's Cannon Street underground station.[30]

(2) While the UK's Kingfisher Group's B&Q big-box home improvement retail business anticipates closing 15 per cent of its space between 2015 and 2016 it is nevertheless adding sixty new omni-channel Screwfix trade counters and launching the Screwfix format in Germany.[31]

(3) One of the most exciting areas of retail real estate investment lies in specialist logistics, where highly specialized property is being developed to support the needs of more integrated omni-channel retailing. The development of online retailing is estimated to have been responsible for 60 per cent of leasing activity in the Dutch logistics-related real estate market and as much as 40 per cent in Germany, Spain, Russia, and the UK.[32] Commercial property services firm JLL puts the take-up of logistics space dedicated to online fulfilment across Europe in 2013 as in the order of 1 million sq.ft.—an increase of 10 per cent over the previous year.[33]

---

[30] Home Retail Group. 2015. Investor Pack, May 2015. <https://www.homeretailgroup.com/media/268370/investor_pack_may_2015.pdf>.

[31] Kingfisher plc. 2015. Prelims and Strategy Update 2015.<http://www.kingfisher.com/files/presentations/2015/prelim15/2015_prelim_presentation.pdf>.

[32] R. Holberton, 'Online Retailing: Impacts, Challenges and Opportunities for European Logistics Markets', *CBRE EMEA ViewPoint*, Dec. 2012.

[33] JLL, *European Logistics and Industrial Investment Market Review*, 2014. <http://www.jll.eu/emea/en-gb/Documents/Capital-markets/Logistics_Industrial_CM_Report_FINAL.pdf>.

The combined effects of technology on conventional retail real estate have been to put pressure on its performance and, therefore, on the profitability of the retail enterprises that operate this space. Investing in complementary facilities such as click and collect, finding more ways of adding experiences into stores, or improving levels of service all add cost. In mid-2015 the UK's John Lewis department store group announced that their highly successful click and collect service would no longer be provided as an entirely free service and that shoppers would instead incur a flat charge of £2 per order of £30 or less, while orders over £30 would continue to be free. Commenting on this change, John Lewis's Managing Director, Andy Street, said that, 'We are sure customers will understand why we are doing this. There is a huge logistical operation behind this system and quite frankly it's unsustainable.'[34] And yet, in the most affected markets, lower sales and profit per square foot/metre have not always been matched by any equivalent reduction in costs of labour or property taxes. The profitability of much retail space is now under extreme pressure. McKinsey estimated that for the typical US retailer, assuming a 5 per cent decline in sales per square foot every year over five years, and without intervention, EBIT (earnings before interest and taxes) would decline by 28 per cent over the period, and return on capital invested would fall by nearly one-third.[35] This reality is a further compelling reason why many, perhaps most, retailers with extensive store networks must look as a matter of urgency at ways to trade more intensively and profitably from existing space; to reconfigure and 'right size' individual stores, and, very probably, exit large amounts of space which is no longer useful and viable and cannot be made profitable.

Regulation

The third driver affecting the scale, nature, and distribution of retail real estate is that of regulation. Such is the centrality of retailing to economies and societies that regulators have taken considerable and increasing interest in both its location and the impact of its trading activity. A broad variety of regulatory interventions have both direct and indirect effects on the physical landscape of the sector. The OECD monitors regulatory conditions in the professional services and retail distribution sectors. Their retail indicators cover barriers to entry, operational restrictions, and price controls.

According to the OECD, the most regulated retail sectors are to be found in European countries, with Belgium and Luxembourg especially highly regulated (Figure 3.5). Across Europe there are many policies at the member state

---

[34] <http://www.theguardian.com/business/2015/jul/01/john-lewis-to-charge-for-click-and-collect>.
[35] McKinsey, 'Making Stores Matter in A Multi-channel World', *McKinsey Quarterly* (Summer 2014), 1–11.

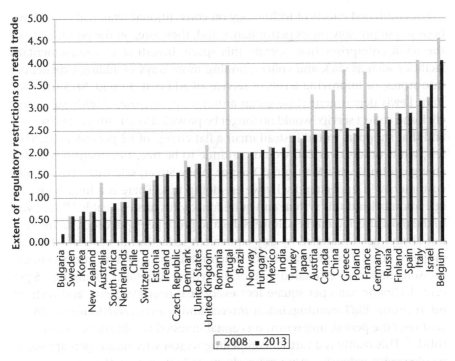

Figure 3.5 Regulatory conditions in retailing: selected countries, 2008 and 2013

Note: Index scale 0 to 6 from least to most restrictive.

Source dataset name: OECD Sector regulation indicators database.

Data source: http://www.oecd.org/eco/reform/indicatorsofproductmarketregulationhomepage.htm#Sources.

Accessed on: 14th August, 2015.

level that are deliberately designed to constrain the development of some physical forms of retailing. This is especially true of the hypermarket sector. Such stores, combining broad assortments of food and general merchandise, are often considered by regulators to have undesirable effects on the locations in which they trade, especially in terms of competitive impacts on other stores and on the viability of traditional urban centres (given their location in edge and out of town locations especially). As a result, some governments—particularly in Western Europe—look at towns and cities more defensively, often seeking to shore up existing investments in retail real estate, and acting in more control-ling ways, further reducing retailers' room for manoeuvre.

In many emerging markets, the principal regulatory driver has historically been a desire to protect domestic retail interests from foreign competition. FDI (Foreign Direct Investment) rules in India, recently relaxed to an extent, provide an interesting example of this. Whether or not to allow multi-brand foreign retailers to take majority ownership of stores became a substantial political football and was only finally permitted by a Congress-led government in 2012. (It is interesting to note that the present party in government, the BJP, despite opposing FDI at the time, has not so far rescinded the legislation.[36]) But sometimes concerns over the socio-economic impact of Western retailing formats have led governments, particularly in emerging markets, to intervene more directly in the physical landscape of retail. For example, the 1Malaysia brand is part of the Malaysian Government's 'people first' initiative introduced in 2010.[37] In addition to promoting 1Malaysia own brands, the government has promoted the growth of a mini-mart format targeted at urban low-income households and which emphasizes providing for consumers' basic food needs. Staples such as oil and rice, in smaller pack sizes, are procured from Malaysian SMEs. The business is operated by the Malaysian MYDIN chain, as an explicit part of its CSR activity.

Regulators have yet to catch up with many of the distinctive features of non-store retail operations. In Europe, the provisions of a digital single market are about sweeping away many regulations that exist at the member state level and work to slow down or prevent the free flow of online services across European boundaries. This liberalization is specifically focused on e-commerce. The European Commission argues that while 44 per cent of shoppers bought online within their own domestic market in 2014, only 15 per cent bought online from other EU countries. It calculates that shoppers could save over US$13 billion (€11.7 billion) if they had access to a full range of EU goods and services.[38]

Consequences for the Physical Landscape of Retailing

We have suggested that the combined effects of urbanization, technology, and regulation are changing profoundly the physical landscape of retailing. The interaction and relative importance of these principal drivers of change is giving rise to much altered retail landscapes in different countries and in different retail sectors.

We discuss here three examples of the broad strategic response of the retail industry: the growth in the need for convenience, the repurposing of the hypermarket, and the implications for shopping centres.

[36] Press Trust of India, 'Government Retains 51% FDI in Multi-Brand Retail, Which BJP Had Opposed', 13 May 2015. <http://www.ndtv.com/india-news/government-retains-51-fdi-in-multi-brand-retail-which-bjp-had-opposed-762655>.
[37] <http://www.1malaysia.com.my>.
[38] European Commission, 'Why we Need a Digital Single Market', 2015. <http://ec.europa.eu/digital-agenda/en/digital-single-market>.

The Rise and Rise of Convenience Retailing

Convenience store, or proximity, retailing internationally continues to demonstrate much greater flexibility and resilience than many other formats, largely as a result of urbanization and lifestyle drivers. This form of retailing appears to be one of the big winners in real estate terms across geographical markets, although positioning and execution varies to a considerable extent:

- In Hong Kong, the 7-Eleven chain operates over 900 convenience stores to serve a population of 7 million located within a predominantly urban territory of just 426 square miles. This equates to one convenience store for every 7,600 citizens. Despite the high costs of operation (with some stores commanding nearly US$1,900 per sq.ft. per month in rental) 7-Eleven trades profitably thanks to relentless innovation in space productivity, innovation in consumer services to meet daily needs, and a willingness to explore trading in any location, including MTR stations, hospitals, universities, and tourist hubs.[39] As Tim Chalk said, when he was Managing Director of 7-Eleven in Hong Kong, 'find a site and I'll find a format'.

- By contrast, in Russia, the Magnit chain has exploited the growth of smaller third-tier cities, where modern retail store formats are largely absent. Where 40 per cent of the family budget is spent on food, Magnit operates over 8,300 simple and straightforward small c-stores of 320 m^2 selling space in over 2,000 cities, with simple layouts and a strong everyday low price positioning.[40]

- In metropolitan Lagos (population 21 million), the biggest city in Nigeria, the growth of convenience stores such as Addide and Valumart (owned by Walmart subsidiary Massmart) has been faster than that of larger formats. This is taking place because smaller convenience stores are able to exploit the high densities of low- and middle-income shoppers to be found in the second fastest growing city in Africa, but with poor infrastructure to support supply chains for large-scale retail formats.

Nor are responses to shoppers' desire for convenience limited to food retailing. IKEA, one of the global icons of large-store retailing, has, in fact, experimented with small-store formats for a number of years, starting with its miniature 750 m^2 shop in 1990s Manhattan, which featured a rotating sample of products available in its larger stores. The opening of its 18,000 m^2 German 'Citystore' in 2014, however, represented a more deliberate attempt to create a more convenient urban offer, with every second visitor expected to arrive

---

[39] T. Chalk, '7–11 in Hong Kong & Macau', presentation to Association of Convenience Stores summit, Birmingham, Apr. 2013.

[40] Magnit, Investor presentation. <http://www.magnit-info.ru/upload/iblock/3ad/3ade588a 8c5e92ccdedb6eb7245ae7a4.pdf>. Data as at Dec. 2014.

by public transport. In mid-2015, IKEA announced its intention to trial in the UK a smaller format of around 2,000 m^2 that will be part order and collect facility and part inspirational studio where shoppers can plan complex purchases such as kitchens. This is part of a global small-store initiative for IKEA with other pilot stores planned in Europe and Scandinavia. As IKEA's UK Country Retail Manager, Gillian Drakeford, said of the trial, 'We need to start testing [different store models]. That is one of the areas where many UK retailers have been at the forefront and now it's IKEA's turn to do that.'[41] Other categories are experimenting with proximity too. In the UK alone, these range from cycling (Halfords' Cycle Republic chain), home improvement (Kingfisher's fast-growing Screwfix trade counter format, now trading in the UK and Germany), pet supplies (e.g. Pets at Home's new Barkers dog care format) and tile retailing (such as Topps Tiles' smaller boutique format).

The Death of the Hypermarket?

By contrast with small-space convenience stores, prospects for large-space, broad-assortment hypermarkets appear mixed at best. In many emerging markets, especially in Latin America and South-East Asia, the format has been the mainstay of much recent modern retail expansion. In Indonesia, for example, there is still extensive growth of the format in a highly competitive market. Local operators Matahari, PT Trans Retail (which acquired Carrefour's interests in 2012), and Hong Kong-based Dairy Farm, trading as Giant, are all expanding their hypermarket operations, especially in eastern Java and northern Sumatra. In India, while modern retailing's market share is still very low, the major domestic modernizers such as Bharti, Future Retail, and D'Mart still plan to grow their hypermarket space. However, even in Asia, notably China and India, saturation in primary cities and strong competition from compact supermarkets, convenience stores, and online is challenging the format.

The situation is rather different in the mature markets of Europe and North America. Here, markets are more saturated with hypermarket space; the format has been affected much earlier by both online competition creating an impact on the general merchandise component of the hypermarket offer, as well as by the growth of price competition from limited line discount grocery retail formats. In the UK, this combination of pressures has led to all the major operators substantially scaling back their previous expansion plans, disposing of extensive land banks, and even cancelling openings of already fully built new stores. The amount of new grocery space under construction in the UK fell by fully 20 per cent in just one year since the end of 2013. Some commentators speak in

---

[41] M. Chapman, 'Ikea to Pilot Range of Small-Format Stores', *Retail Week*, 26 June 2015, 3.

apocalyptic terms about the prospects for the sector: 'the changes we are seeing in grocery markets currently are the most fundamental in a generation'.[42]

Attempts to revitalize the format are being focused in particular on adding more services into the offer and creating destination environments that shoppers will be motivated to visit in an environment where they no longer need to. Tesco's efforts to revitalize the format are a case in point. The company's UK Managing Director, Chris Bush, set out the nature of the challenge when he said that, 'In the past, large hypermarkets were popular because they offered a massive range of products and people liked being able to buy everything under one roof—it made life easier. The internet has changed all that—people don't even need to leave their homes to go shopping and more people are using convenience stores for regular top-up shops.'[43] Two of Tesco's new UK large-store openings in 2015 included free community spaces for local groups, family-friendly cafes and restaurants, hair salons, cookery classes, gyms, and soft play areas for children.[44]

Similarly, in France, much attention is being focused on the future of the hypermarket. This is not surprising given that it was in France that the format was first developed. Carrefour's Chairman and CEO Georges Plassat does not believe the format is in inevitable decline, but rather it needs to do better in meeting customer's changing expectations. For him, the contemporary hypermarket 'has become a big convenience store' as it leads with deeper food ranges, good prices, and (crucially) local adaptation, combined with online integration.[45] To this end, the renovation and repositioning of the format continues. Carrefour's new store in Auteuil, Paris, opened in March 2014 with substantial local adaptation in terms of range of products and services, with the objective of meeting the needs of the upscale clientele of the 16th arrondissement. Carrefour's Auteuil store is, in its early days, one of the best performing in Carrefour's network and is an example of the business's efforts to revitalize both the hypermarket format and its own performance through a 'multi-local' strategy which emphasizes local adaptation rather than slavish conformity across all stores.

Will such initiatives prove sufficient to re-energize the format in the mature markets? No one can, in truth, be entirely sure. But certainly these types of initiatives are a necessary step to recognizing that the format can only retain its relevance in the mature markets if it provides services and experiences

---

[42] Phil Cann, head of UK retail, CBRE, quoted in CBRE Global Research & Consulting, 'UK Grocery Markets in the Pipeline, Marketview', 2014.

[43] Chris Bush, quoted in <http://www.independent.co.uk/news/uk/home-news/yoga-classes-and-hair-salons-every-little-helps-for-tesco-8737332.html>.

[44] <http://www.tesco.com/store-locator/uk/?bID=3372>.

[45] Georges Plassat quoted in 'L'hypermarché est devenu un grand magasin de proximité', *Les Echos*, 13 June 2013. <http://www.lesechos.fr/13/06/2013/LesEchos/21456-082-ECH_georges-plassat>.

which are complementary to the online alternative as well as integrated into it (naturally Tesco's new-style hypermarkets have order and collection points for online orders).

The Changing Role of Shopping Centres

It is in shopping centres, whether managed or not, that we see the combined effect of the rise of e-commerce and, in some markets, the long-term effects of the global financial crisis. One consequence of (adverse) changes in retail firm viability and rationalizing physical store networks has been the reduced requirement for some more traditional types of physical retail real estate in many of the mature retail markets of Europe and North America. In Europe in 2012, vacancy rates for all types of retail property in centres (whether managed or not) varied from 6 per cent to as high as 15 per cent in Spain, 14 per cent in the UK, and 10 per cent in Belgium.

For managed shopping centres in mature markets, the consequence has been a focus on renovation, refurbishment, and extensions to existing centres in order to meet shoppers' changing needs, alongside a slowdown in new developments. In France, much of this extension and refurbishment is taking place in small- and medium-sized centres and in the UK 40 per cent of shopping centres are planning refurbishments over the period 2014–17.[46] However, a 'squeezed middle' of smaller, secondary managed centres in the UK has proved hard to let to retailers who are more concerned with closing stores in secondary space and focusing on fewer stores in larger centres. In North America, too, whilst some commentators have talked about the death of the US shopping mall, this looks exaggerated.[47] Much of the pain is focused on centres in suburban locations that have been either poorly specified and tenanted or have been fundamentally unsuccessful in evolving their role as shoppers have returned to downtowns or shopped increasingly online. But elsewhere in the US, regional malls are successfully repositioning themselves to match the changing composition of the cities in which they are located and the changing expectations of shoppers in those catchments. One of the more overt attempts to localize a shopping centre in an effort to re-energize it is La Gran Plaza in Fort Worth, Texas, which has attempted to remodel itself as an overtly Hispanic-oriented centre, reflecting the catchment in which it is located.

A major challenge for shopping centres seeking to adapt and reinvent is the sheer inertia of the built form and the constraints in many markets, especially

---

[46] College of Estate Management, *UK and Ireland Shopping Centre Management Sentiment Survey 2013*, 2014. <http://www.cem.ac.uk/media/73849/shopping_centre_survey_op-110814.pdf>.

[47] D. Uberti, 'The Death of the American Mall', *Guardian*, 19 June 2014. <http://www.theguardian.com/cities/2014/jun/19/-sp-death-of-the-american-shopping-mall>.

in Western Europe, over new physical development. There is a growing mismatch between, on the one hand, the investment timescales of real estate owners and, in some locations, the extended timescale for planning authorities to approve (or not) new developments and, on the other, the ever-shortening life expectancy of retail formats as a consequence of the profound changes that are a central theme of this book. Temporary pop-up shopping centres and a move to 'semi-permanent' centres might be one answer. One, amongst a fast-growing number, is the Boxpark development opened in 2011 in uber-trendy Shoreditch, east London. Constructed from stripped and refitted shipping containers, Boxpark has created low-cost, low-risk pop-up stores, a number of which trade rent-free for three months. The key feature, however, is that Boxpark was only proposed to be open for four years (although it is still trading at the time of writing). The development places local and global brands side-by-side and the owners engage in very active tenant management, with the focus on interest and diversity. Boxpark's Founder and CEO Roger Wade says: 'Some of the biggest retailers in the world have approached Boxpark and said they would bend over backwards to come here but we've said we feel there are enough places for them.'[48]

Throughout Europe, the recent new-build focus has mainly been on the creation of a few, very large, destination shopping centres where a substantial proportion of floorspace is allocated to leisure and hospitality services. Germany's 76,000 m^2 Mall of Berlin, the 100,000 m^2 Mall of Scandinavia, and extensive new developments in Turkey and Russia speak to developers' intentions to create iconic experiences for consumers. Their different composition also reflects the different roles of shopping centres in the minds of shoppers. For 54 per cent of East European shoppers, large purpose-built covered shopping centres were destinations of choice, compared to 35 per cent in Western European countries, where uncovered centres or high streets were likely to be as important.[49]

Case 3.1 THE TRIUMPH OF THE LUXURY OUTLET MALL—VALUE RETAIL

Those who say that the shopping mall is dead or dying should try to visit Bicester Village in high season, a retail development that attracts over 6 million visitors a year. Bicester Village, a 'chic outlet shopping village', based on the edge of an unprepossessing market town in northern Oxfordshire, UK, was the first site to be developed by the luxury outlet

---

[48] N. Sam-Daliri, "World's First Pop-Up Mall, Boxpark, Opens in East End', *The Docklands & East London Advertiser*, 5 Dec. 2011. <http://www.eastlondonadvertiser.co.uk/news/world_s_first_pop_up_mall_boxpark_opens_in_east_end_1_1145311>.

[49] CBRE, 'How Consumers Shop 2014'. <http://cbre.eu/retail>.

shopping enterprise, Value Retail. Since its inception in 1995, Value Retail has sought out locations within easy reach of what it calls 'gateway cities'. Its nine villages trading in Europe (in Germany, France, Spain, Ireland, Italy, and the UK) attracted 33 million visitors in 2015 and further villages will open in China.

Value Retail's proposition is to bring together a distinctive range of international retail brands with a small number from each domestic market in which it operates.[50] It has proved an extraordinary recipe for success. At Bicester Village the average length of a visit is three hours and the typical customer spends more than US$750 in its 130 stores. The best tenants at Bicester achieve nearly US$4,000 per sq.ft. per year in sales. Signs at the local railway station, recently renamed Bicester Village out of homage to this retail phenomenon, are in both Mandarin and English. Value Retail founder and Chairman Scott Malkin says: 'We are not in the outlet business, we are in consumer travel.' The Mandarin station signs provide the clue: over 9,500 buses a year deliver Chinese tourists to the Bicester site. Rather than taking in the 'dreaming spires', tourists arrive in Oxford asking for directions to Bicester Village (some ten miles to the north of the city).[51]

A key part of the success of Value Retail's business model is an active approach to tenant management, which is around licensing rather than renting and which keeps the tenant mix fresh and the experience attractive for customers. Malkin sees retail brands as partners and employs an approach to designing and managing the tenant mix that is more akin to how a department store works with its brand partners rather than the norm for a shopping centre operator.

Value Retail presently has two ventures in China. The 35,000 m² Suzhou Village opened in 2014, and Shanghai, which, at 50,000 m², will open in 2016. Similar principles have been followed. Suzhou city itself attracted an almost unbelievable 94 million visitors in 2013 (the vast majority domestic tourists) who spent over US$23 billion.[52]

Conclusion

The ways in which retailing around the world physically manifests itself has always been in flux, both in response to and in anticipation of social and economic forces: notably of shoppers' behaviours, as well as a result of competitive and regulatory pressures. Inevitably, there are time lags—often considerable—between the changing demands and expectations of shoppers and the ability of retail real estate to respond to these changes. The supply of physical stores, store networks, and shopping centres reflects the scale and nature of demand at the time in a complex feedback loop. One consequence of this has been the emergence of relatively stable, replicable, trading formats, such as hypermarkets, department and convenience stores as well as managed integrated shopping centres themselves. These formats have historically created an equilibrium in that they reflect both the reality of inertia in retail real

---

[50] <https://www.valueretail.com/who-we-are/about-value-retail/about-value-retail>.

[51] G. Ruddick, "The Unlikely Spot for Designer Holidays Where the World Shops', *Daily Telegraph*, 18 Apr. 2015. <http://www.telegraph.co.uk/finance/newsbysector/retailandconsumer/11547400/The-unlikely-spot-for-designer-holidays-where-the-world-shops.html>.

[52] <https://www.valueretail.com/the-villages/suzhou/sv-facts>.

estate development as well as the need for longer term commercial stability and predictability in the business models of the developers, operators, and occupiers of such space.

This chapter makes clear that many of these bets are now off and the previous equilibrium is being significantly destabilized. Accelerating urbanization, particularly in the world's fastest growing economies, is being paralleled by modernization in lifestyles, new technological and competitive pressures, and increased regulatory attention being given to the sector. The implications of these combined forces of change are very considerable for the physical landscape of retailing and, in consequence, for the locations and communities within which physical retailing is to be found. At a headline level, much has been made of the need for retailers in omni-channel markets (be they in mature or emerging economies) to radically reconsider their property portfolios and often scale back the total amount of space they operate and substantially change the role and physical nature of that which remains. Certainly, we also believe this to be true. But, as ever, the picture is far more nuanced and complex than the headline alone.

In the new (physical) landscape of retailing, shopping centres will continue to be built and valued and some physical formats seem likely to flourish—especially where they deliver enhanced convenience to the shopper and/or an experience that cannot be delivered by online alone. But simultaneously other shopping centres will close and many stores will close, while the continued relevance of some formats will be challenged. Often it was department stores that were thought especially vulnerable to competitive pressures. Today, it is hypermarkets in particular that have lost their assortment advantage (compared with the world of almost infinite choice online) and must look to reinvent—or else radically scale back and close. In the new landscape of retailing, the total global stock of retail space seems likely to reduce, probably very considerably in the mature geographies of Western Europe and North America especially. Much of what remains will be very different in location, scale, usage, and in its physical form. This is the logical, and inevitable, consequence of a new landscape where the act of retailing is no longer synonymous with physical retail stores alone. The resultant challenges are considerable for those tasked with maintaining, let alone enhancing, the vitality of urban areas where traditionally the majority of commercial space was given over to retailing.

4

New Dimensions in Retail Industry Internationalization

A New Internationalization Narrative

For most of the era of modern retailing, the prevailing orthodox view has been that retail businesses do not travel at all well; that retailing is defined, above all else, by its essential nature as a customer-centric activity which must, therefore, be conducted at a local level by retailers which are located in and understand the very specific nature of those local markets. Furthermore, the record of many retailers that have tried to extend their businesses internationally has been a sad story of unfulfilled ambitions and unrealized returns—which serves only to strengthen the orthodox view that retail businesses really don't travel.

In the new landscape of retailing, a reappraisal is necessary. There is a new narrative which holds that retail enterprises operate now in a largely border-less world and engage with shoppers converging to common global norms in their behaviours, their attitudes, and their access to information. Today, 'going international' can appear to involve nothing more complex than operating a website—local language if you wish—and being able to fulfil orders that have been placed in remote locations. International expansion can seem now to occupy the 'easy, low cost, high return' part of the matrix of expansion opportunities, not the 'difficult, high cost, low return' territory of an earlier era. But this is not even a reasonable approximation of the truth. International expansion for retail enterprises has not become easy overnight in the internet era. In fact, it has become more complex because the geographic canvas of possibilities is so much broader, the means of market entry so much more diverse, the nuances of shopper behaviour so much harder to identify underneath the headlines of the global themes, and, not least, because the competitor set is itself rapidly globalizing. The challenges of establishing successful, enduring, and profitable businesses outside domestic markets are, in our opinion, greater than ever because they are very different and less well understood than those of the past and because they exist behind a façade that 'going international' is as easy as 'putting up a website'.

In this chapter we provide a brief history of internationalization in the retail sector, before considering the newly emerging landscape, in which we explore the extent to which the internet is a facilitator of globalization, its impact on changing international growth strategies, and the emergence of disruptive, global web-based enterprises. The directions of travel for the continued internationalization of the sector are more complex and multi-directional than ever before, leading to the modernization of markets in ways that are quite different from those that took place in the West.

Context: A (Brief) History of Retail Sector Internationalization

By comparison with many other sectors of activity, the retail industry has been relatively slow to internationalize, at least in the sense of retail enterprises expanding their store networks beyond their domestic markets. The top 250 retailers worldwide still only generate just over 23 per cent of their sales revenues from non-domestic markets.[1] In contrast, leading FMCG brands in such categories as grocery, health & beauty, and electronics developed international reach and brand familiarity while the retailers to which they were supplying remained for the most part highly localized—often even within their domestic markets.

It is important to recognize, however, that while retail enterprises have historically been slow to internationalize their businesses, the mobility of retail ideas, formats, and techniques—and indeed of leadership talent—has been far more fluid. We discuss this theme later in this chapter. There are several reasons why retail enterprises have been, and in many cases still are, reluctant to internationalize. Many have considered retailing to be an essentially local activity and that understanding the very specific nature of local consumer markets and local operating conditions is just too fraught with difficulties to make the idea of expansion outside domestic markets appealing, by comparison with other routes to growth such as domestic organic growth, diversifications, or acquisitions. There are countless examples of retailers which have failed to understand local tastes and preferences—that pillows are a different shape in Germany than the UK or that Chinese shoppers typically prefer to buy fish live and so on and so on. As Sir Ian Cheshire, then CEO of UK-based Kingfisher Group, said when reflecting on the relatively

---

[1] Deloitte, *The Global Powers of Retailing*, 2016. https://www2.deloitte.com/content/dam/Deloitte/global/Documents/Consumer-Business/gx-cb-global-powers-of-retailing-2016.pdf.

disappointing performance of the Group's B&Q home improvement business in China: 'We just have to be that much more Chinese in China.'[2] (A point of more universal applicability than to either China or home improvement alone.) Moreover, the challenge of aligning an offer with the very particular and specific needs of shoppers outside familiar domestic markets is heightened by both the difficulty of exercising management control over remote operations and by the operational effort required. There are many instances where the management attention that has needed to be given to international operations has been far in excess of the contribution of those operations and has been materially damaging to the business at home. For Walmart, for example, attempts—ultimately fruitless—to resolve the challenges of the Wertkauf business that it acquired in Germany required the attention of several hundred US executives. Why embark on risky international adventures when there are unrealized opportunities in familiar domestic markets has been the mantra for many. Many US retailers have taken this view for obvious reasons of geography and domestic market opportunity, so that the top US retailers derive only 14.6 per cent of their revenues from non-domestic markets, compared to 45.1 per cent in the case of the top French retailers.[3]

In discussing the internationalization of retail enterprises, it is helpful to distinguish between those enterprises which have been only reluctant to grow their presence internationally and those more ambitious, confident enterprises convinced that their brand, format and/or operating system was sufficiently different and better than those which existed outside their domestic market as to make international expansion highly attractive.

Reluctant Internationalists

What might be called reluctant internationalists have only been tempted to extend their reach beyond domestic borders when those home markets looked far less appealing as they matured and growth opportunities diminished, competitive intensity increased, costs of doing business rose, and the sustainability of acceptable returns came under pressure. When these conditions started to emerge, the response of many retailers was often still to seek to leverage their expertise by growing into new categories domestically rather than expanding internationally. This preference for domestic extension over international expansion reflects, in particular, perspectives of and appetite for risk taking. We discuss in Chapter 10 the question of appetite for and

---

[2] A. Felsted and R. Blitz, 'Kingfisher Seeks Partner for STRUGGLING CHINESE BUSINESS', *Financial Times*, 25 Mar. 2014. <http://www.ft.com/cms/s/0/492c9cf0-b3f5-11e3-a102-00144feabdc0.html>.

[3] Deloitte, *The Global Powers of Retailing 2016: Navigating the New Digital Divide*. <http://www2.deloitte.com/global/en/pages/consumer-business/articles/global-powers-of-retailing.html>.

evaluation of risk. When international expansion did—eventually—rise up the corporate agenda, retailers often sought out countries perceived to have fundamental similarities to their familiar domestic environments, or were immediately adjacent to them (so-called 'border hopping'). So, for example, the Benelux retailers tended to stay within Benelux, Scandinavians within Scandinavia, Latin American retailers within LatAm, and so on. Nor were there any guarantees of success here, as Target's recent experience in Canada bears witness.[4] For UK and French retailers, the geography of their international endeavours tended often to focus on their former colonies, perceived as they were to have inherited helpfully familiar characteristics (and shoppers) from their 'mother' countries. Geographically such moves were international but culturally and psychologically they can more accurately be thought of as being rather more 'pseudo-domestic' in nature.

Confident Internationalists

The other group of international retail enterprises in the pre-internet era are what could be called 'confident internationalists'. Characteristically, such businesses considered themselves to have a proposition that would be relevant and well-received internationally, a store format very different to (and presumed to be better than) anything that existed in their target growth markets, a competitive advantage derived from their operational capabilities, or some combination of all three.

IKEA is an obvious example. Now that IKEA is such an established and familiar part of the retail landscape in so many countries, it is difficult to imagine just how disruptive their early international market entries were: into Switzerland (1973), Germany (also 1973), Japan (1974), Australia (1975), France and Spain (1981), Canada (1982), Belgium (1984), the United States (1985), the United Kingdom (1987), Italy (1989), and Poland (1991). Or consider also Sephora which, for a few years in the mid-1990s, was very possibly *the* hottest retail format on the planet and has a genuine claim to have reinvented an entire category—in their case health & beauty—when their iconic Champs-Elysées flagship store opened in 1996 (and which still attracts around 6 million visitors a year—the nearby Eiffel Tower averages only around 1 million more[5]). Today, Sephora has around 1,900 stores in twenty-nine countries[6] and it is difficult to imagine how dull and uninspiring much of the health & beauty category was before Sephora changed everything. And, of

---

[4] P. Wahba, 'Target's Loss is Wal-Mart's Gain in Canada', *Fortune*, 8 May 2015. <http://fortune.com/2015/05/08/walmart-target-canada>.

[5] <http://www.toureiffel.paris/en/everything-about-the-tower/the-eiffel-tower-at-a-glance.html>.

[6] <http://www.sephora.com/about-us>.

course, premium luxury fashion brands in many categories have had global footprints almost since their inception, enabled by both their own brand heritage and the international appeal of what their city or country of origin represents in terms of style, heritage, and craftsmanship. Premium luxury brands were amongst the first enterprises to recognize explicitly that their best growth opportunities were in engaging with consumers internationally that shared similar attributes. Many such brands exist within Sephora's parent company, the LVMH Group, which owns Louis Vuitton, Céline, Marc Jacobs, and Givenchy amongst other premium luxury brands.

More recently, much attention has been focused on the 'fast fashion' apparel retailers such as Topshop, Uniqlo, H&M, and, above all, Zara and the speed and confidence with which these businesses have expanded their reach into a great diversity of international markets from their domestic origins in the UK, Japan, Sweden, and Spain respectively. Zara's widely admired supply chain expertise in bringing new ranges to market in a geographically targeted way far more quickly than was the norm in its category has perhaps been the single most important reason for this business achieving such widespread presence so quickly. Zara has also been something of a catalyst for the growth to prominence of other retailers seeking (either deliberately or in concept) to occupy a somewhat similar positioning including, for example, Renner (Brazil), Forever 21 (US), and H&M (Sweden). This illustrates a wider theme also; namely that retailing is a highly visible industry where techniques are easily replicable, an environment of what strategy academic David Teece refers to as 'low appropriability' (i.e. lower barriers to imitation, at least in principle if not always in actuality).[7] The global transfer of limited assortment discount grocery retailing, exemplified by Aldi and Lidl both from German origins, is similarly illustrative of the mobility of retail operating models as well as of brands and businesses themselves.

While the retail sector has, in general, been relatively slow to internationalize—the efforts of the confident internationalists notwithstanding—the movement of retail formats and practices has been far more fluid. Department store retailing illustrates the point and is very much a story of charismatic individuals exporting their business or being inspired by an iconic department store in another market. Harry Gordon Selfridge's experience is amongst the best known. His background with Marshall Fields in Chicago led directly to the establishment of Selfridge's instantly iconic store on Oxford Street, London, in 1909, which continues, over 100 years on, to be held up (including by us) as an exemplar of what a creative and hugely theatrical playground retailing can be. Perhaps a little more prosaically, the global adoption of the hypermarket

[7] D. Teece, 'Profiting from Technological Innovation: Implications for Integration, Collaboration, Licensing and Public Policy', *Research Policy*, 15 (1986), 285–305.

format was led by both the internationalization efforts of Carrefour, its originator, and the imitative activities of many others, not least Walmart whose supercentre format owes its origins to the French original. Similarly, the international adoption of the shopping mall format was driven by a number of notably ambitious property developers visiting the US in the 1950s and 1960s especially and then developing malls in their own countries. One of the most influential of these 'early imitators' was Frank Lowey who brought the format back to Australia (his adopted home country after the Second World War) where he built his earliest centres and then spent the next sixty years re-exporting the format across much of the rest of the world, not least back to the US itself.

Two factors have been especially important in promoting the internationalization of retail enterprises. The first is property developers, given their desire to bring new names and formats into their developments in order to provide points of differentiation. In terms of the retail brands which are present (as well the quality of the physical environments being created), there is a strong case to argue that today some of the most competitive and complete shopping centre environments are in the Middle and Far East, as these are home to both leading European and US retailers as well as to established—and often very impressive—local operators. Second is the easing of restrictions on enterprise establishment and ownership in overseas markets as part of initiatives towards greater economic integration and the establishment of free trade areas, where the extent of regulation in both OECD and leading non-OECD countries fell by one-third between 1998 and 2013.[8] The European Union project is the most ambitious in its scope and reach—although it would be a mistake with potentially disastrous consequences to consider Europe as anything approaching a single market from an operational or shopper perspective.[9] Initiatives similar in concept, if not in scope, in North America (NAFTA), Asia (ASEAN FTA), Africa (COMESA), South America (MERCOSUR), as well as smaller regional and sub-regional groupings, further facilitate internationalization moves, not just by retail enterprises.

It must be acknowledged also that impediments to the international ambitions of retail enterprises remain very real and considerable in many markets. India is a particular case in point where a market with huge potential and attendant appeal for many has been very cautious in allowing foreign direct investment to come into its retail sector. In 2012, the Indian Government

[8] OECD, *STRI Sector Brief: Distribution Services*, 2014. <http://www.oecd.org/tad/services-trade/STRI_distribution_services.pdf>.

[9] J. Reynolds and R. Cuthbertson, *Retail and Wholesale: Key Sectors for the European Economy*. Brussels: Eurocommerce, 2014.

allowed 100 per cent foreign ownership of single-branded retailers, but continues (at the time of writing) to restrict to 51 per cent foreign direct ownership of multi-branded retail businesses—and even then, with significant pre-conditions around sourcing, store locations, and, perhaps most importantly, state government approval.[10] Indeed, the present BJP government, whilst it retains the FDI policy on paper, has indicated that it is unlikely to grant any applications whilst in office. (According to the World Bank, India ranks 142—a little behind Ethiopia and Iran—out of 187 countries in terms of ease of doing business.[11]) We are not making here any judgement of the 'open markets are good and regulation is bad' variety—or indeed the reverse. Rather we seek simply to point out that retail enterprises should not assume that access is unfettered to markets that might seem attractive to them.

Neither have the efforts of retailers to extend their businesses internationally been anything approaching universally successful. Very far from it. Indeed, the relative lack of success of many retailers internationally—often businesses highly regarded and highly adept in their home markets—has unquestionably contributed to the reluctance of others to attempt international expansion. As Marcel Corstjens and Rajiv Lal observed in the context of grocery retailing, '(And) every grocery retailer that has ventured overseas has failed as often as it has succeeded... Some industries clearly can't travel across borders as well as others.'[12] Neither are the challenges of expanding internationally confined to grocery and basic needs categories.[13]

There are several reasons for the often-poor performance of retail enterprises outside their domestic markets. These resolve into two main groups—those factors which are internal to the enterprise and those that are external and related to the challenges of a new operating environment. Prominent amongst the former are considerations of management capability and focus; the extent to which perceived competitive advantages are, in fact, relevant and transferable; and, on occasion, unrealistic expectations. External factors resolve largely around a failure to fully understand the challenges of a new operating environment, including levels of competitive intensity; the extent to which an offer needs to be adapted to suit local expectations;

---

[10] A. T. Kearney, 'Global Retailers: Cautiously Aggressive or Aggressively Cautious? 2013 Global Retail Development Index', 2014. <http://www.atkearney.co.uk/consumer-products-retail/ideas-insights/article/-/asset_publisher/BHhEu3OEUtE7/content/2013-grdi/10192?>.

[11] World Bank, 'Ease of Doing Business Index', 2015. <http://data.worldbank.org/indicator/IC.BUS.EASE.XQ/countries/1W?display=default>.

[12] M. Corstjens and R. Lal, 'Retail Doesn't Cross Borders: Here's Why and What to Do about it', *Harvard Business Review*, Apr. 2012. <https://hbr.org/2012/04/retail-doesnt-cross-borders-heres-why-and-what-to-do-about-it>.

[13] See e.g. Christoph Schröder, *The Replication of Retail Fashion Formats into Foreign Countries: A Qualitative Analysis* (Google eBook, Springer, 2015, which discusses the challenges several fashion retailers have faced.

and difficulty in securing the right locations and reliable sources of product supply.[14]

The Emerging Landscape of Retail Internationalization

The historical narrative of retail sector internationalization will be a familiar one for many: FMCG brands running some considerable way ahead of retailers in their international ambitions and achievements; formats and techniques migrating rather more easily than retail businesses themselves; a desire of many to exhaust opportunities domestically before taking on risky international adventures and the ambition of others to 'change the world' with highly differentiated propositions.

Today, we are in the early stages of a new and much more dynamic era in the true globalization (as distinct from internationalization) of the retail industry. We are moving from the notion of a retail sector internationalizing somewhat incrementally and reluctantly to an industry that is globalizing rapidly and often with great vigour and enthusiasm. Not only is this an emerging internationalization of retail enterprises, it is also an accelerating globalization of different retail approaches, enabled by technology and consumer change being played out on a global scale. It will not be without its challenges and there will certainly be casualties, but we are confident in asserting that the landscape for retailers and of the retail sector is entering an era of accelerating change. Before we discuss how this change is taking place, there are some important caveats to make. First, this should not be taken to imply that all retail enterprises are now highly motivated to globalize their operations. Clearly, many are not and for good reason. Secondly, retail sector internationalization has something of the feel of Newtonian Laws of Motion about it. To misquote his Third Law: 'For every action there is an *un*equal but opposite reaction.' Some retailers will continue to pull back their international presence for reasons of either change in strategic priorities or else in response to trading difficulties either in their international or domestic operations—or both. Thirdly, our assertion that we expect to see a material acceleration in the scale of internationalization in the retail sector should not be taken to imply that we expect also to see a convergence across markets in the ways in which retailing is conducted such that everywhere will essentially look like everywhere else. We do not. As we have discussed already, differences in shopper

---

[14] For a fuller discussion of the challenges of achieving success in international markets see e.g. J. A. Dawson and M. Mukoyama, *Global Strategies in Retailing: Asian and European Experiences*. Abingdon: Routledge, 2013.

behaviours and expectations between countries look likely to endure in many sectors and will require different responses to similar drivers in others.

The internet is a critical enabler of the step change that is now taking place. We are certainly not dismissive of the importance of other factors, and we discussed earlier the greater permeability of some former barriers to internationalization in the form of the emergence of regional trading blocs and the globalization of media content and social media platforms. But it is the internet especially which is doing most to change the scale, approach, geography, and ambition of the retail sector to internationalize. Indeed, regional trading blocs recognize this pre-eminence: the European Commission, in its new emphasis on a digital single market, has estimated that if properly implemented this would add US$455 billion per year to the European economy and create 3.8 million jobs.[15]

The Internet as Facilitator of Globalization: From Nodes to Networks

The transformative nature of the internet lies especially in the reach that shoppers with reliable high-speed access now have to global networks, information, and influence. In earlier eras, shoppers' purchase behaviours were influenced overwhelmingly, and very often solely, by the influences to which they were exposed within the localities (or nodes) in which they lived. The internet has transformed the geography of engagement in a process sometimes described as the 'death of distance'.[16] Today, for many shoppers the networks that connect nodes together matter more than the nodes themselves. This is true especially of the Millennial Generation shoppers that we discussed in Chapter 1. So today it is perfectly simple for people who do not live in or visit, say, 5th Avenue, New York City; The Bund in Shanghai; or the Avenue des Champs-Elysées in Paris to nevertheless have access to the retailers that are present in these locations, to the new lines of merchandise they are ranging, and to the promotions that they are running.

The greater importance of networks over nodes should not be taken to imply that the direction of travel of ideas and influence is uni-directional and *only* extends outwards from nodes of high influence to the rest of the world. One of the attributes that makes the new networks of shopper engagement so stimulating and, frankly, so difficult to navigate is that ideas and trends do not start in just a few locations and extend from those locations in a single direction of travel only. Certainly, some locations—the global centres of creativity such as Tokyo, New York, London, Berlin, and so on—are

---

[15] <http://ec.europa.eu/priorities/digital-single-market>.

[16] F. Cairncross, *The Death of Distance: How the Communications Revolution is Changing our Lives.* Cambridge, MA: Harvard Business School Press, 2001.

considerably more influential 'trend shapers' than are other population centres. But apparently small ideas can quickly become global trends irrespective of their geographic starting point. The key point is that increasingly these processes are volatile and unpredictable—as well as often accidental and sometimes short-lived. (One recalls, albeit with only great reluctance, the global phenomenon that was Seoul-based Psy's Gangnam Style video in 2012—2.5 billion YouTube views and still counting.)

Case 4.1 LEVERAGING LEARNING ACROSS BORDERS: THE EXAMPLE OF SPAR

The global food retailer SPAR provides an interesting example of the power of transferring learning from one country in order to develop a presence in others. At the start of 2015, SPAR members operated around 12,500 stores in forty countries on four continents, SPAR operates multiple formats ranging from small convenience stores to full-scale hypermarkets. In China, SPAR had 299 stores and 955,000 m^2 of selling space at the end of 2014. Hypermarkets still account for 80 per cent of SPAR's selling space in that country. The company looked to its operations in Austria to define the key elements of the format for China, putting a focus on freshness, service, choice, and value. China is now 14 per cent of SPAR's global sales and a growing middle class in particular is fuelling growth there. To target this audience SPAR is introducing new categories into its hypermarkets, including bakery and wine, which are based on its European operations. SPAR is also now developing convenience stores in China. This format borrows heavily from SPAR's experience with c-stores in Ireland. As Tobias Wasmuht, MD of SPAR Asia, explains it: 'The principles are just the same but the experiences are very local.' In Indonesia, SPAR's operations are shaped in particular by its experiences in South Africa where SPAR has, in Wasmuht's words, learnt to 'sell to the top and the bottom of the pyramid'. Indonesia, like South Africa, has both a small affluent 'top of the pyramid' and a very large 'bottom of the pyramid'.[17]

Online Changing International Growth Strategies

In the pre-internet era retailers with international ambitions could only realize those ambitions by having a physical store presence in new markets. Of course, the traditional mail order operators, most notably Otto Group of Germany and La Redoute from France, are exceptions and store-based retailers could mitigate at least some of the risk and cost associated with international growth by employing entry options such as franchising and licensing. But the present and future era of globalization of retailing is very different. We have noted already that retailing is no longer synonymous with physical stores and this proposition is as true at a global scale as it is domestically.

Today, the extension of retailers' trading capabilities outside their domestic markets is typically proceeding in broadly three stages.

---

[17] Tobias Wasmuht, Presentation to Retail World Asia Pacific Congress, Singapore, Mar. 2015.

1. BUILD AWARENESS

Awareness of retail businesses and brands is being built at a speed and of a scale that was simply not possible in previous eras. While the internet plays, as we have suggested, a central role in bringing awareness of retail brands to many more shoppers much more quickly than has been possible in the past, it is not the only driver. The globalization of media, celebrity, movies, video gaming, and personal contact networks all contribute to a growing awareness of and engagement with 'non-domestic' retail brands and businesses. Fashion designers and brands have also acquired global reach, and this must go some way to explaining the particular success of monobrand fashion retailers internationally. A further contributor has been the greater mobility of labour across national boundaries and the greater ease of international travel for many. In a previous era, it would have been impossible to imagine the contribution that shoppers from mainland China are now making to retail sales in London, Paris, and New York, for example. Globally, the number of Chinese tourists travelling abroad increased from 10 million in 2000 to 120 million in 2015. About half spend more than £3,000 a trip and account for 25 per cent of sales of luxury goods around the world, according to the World Tourism Organization.[18] Furthermore the number of Chinese travelling abroad is forecast to increase further to 200 million by 2020.[19] Going shopping in particular places forms part of their foreign travel experience. For example, the phenomenally successful Bicester Village outlet shopping centre (profiled in Chapter 3)—home to 130 luxury outlet boutiques–100 km north-west of Central London is the second favourite place for Chinese tourists in the UK to visit (after Windsor Castle).[20] Almost unbelievably eight in ten Chinese tourists going to London visit Bicester Village during their stay.[21] Amongst the attractions are Clarks' shoes—made in China—which Chinese visitors take back to China with them.

2. CREATE ACCESS

After awareness comes access. It is in this respect that the internet is perhaps of most importance. Now that retailing is an activity no longer confined to physical stores alone, the number of retailers with an international presence through transactional websites has exploded. So too has the proportion of sales being derived from international markets for many retailers, as Table 4.1 shows. Clearly, it is the higher fashion categories and retailers with strong

---

[18] Data for 2015 from <http://www.travelchinaguide.com/tourism/2015statistics/outbound.htm> and expenditure quoted in <http://www.theguardian.com/money/2013/oct/14/uk-retailers-relaxed-visas-chinese-visitors>.

[19] CLSA brokers report in http://www.economist.com/news/briefing/21595019-market-growing-furiously-getting-tougher-foreign-firms-doing-it-their-way>.

[20] <http://fashion.telegraph.co.uk/article/TMG10968123/Bicester-Village-heads-to-China.html>.

[21] <http://www.independent.co.uk/news/business/analysis-and-features/chinese-pack-their-suitcases-at-bicester-8209793.html>.

Table 4.1 Proportion of sales from overseas markets, selected retailers, and sectors

Top 250 rank	Name	Country of origin	2014 Retail revenue (US$mn)	No. countries of operation	% retail revenue from foreign operations
1	Walmart Stores Inc	US	485,651	28	28.3
2	Costco Wholesale Corporation	US	112,640	10	28.6
3	The Kroger Co	US	108,465	1	0.0
4	Schwarz Unternehmenstreuhand KG	Germany	102,694 (est)	26	59.2
5	Tesco plc	UK	99,713	13	30.0
6	Carrefour SA	France	98,497	34	52.7
7	Aldi Einkauf GmbH & Co. oHG	Germany	86,470 (est)	17	57.1
8	Metro Ag	Germany	85,570	32	59.3
9	The Home Depot Inc	US	83,176	4	10.2
10	Walgreen Co.	US	76,392	4	10.2
	Top 10		**1,339,267**	**16.7**	**31.5**
	Top 250		**4,478,205**	**10.4**	**23.4**
	Apparel & accessories			*25.9*	*31.6*
	Fast-moving consumer goods			*5.3*	*22.2*
	Hardlines & leisure goods			*8.1*	*24.5*
	Diversified			*11.4*	*22.2*

© Deloitte, 2016.
Sources: Deloitte, Planet Retail, 2016. <http://www2.deloitte.com/global/en/pages/consumer-business/articles/global-powers-of-retailing.html>.

brands with global appeal within those categories that have the potential to grow their international sales most strongly through their online presence. In other words, high levels of global brand awareness are now being converted into global sales.

The ways in which retail businesses are employing the internet to extend their reach internationally varies widely and no single model has emerged as optimal or preferred. This is unsurprising. The way in which different retailers and brands use online in international markets is (or should be) a function of several considerations:

- the positioning they wish to occupy
- the desired level of local adaptation versus global consistency
- the way in which they want their brand to be presented
- how they wish to address localized issues of fulfilment and pricing
- the channels that shoppers are using, and
- the level of investment and timescale for return that they are seeking.

These considerations resolve in different ways for different retailers. And so within the same category—such as fashion apparel—for Superdry the preferred solution is for around 85 per cent of the merchandise assortment to be globally consistent because 'the global consumer has amalgamated itself into more of a consistent consumer. You have to take a globally consistent approach to the brand.'[22] By contrast for ASOS, country-specific websites offer merchandise tightly tailored for individual markets and, since 2014, the business has progressively rolled out zonal pricing—that is, different price points in different countries. There is no single right way of using the internet to facilitate the development of an international trading presence and, as such, there is no single model of how to do this.

3. DEVELOP A PHYSICAL STORE PRESENCE (FOR SOME)

For many retailers, creating and fulfilling demand that originates internationally without ever developing physical points of presence outside domestic markets will be their preferred modus operandi. But for others there is a third phase to the realization of their international growth ambitions which does take the form of a physical store presence in new markets once demand has been created, proven, and fulfilled through an online transactional presence. This creates a new strategic route to internationalizing a retail business—start online, build visibility and demand, and only then progress to opening physical stores.

The impact of online is also leading many retailers with existing international store networks to reconsider whether those networks can continue to be the most appropriate way of going to market. One example is M&S, a retailer with a long history of trading internationally through a wide range of store types and ownership models. In April 2014, M&S announced that its strategy in China would shift to focusing on flagship stores in Tier 1 cities, closing smaller stores outside those locations, and fulfilling demand elsewhere in China through a localized website delivered through Tmall, the Chinese-language website for online retail owned by Alibaba Group and, by some way, the largest retailer in China.[23] (As a point of context Suning, China's biggest store-based retailer, achieved 2013 sales of around US$17 billion, while sales transacted on Tmall were around half that in just one day—the huge and hugely important 'Singles' Day' sale event.[24]) Likewise in France, M&S's changed approach to that market involves operating a relatively small number of flagship stores supported by franchised food-only outlets and an online offer which includes using the approximately 5,000 order collection points operated by Point Relais.

For other retail brands, web hosting platforms are being used as an addition to rather than a replacement for their existing international store presence. Zara in China is a case in point. Zara has had an e-commerce website serving

[22] Susanne Given, COO Superdry, Retail Week Conference UK, Mar. 2014.

[23] <https://www.techinasia.com/Alibaba-tmall-heads-list-china-top-100-retailers>.

[24] <http://www.uk.businessinsider.com/r-mega-retailers-battle-to-survive-as-e-commerce-booms-in-china-2014-12>.

China since 2012 and around 450 stores in the country also. It nevertheless began offering its products on Tmall in late 2014 to support these existing activities and to extend the reach of Zara into Tier 3 and 4 cities where it does not have a physical store presence and where the Tmall tie-up will add considerable credibility as well as reach.

Disruptive Global Web-Enabled Enterprises

The third defining theme of the web-enabled acceleration of the globalization of the retail industry is the rapid emergence of entirely new and disruptive online businesses whose ambition from the start is to create an extensive international presence. Indeed, many such enterprises are not easily associated as having originated in any one country at all. Rather, they self-identify as being in the business of creating globally connected networks of people and shoppers and not at all with the traditional notion of exporting a format from a domestic market into international markets. ASOS, the hugely popular and influential online fast fashion retailer, is an obvious case in point. Not only does this business not identify with the notion of being a UK retailer with an international reach, it does not even identify especially with the idea of being a retailer. As James Hart, at the time a Director of ASOS, said, 'We don't see ourselves as a retailer. We see ourselves as a community. Ultimately we want to create a personalised, seamless, connected experience for anyone, anywhere in the world.'[25] ASOS cites its ambition as 'To become the number 1 fashion destination for 20-somethings globally.'[26]

Amazon is perhaps the ultimate expression—so far—of a web-enabled online business with a wholly global outlook. The business's mission statement encapsulates the notion that Amazon does not identity itself as being either a retailer or of any particular geography: 'We seek to be Earth's most customer-centric company for four primary customer sets: consumers, sellers, enterprises, and content creators.'[27] Neither is this business challenged by the need to carefully edit and tailor merchandise assortments to non-domestic markets: 'No walls means no stock limits' being the mantra for many online businesses. (Brad Stone's 2013 book, *The Everything Store,* is a skilfully detailed account of the creation and rise of Amazon.[28] It is interesting to reflect that the motto of Harrods, the iconic London department store, has for over 180 years been *Omnia Omnibus Ubique*—All Things for All People, Everywhere. The difference is that, in the internet age, Amazon can get very much closer to—literally—delivering this vision than could Harrods when it was founded

---

[25] James Hart, Former Director ASOS, *Drapers Magazine*, 8 June 2013, 17.
[26] <http://www.asosplc.com>.   [27] Amazon Company Accounts.
[28] Brad Stone, *The Everything Store*. Boston: Little, Brown & Co., 2013.

in 1834.) In 2014, Tim Steiner, CEO of Ocado, the largest specialist online grocery retailer in the UK, said that, 'If you were to ask who our biggest competitor in online grocery retailing in 20 years' time [will be]...I'd place my money on Amazon.'[29] What makes this observation especially interesting is that at the time Amazon did not sell groceries at all in the UK. But by September 2015, the launch of Amazon Fresh into the UK had been announced, following earlier investments made by Amazon in warehousing to support an online grocery fulfilment operation.[30]

Case 4.2 ALIBABA AND THE INTERNATIONALIZATION OF RETAILING IN CHINA

When we talk of the disruptive impact of online in accelerating the growth of international retailing from often-reluctant extensions into proximate markets into a truly global scale of expansion, no one is more disruptive than Alibaba in its transformative impact upon shopping behaviour and on the entire retail industry in China. Certainly, the numbers are extraordinary.[31] Founded in Hangzhou, Eastern China, in 1999, as of May 2015 Alibaba had over 350 million annual active buyers in China, annual transactions worth in excess of US$394 billion, an increase of 46 per cent over the previous year (and a total bigger than Amazon and eBay combined) and net income in 2014-15 of US$3.9 billion. Then there was the 'mega IPO' in New York in September 2014 which was one of the largest and most keenly anticipated of all time that valued Alibaba at over US$200 billion and felt much more like the start of the next phase of growth for this extraordinary business than the culmination of what had been achieved so far.

There are many facets to what makes Alibaba so disruptive. Clearly, it is in the vanguard of the transformation of retailing overall in China. But more than this Alibaba is leading the transformation of consumer markets themselves in China by not only putting online at the centre of the new shopping landscape but also with its C2C, B2C, and B2B platforms (Taobao, Tmall.com, and Alibaba.com respectively) that have enabled a plethora of international brands to quickly build a presence in China. As at the end of 2014 more than 4,000 international brands from forty-five countries were using Tmall.[32]

It seemed a highly significant barometer that, after years of trying to establish a meaningful presence independently in China, Amazon announced in March 2015 that it would open on Tmall, Alibaba's B2C platform (and majority owned by Walmart). As Sucharita Mulpuru, an analyst at Forrester Research, observed: 'Everyone knows that Chinese e-commerce is dominated by Alibaba and at some point you go fish where the fish are.'[33]

---

[29] Tim Steiner, Retail Week Conference, London, Mar. 2014.
[30] <http://www.retail-week.com/sectors/food/analysis-how-amazon-fresh-could-take-a-slice-of-the-uk-grocery-pie/5077953.article>.
[31] http://www.alibabagroup.com/en/ir/financial_fullyear. See <http://hbswk.hbs.edu/item/7534.html> for a fuller analysis of Alibaba.
[32] <http://usa.chinadaily.com.cn/epaper/2014-10/14/content_18736828.htm>.
[33] <http://www.bloomberg.com/news/articles/2015-03-05/amazon-opens-store-on-Alibaba-s-tmall-to-reach-chinese-shoppers>.

Nor is it only the Amazon and Alibaba behemoths that are reshaping the globalization of the retail sector and the modernization of retail markets. A large and growing number of web-enabled platform providers, many with regional footprints, are acting as hosts for international retailers. A number of these enterprises are, ultimately, owned by Rocket Internet AG based in Germany which has, since its formation in 2007, been very aggressive in establishing and rapidly growing several such businesses, including Jabong (India), Lamoda (Russia), ZALORA (SE Asia), and Jumia (Africa).

A further group of businesses to enter the global retail landscape with disruptive web-enabled operations are enterprises whose origins lie entirely outside the retail sector and whose self-defined objective is to usurp and bypass the role of traditional retailers. We discuss in Chapter 5 the emergence of such businesses and the challenges they present to established retail enterprises. One such business (amongst many globally) is Redmart.com in Singapore. At a commercial level, Redmart is an online grocery retailer, which has been operating in Singapore since 2011. But in concept and heritage Redmart is, as Todd Kurie their Marketing Director, says, 'a technology company that happens to sell groceries'.[34] Singapore is, for several reasons, an excellent environment in which to test the operations and enabling architecture of a new, technology-driven online business: a highly connected, technology-embedded young and educated population; a lifestyle and urban infrastructure that could have been created with remote shopping in mind; and a self-contained affluent market. For Redmart, Singapore is less the business's home market (the founders are from the US and India) than its test market ahead of an anticipated rollout to other major cities globally.

Case 4.3 AUSTRALIA: A MARKET BEING TRANSFORMED BY RETAIL GLOBALIZATION

Australia provides an interesting example of just how impactful and intrusive internationally aggressive online enabled retailers can be on a domestic market. The changes taking place in clothing and homewares retailing especially demonstrate the impact that internationalization is having on a country which in a previous era was protected almost entirely from overseas competition for obvious reasons of geography. However, the protection afforded by geographic isolation has disappeared now that retailers with a transactional presence online are able and willing to fulfil orders from shoppers in Australia.

The Australian market has considerable appeal for many specialty retailers especially. The economy survived the 2008/9 Global Financial Crisis far better than most, many of its 23 million population are well-travelled and very familiar with leading retailers in other

---

[34] Todd Kurie, speaking at Singapore Retail Association Congress, Singapore, Oct. 2014.

markets, and the country is a major destination for affluent Asian tourists. In fashion apparel, H&M, Zara, Hollister, Miss Selfridge, Victoria's Secret, Topshop, and Uniqlo have all opened stores in recent years after satisfying themselves through their web presence that there is strong demand for their merchandise. As Paul Gould, International Development Director of Arcadia Group (owners of Topshop), has said, 'We knew from the success of our online business that brand awareness was strong, and that's always a great position to be in.'[35] Still more seem likely to follow. Between 2014 and 2016, a further sixty international brands were expected to enter Australia, especially in fashion, and including Fendi, Alexander McQueen, Tom Ford, The Kooples, and Reiss.[36]

Topshop's physical presence in Australia is illustrative of the strategies being pursued by others also. The company is not aiming for anything close to national coverage with its store portfolio. Rather, the intention is to open a relatively small number of large flagship stores in the highest traffic and most impactful locations and to fulfil demand elsewhere through an online presence only. This strategy goes some way towards explaining why retail rents in Sydney's best location (Pitt Street) ranked as the fifth most expensive in the world at the end of 2014 and were the fastest growing of all major capital cities.[37]

Neither is the strategy of creating demand online ahead of opening physical stores confined solely to the fashion category. Williams Sonoma, the great US homewares retailer, has opened flagship stores in Sydney (2013), Melbourne (2014), and Brisbane (2015) for all four of its main brands (Williams Sonoma itself together with Pottery Barn, Pottery Barn Kids, and West Elm) on the back of Australia already being its largest market outside North America through its e-commerce site.[38]

The pureplay online-only retailers have also targeted Australia. So, for example, for ASOS Australian orders contributed some 50 per cent of revenues outside the UK, US, and Europe in 2014, although it was required to reduce prices by 20 per cent in 2015 partly because of currency fluctuations and partly to remain competitive.[39]

There is one important final component to this brief profile of the Australian experience. Local sales tax in Australia (the GST—Goods and Services Tax) is 10 per cent on almost all goods and services. However, no sales tax is levied on purchases of less than Aus$1,000 (around £500 or US$650 at the start of 2015) that have been ordered online and are fulfilled from overseas. As the amount of sales being 'lost' to online increases, so the pressure from established local retailers to end this anomaly has continued to strengthen. Indeed, one high-profile Australian retailer, Just Group in fashion apparel, has suggested that it will investigate fulfilling orders from overseas locations in order to level the playing field and restore its price competitiveness.[40]

The wider issue is that, as borders between geographic markets become ever more permeable, so the pressure will intensify for local sales tax rates to be harmonized down

(continued)

[35] <http://www.ft.com/cms/s/0/c37495d0-bb84-11e3-8d4a-00144feabdc0.html#axzz3PStsd0vc>.

[36] Charlotte Rogers, 'The Beautiful South', *Drapers Record Property Special*, 2–12 Sept. 2015, 15–17.

[37] <http://www.costar.co.uk/en/assets/news/2014/November/MAPIC-2014-The-worlds-most-expensive-retail-locations>.

[38] <http://www.smh.com.au/business/homewares-giant-williamssonoma-joins-rush-to-australian-retail-20140316-34vgu.html>.

[39] <http://www.smh.com.au/business/asos-gets-its-mojo-back-in-australia-after-cutting-prices-20150313-142xwv.html>.

[40] <http://www.theguardian.com/australia-news/2014/dec/05/large-local-retailer-announces-plans-to-sell-to-australians-from-overseas>.

Case 4.3 Continued

to those of the lowest and for online sales to be treated in just the same way as store-based sales for tax purposes. In August 2015, the Australian Federal Government announced that, from mid-2017, the Aus$1,000 sales tax-free threshold would end and tax would be levied on all purchases made overseas. But this issue is not confined to international cross-border web-enabled transactions. In the US, online retailers have until recently not had to pay sales tax in states where they do not have a physical presence. Given that sales taxes are set at a state level and vary from 3 per cent to almost 8 per cent, this represents a significant price advantage for the online operators. In consequence several states have now enacted legislation—often called 'Amazon laws'—that require online retailers to levy sales tax when sales are made to a state where they do not have a physical presence. The US Federal Government continues also to discuss the issue but, at the time of writing, no resolution seems imminent; meanwhile the State Governments estimate that they are losing $23 billion a year in uncollected sales tax on goods purchased online.[41]

New Directions of Travel in Retail Internationalization

As we have suggested, it is today inappropriate to see the accelerating globalization of retailing as being in the hands solely or even mainly of traditional retail businesses or as taking the form of a single direction of travel outwards from the mature European and North American markets and into the emerging markets. Anyone who has spent time in the major cities of the Middle East, Far East, and Latin America could not possibly mistake such environments as in any sense underdeveloped. They have already emerged—and very strongly.

Directions of travel in the continued internationalization of the retail sector are notably more complex and multi-directional than those that have gone before. In this regard, one of the most important themes in the new era of retail globalization looks likely to be the accelerating ambition of consumer brands from China to achieve international prominence. The Chinese economy is being transformed at a hugely impressive rate from one driven by low-cost manufacturing to one driven by consumer consumption. Certainly, we should not assume that the Chinese economy will achieve double digital annual growth in perpetuity. No economy works that way and the unique complexities of China mean that there will always be elements of uncertainty about the scale and forms that growth and modernization will take. Nevertheless, Karl Gerth, an expert on Chinese consumption at the

---

[41] <http://www.reuters.com/article/2014/03/12/us-usa-tax-Internet-idUSBREA2B20120140312>.

University of California, is right to say that: 'the future of the world will be profoundly shaped by China's rush toward consumerism'.[42]

For some Chinese consumer brands, which have grown to prominence domestically, the next phase may well be to extend their reach internationally. In FMCG categories, several have done this already, most notably in consumer electronics with Lenovo being particularly prominent. When Lenovo acquired IBM's PC business in 2005 it felt as though a torch had been passed not just between two businesses but between two economies also. Since 2005, there have been many further acquisitions and Lenovo is today a truly global brand. The internationalization of Lenovo has been considerably facilitated by what David Roman, Lenovo's Chief Marketing Officer, refers to as a 'global consuming class' which has more in common across borders than within them. The organizational expression of this notion has seen the establishment of a global marketing hub in Bangalore and a global social media hub in Singapore.[43] In the automotive sector, the emergence of Chinese auto brands, such as Great Wall, as internationally credible looks set to be one of the defining themes in the auto industry for many years to come and has strong parallels with the international growth of Korean brands, notably Hyundai and its Kia sister brand, in an earlier era. Twenty or more years ago Korean cars were often dismissed as cheap, poor-quality 'white goods on wheels'. No one in the auto industry is dismissive of Korean cars now.

So should we expect to see Chinese retail businesses following consumer brands and extending their reach internationally? Conventionally, the enormous scale of growth opportunities within China might suggest not. Yet it seems to us entirely realistic to suppose that several will, driven by some combination of a desire to acquire retail brands with global as well as Chinese appeal and to establish branded outlets internationally that both confer prestige domestically as well as engage with Chinese shoppers overseas. When Bosideng, the clothing retailer with over 10,000 stores in China, opened its first store overseas in a prime central London location in 2012 it felt like a very brave venture that could presage a much bigger movement. Considerable further momentum was given to this thought when, in April 2014, the Chinese conglomerate Sanpower purchased the UK's House of Fraser department store group for £480 million.[44] As well as the internationalization of retailing practices and ideas no longer being uni-directional, so too is the movement of retail capital.

---

[42] <http://www.economist.com/news/briefing/21595019-market-growing-furiously-getting-tougher-foreign-firms-doing-it-their-way>.

[43] <http://www.marketingmagazine.co.uk/article/1218096/lenovos-ajay-kaul-digital-millenials-mobile-expansion-marketing-hubs>.

[44] <http://www.bbc.co.uk/news/business-27009359>.

Globalization and Modernization

One of the most important features of the new landscape of global retailing is that modernization of markets is proceeding at a pace and in directions which are quite different to the ways in which the retail markets of Western Europe and North America have evolved in earlier eras. This should not surprise. In an era of profound and discontinuous change it would be improbable if the development trajectories of the presently less mature markets followed even at all closely the experiences that have gone before in the now mature markets.

Amongst the academic community studying the retail industry, the modernization of retail markets has often been presented as progressing through a series of stages, which are predictable, sequential, and discrete (Figure 4.1 shows one example amongst many). While this has the benefit of simplicity and might have been a useful approximation of the experiences of Western Europe and North America (although many doubt even this[45]), it is certainly not a realistic representation of what is actually happening in the newly modernizing markets. At a headline level, what is in fact taking place is a rapidly accelerating drive to modernization, enabled by a highly informed, globally aware shopper whose perspectives and behaviours are being influenced especially by the technology that is increasingly embedded in their lives. As we noted in Chapter 1, these behaviours are shaped more by the

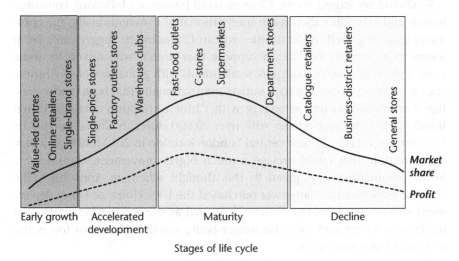

Figure 4.1 The 'retail life cycle' of North America
Source: Kerin, R., et al., 2014, Marketing. McGraw Hill Education.

[45] See e.g. M. Mukherjee, R. Cuthbertson, and E. Howard, *Retailing in Emerging Markets*. London: Routledge, 2014, ch. 11 'Conclusion—Public Policy and Retail Strategy'.

networks that shoppers are part of than they are by the locations in which they happen to reside.

Consider the enabling role of the smartphone. Everywhere that shoppers have smartphones, they expect to be able to use them for shopping—if not to actually make a purchase, then to view promotions, seek product reviews, receive information, share reviews after making a purchase, and so on. A 2015 survey by management consultants PwC (Table 4.2) showed that the proportion of shoppers who have used a smartphone to make a purchase was already far higher in China (77 per cent) and India (69 per cent) than the global average (43 per cent). This points to an important feature of the new landscape of retail: the emerging markets are already amongst the most dynamic globally and technology in the hands of the shopper is central to how they are being transformed. Moreover, the rapid take-up of mobile devices in particular seems certain to accelerate the modernization of retailing beyond major urban areas and into less developed rural hinterlands also. As Alibaba's Ken Ma has noted: 'There's huge opportunity for online in rural areas [of China] too now that you can buy a mobile phone for less than US$100.'[46]

Case 4.4 NIGERIA AND THE E-COMMERCE LEAPFROGGING OPPORTUNITY

Nigeria has a population of around 180 million people but relatively few modern retail outlets and internet penetration of over 30 per cent and growing quickly, especially amongst a fast emerging middle class with disposable income. In this environment, online commerce is flourishing. Locally established websites Konga and Jumia were each fulfilling over 1,000 orders a day within six months of being established. It is, in particular, the relative absence of shopping centre alternatives that has accelerated the emergence of e-commerce. Nigeria's largest city, Lagos, has a population of around 17 million people but just two shopping centres of more than 20,000 m². (Johannesburg by comparison has seventy-four serving a city of 4 million people.) As Sim Shagaya, founder of Konga in mid-2012, puts it, 'It's not so much that there's this appetite for online shopping, as that there's an appetite for shopping. Retail here is still mostly informal, fragmented and inefficient. People want convenience, which gives us the opportunity to leapfrog with e-commerce.'

If Alibaba is often referred to as e-commerce with Chinese characteristics, then Konga is online retailing with Nigerian characteristics. Many Nigerians do not have bankcards so payment of online orders is typically made in cash at the point of delivery. (Interestingly, Germany has evolved much the same model for much the same reason.) In view of the unpredictability of the postal service, many vendors have developed their own courier fleets comprising motorbikes, vans, and tuk-tuks. These are early days in the development of e-commerce in Nigeria and buying online is still mostly in the hands of

(continued)

---

[46] Ken Ma, speaking at Retail Congress Asia Pacific, Singapore, Mar. 2015.

Case 4.4 Continued

early adopters. But as Olumide Olusanya, a doctor and founder of several e-commerce websites says, 'Everything has come together at the right time for e-commerce here. We are still paddling ahead of the wave but, when it comes, it is going to be huge.' It seems unlikely that Nigeria will add a great deal to its stock of shopping centres as e-commerce growth continues to accelerate.[47]

Table 4.2 Top regions globally for mobile phone shopping (responses to statement 'My mobile phone will become my main tool from which to purchase')

Region	% strongly agree	% strongly disagree
China	24%	3%
India	24%	4%
Middle East	13%	6%
Global Average	17%	9%

Base: 19,068 interviews across 19 territories in Aug./Sept. 2014

© PwC, 2015

Source: PWC Global Total Retail Survey 2015.
<http://www.pwc.com/gx/en/retail-consumer/retail-consumer-publications/global-multi-channel-consumer-survey/assets/pdf/total-retail-2015.pdf>

But the transformation and accelerating modernization of emerging markets is not just a phenomenon of the internet age. Physical store development continues to contribute considerable momentum to the modernization of retail systems in markets globally. For example, in China the global grocery retailer SPAR focuses its expansion on Tier 2 to 5 cities rather than the Tier 1 cities (Shanghai, Beijing, etc.), which tend to get a disproportionate amount of attention. Moreover SPAR is now moving further down, not up, the urban hierarchy and targeting cities of around 250,000 people where, according to Tobias Wasmuht, MD of SPAR Asia, SPAR is giving shoppers in these locations their 'first access to modern retail'.[48]

Shopping malls also continue to have high appeal to many shoppers in many emerging markets (we discuss the development of mall space in emerging markets in Chapter 7). In fact, it is often the case that, as online shopping increases, so too does the amount of shopping taking place in modern mall developments and the majority of new shopping centre space being developed globally is in emerging markets. The rapidly modernizing retail sector in

---

[47] Content for this example was taken from an article by Xan Rice, 'Nigerian Shoppers Buy into E-Commerce Boom', *Financial Times*, 15 May 2013, 9.
[48] Tobias Wasmuht, speaking at Asia Pacific Retail Congress. Singapore, Mar. 2015.

Vietnam is a case in point. Amongst several large and impressive malls in that country, the Royal City Mega Mall in Hanoi, opened in 2013, is the largest at 230,000 m^2 GLA (Gross Leasable Area)[49] and is tenanted with an impressive array of local, regional, and international retailers. This is a centre that would certainly not look out of place in Europe or North America.

Despite the rapid emergence of online, there are good reasons to believe that modern shopping centres will continue to hold high appeal for many shoppers in emerging markets. They clearly play important and valued social, leisure, and entertainment roles that extend well beyond serving as purely functional centres for making purchases. The Philippines provides an especially persuasive example of just how powerful a force of modernization the shopping centre developers can be. The huge SM Group alone has been responsible for the development in greater Manila of three of the ten largest shopping malls in the world by gross leasable area.[50] Each is anchored by SM operated formats, usually a hypermarket and a department store, while substantial amounts of mall space are tenanted to international brands, including H&M, Uniqlo, and Crate & Barrel, all of which have been introduced to the Philippines by the SM Group.

While the accelerating globalization of information and retail techniques as well as businesses and brands themselves is having a transformational impact on retail landscapes in emerging markets, this should not be taken to imply that modernization is sweeping aside all of the traditional approaches to how retailing is conducted in emerging markets. Very far from it. As Mukherjee et al. have observed, 'Consumer demand for traditional retailing and regulatory intervention and impediments ensure the coexistence of traditional and modern retailing in these markets.'[51] This coexistence of traditional and modern is an enduring feature of retail landscapes in emerging markets and one that we expect to continue for many years to come. Thus, for example, Landmark's Max Fashion business in India transacts approximately 60 per cent of its sales in modern malls, 20 per cent in shopping strips, and a further 20 per cent in traditional markets.[52] This juxtaposition has created very complex distribution and shopper engagement landscapes characterized by overlapping layers of engagement that extend from traditional hawkers and market stalls, through modern shopping centres, to global e-commerce platforms. Navigating through this complexity in order to create and execute the go-to-market strategy best aligned to a business, its brand positioning, and its

[49] <http://www.vincomshoppingmall.com/Uploads/04_VincomMegaMall_RoyalCity/VMM%20Royal%20City%20-%20Presentation%20ENG%2013102012.pdf>.

[50] <http://en.wikipedia.org/wiki/List_of_largest_shopping_malls_in_the_world>.

[51] Mukherjee et al., *Retailing in Emerging Markets*.

[52] Vasanth Kumar, speaking at Asia Pacific Retail Congress, Singapore, Mar. 2015.

target customer audiences will continue to be a major challenge for retailers in these markets.

Conclusion

It is generally true to say that retailing has been amongst the more reluctant economic sectors to reach outside domestic markets and to internationalize its enterprises. Certainly, there has historically been far more fluidity of movement of retailing techniques (such as self-service grocery stores) and formats (such as convenience, hypermarket, and department stores) than there has been of actual retail enterprises themselves. In the new landscape of retailing this is changing quickly. The internet in particular is giving far more impetus to the internationalization of the sector by making it quicker, easier, and less costly to establish a trading presence in non-domestic markets, or at least to fulfil demand created in international markets by the far greater fluidity across country borders of trend awareness and subsequently of demand. A growing number of retailers are now emboldened and able to take an 'internet-first, stores maybe' approach to extending their reach internationally. Entirely new enterprises, most notably global and regionally important online trading platforms such as Amazon and Alibaba, are adding very considerably to the impetus for international expansion in the new landscape of retailing. Country markets and categories within those markets are being transformed increasingly rapidly by the combined effects of the accelerating internationalization of shopper demand on the one hand and the global reach of retailers and the means of fulfilment on the other.

Historically, it was broadly appropriate to conceive of the internationalization of the retailing sector as a migration that predominantly took place from the mature markets of the West (and Europe especially) and into the emerging markets of the Far East, Africa, and South America. Today this is most definitely not the case. In fact, in many cases it is the so-called emerging markets that are changing faster than the West European and North American markets as they modernize far more quickly and, indeed, cut out entirely stages of development through which the Western markets have progressed. In consequence, there is a case to argue that some of the most innovative activity in retailing is now taking place in the emerging markets. The great fluidity of ideas and techniques and the lack of clear patterns of movement is one of the defining features of the internet-enabled age of retailing.

This should not, however, be taken to imply that the new global landscape of retailing is a landscape defined by a world converging rapidly towards global uniformity in demand, in retailing techniques, and in retailing formats. In fact, the opposite appears to be more true. Happily, from our perspective, the world of global retailing is becoming less uniform and more diverse as the emerging markets in particular develop very complex and distinctive new retail landscapes which combine the traditional (market stalls and so on) with the physical modern (shopping centres and so on) and the fast emerging digital modern (online platforms, digital stores and so on). We say 'happily' because, philosophically, diversity and differences are surely to be welcomed and because, practically, complex landscapes are rich in opportunity for those able to embrace the differences, understand the nuances, and navigate through the complexities.

5

The Emergence of New Business Models

What is a Retailer Anymore, Anyway?

The act of retailing is no longer being conducted solely by traditionally thought of retail businesses (although we are happy to acknowledge the tautology that engaging in the act of retailing makes any enterprise by definition a retailer). Well-established value chains where participants knew their role and did only that—manufacturers made things, logistics businesses delivered them, and retailers sold them—are a thing of the past. In the new landscape of retailing it can seem that everyone is now aspiring to be a retailer. It is established retail enterprises themselves that now face the greatest risk of disintermediation—that is, of being bypassed within the value chain or having their relationship with the end shopper usurped by intrusive newer entrants who aspire to build strong, direct relationships with the shopper.

Vendors are 'going direct' (it is easy to forget that Apple is still a consumer technology company much more than it is a retail business). Logistics businesses aim to 'own the customer relationship' because in an online world they are often the most visible actors in the delivery chain to the shopper. Payment providers have moved from the background to the foreground as they seek more prominence and visibility with the shopper. Comparison websites threaten to usurp conventional retailers. Technology companies are setting up retail enterprises online because they believe that they can deliver a better and/or more efficient experience than conventional retailers. Pureplay online-only enterprises are growing to huge scale with (almost) borderless reach and (almost) limitless assortments. The new behemoths of globally connected retailing are not Walmart, Carrefour, and Tesco; they are Amazon, Alibaba, and eBay. Yet simultaneously some of the formerly online-only enterprises are themselves discovering the 'joy of shops' and opening their own physical spaces. In the new landscape of retailing it is entirely possible and increasingly likely that, for an established retailer, major channel partners are also at the same time major competitors. (Walmart may be Proctor & Gamble's major retail partner globally but that has not deterred P&G from establishing trans-actional websites in some key geographies.)

In this chapter we explore the nature and implications of new sources of competition for established retailers, we discuss some of the more radical departures from 'business as usual' that these businesses might explore, and we examine some of the consequences of a changing cost model for the retail enterprise.

Everyone's a Retailer Now

One of the defining features of the new landscape of retail is that the act of retailing is no longer the preserve solely of traditional retail enterprises. Indeed, it can reasonably be argued that many of the most innovative and far-reaching developments to have taken place in retailing in recent years have *not* been made by traditional retail enterprises at all. A group of Harvard Business School graduate students advised Jeff Bezos after he spoke to them in early 1997 that his business, Amazon, had little chance of surviving when established retailers moved online and the best thing he could do was sell to Barnes & Noble. Bezos's response was, 'I think you might be underestimating the degree to which established brick-and-mortar business, or any company that might be used to doing things a certain way, will find it hard to be nimble or to focus attention on a new channel. I guess we'll see.'[1] Well, we've certainly seen. But this is not a story of online killing a long-established brick and mortar business. Barnes & Noble may be the last business standing as a national bookstore chain in the US (Borders having succumbed in 2011), but its 650+ physical retail stores are still significantly profitable at an operat-ing level.[2] Meanwhile, Amazon has developed a more recent enthusiasm for physical space in the form of secure kiosks and, since early 2015, staffed collection points on US university campuses.[3] In another geography, the spectacular transformation of the retail landscape in China has its most visible expression in the proliferation of megamalls tenanted by a plethora of globally recognized retail brands. (When visiting malls in Shanghai and Beijing it can be truly difficult to know whether you are in China, the US, or Europe.) But of ultimately more importance in the transformation of retailing in China are Alibaba and Tmall, because of their extraordinary reach into the lives of so many shoppers not just within but also beyond the megacities. Alibaba is like many of the other platform providers and pureplay online retailers in that

[1] B. Stone, *The Everything Store*. London: Corgi Books, 2014.

[2] <http://barnesandnobleinc.com/press_releases/6_25_15_2015_FYE_Q4_earnings.html >.

[3] <http://www.theguardian.com/technology/2015/feb/03/amazons-first-store-opens-indiana>.

they are technology companies that are in the business of retailing. In the opposite direction of travel, traditional retail businesses of long standing are having to evolve from store-only to omni-channel enterprises to such an extent and requiring such very different enterprise competencies that even they are not always sure whether they are still retail enterprises any more. As Katy Gotch, Head of Group Strategy at Home Retail Group, the parent company of the UK's general merchandise retailer Argos, told us, 'We spend quite a lot of time asking ourselves if we're even a retailer any more or whether we are in fact a logistics company.'

Does any of this matter or is it all irrelevant semantics to even be discussing a distinction between retailers and retailing? Surely, the very act of being in retailing makes an enterprise a retailer irrespective of their starting point—as a tech company, a logistics company, an FMCG company, or whatever. In some ways it does not matter at all but in other ways it matters a great deal.

From a shopper's point of view, the starting point from which an enterprise entered the business of retailing is largely irrelevant. Whether the groceries are delivered to a household in the UK by a company that defines itself as a retailer (Tesco), or a technology company (Ocado), is irrelevant. What matters is that the order is delivered in full, on time, competitively priced, and by a pleasant delivery driver. *Plus ça change, plus c'est la même chose* indeed. (The more things change, the more they stay the same.) Neither can traditional retailers fall back on the 'heritage of my business and brand' defence. In environments of great change and intense competition, strong brands with real equity to the shopper matter more than ever (a theme we discuss in Chapter 9). But a brand only achieves strength and becomes valued by shoppers when the business behind it delivers consistently on or beyond the shopper's expectations for it. And strong brand equity in retailing is by no means the preserve of traditional retail enterprises alone. One thing that the internet age has shown with great clarity is that brands with wide reach and strong customer equity can be established very quickly and are in no sense less well thought of than are their traditional counterparts. Think Zappos (shoes and accessories), ASOS (fashion apparel), and Amazon (everything). Indeed, there is a strong sense in which, for younger customers especially, it is the newer brands without the heritage (or baggage depending on one's perspective) of a traditional retail past that have the strongest appeal.

The counter-argument is that the starting point of enterprises that are engaged in retailing is of great importance because the competitive landscape is being so rapidly transformed by enterprises that in their culture, competencies, business, and financial models look and behave in ways which are so different to the conventional competitive set faced by retailers in an earlier era. When hypermarkets began usurping supermarkets, which in turn had usurped counter service food stores, the fundamental operating principles and financial model were not overturned. Rather they were refined and made more efficient, but trade still took place in stores, shoppers still had to visit those stores, the line items in the enterprise financial model were still the same (it was the numbers set against them that were different). But the new landscape of retailing is not just a competition between businesses with fundamentally similar models. It is an intense clash of cultures, philosophies, enterprise capabilities, and operating models, and it is being played out at a global scale.

Case 5.1 WECHAT SHOP: EVERYONE'S A RETAILER NOW

WeChat (developed by Tencent and launched in January 2011) is the dominant mobile messaging platform in China. Growth has been remarkable. As of September 2015, WeChat had 650 million monthly active users (MAUs), a year-on-year growth of 39% of which at least 30 million are outside China. WeChat users skew around two-thirds male, one-third female, and three-quarters of users are 20 to 30 years old. Thirty-four per cent of users say that they go onto WeChat as their first act in the morning, 24 per cent say that their purchase decisions are influenced by their friends on WeChat, and 12.5 per cent make a purchase via WeChat.[4] It is this extraordinary level of connectedness and influence that has enabled WeChat to quickly morph from being a social messaging site into an indispensable part of the lives of many of its users. In very short order, WeChat has gone from mobile messaging app to ubiquitous electronic wallet.

In early 2014, WeChat created WeChat Shop—in-app stores created for free to a basic common template with the objective of bringing small enterprises across China into WeChat. Enterprises have to use WeChat's own payment platform if they are to trade on WeChat Shop. WeChat's strategic objective is to take market share in China's burgeoning e-commerce market where Alibaba dominates. What WeChat is doing is giving small enterprises throughout China the ability to engage with a huge and very active audience of WeChat users without ever leaving the WeChat app to find products and services, seek advice from social networks, and, finally, make payment.

It is most useful to think of WeChat as a facilitator of engagement and connectivity. WeChat could be described as a social networking site, a gaming site, and now a retailing site. It could also be described as a digital payment provider, a digital shopping mall developer, and a digital SME (Small & Medium Size Enterprise) incubator. It is all of these things, but none of these descriptions brings to life the full scale, reach, and ambition of WeChat. (Even the Chinese government uses WeChat as a communication platform.) In the new landscape of retail, the old language is far too constrained and trying to understand and define the new digital landscape by seeking analogies with the old, pre-digital world is irrelevant.

Neither is WeChat unique. Whatsapp is often compared with WeChat, not least because both started out as mobile social networking apps and have quickly developed huge user bases. Whatsapp is larger, with around 900 million MAUs (Mobile Active Users) sending an almost unfathomable 34 billion messages a day.[5] (Whatsapp went

(continued)

---

[4] <https://www.techinasia.com/wechat-650-million-monthly-active-users>.
[5] <http://fortune.com/2015/09/04/whatsapp-900-million-users>.

Case 5.1 Continued

from 800 million to 900 million MAUs in a little over six months.) WeChat is further down the track in extending the reach of its platform but it is difficult to imagine that Whatsapp will not look to follow a trajectory that is at least as ambitious. Commercializing—into banking, retail, and elsewhere—this huge user audience was surely part of the reason that led Facebook to make Whatsapp its largest acquisition to date when it paid US$19 billion for the business in February 2014.[6]

Thinking—and Executing?—the Unthinkable

For established retail enterprises, business leaders need to allow themselves the freedom to 'think the unthinkable'. (Doing the unthinkable is different entirely. We discuss in Chapter 9 the risks of making too much—and indeed too little—change.) Very often this is easier to do in enterprises which are underperforming and where often radical change is essential to the very survival of an enterprise. It is often much harder to consider and execute change when an enterprise is successful, especially when that success breeds a sense of entitlement, complacency, insularity, or all three. It is crucial to guard against any such tendencies. As Sir Charlie Mayfield, Chairman of the very successful John Lewis Partnership in the UK (department stores and grocery), has said, 'It's not about running the same business model. It's about changing it in flight in order to serve customers in the way they want to be served in the future.'[7]

Thinking the unthinkable can feel very uncomfortable. But it also offers up the possibility of delivering something genuinely different and better than the competition, engaging to the target audience and profitably differentiating for the enterprise. Here we discuss some possibilities for established retailers to contemplate very different approaches to engaging their audiences.

Stores Without Staff

Many financial services businesses have long been of the view that shoppers like physical outlets but do not like interacting with sales staff. Some retailers have come to the conclusion that the best way to try to reinvent and retain the relevance of store-based retailing is to remove staff (and therefore staff costs) and deliver an experience more akin to a physical interpretation of an online experience.

---

[6] <http://newsroom.fb.com/news/2014/02/facebook-to-acquire-whatsapp>.
[7] Sir Charlie Mayfield, quoted in *The Times*, 7 Mar. 2014.

One such business is Hointer, based in Seattle. Hointer is part tech start-up (it sells its operating system to other enterprises) and has created what its founder describes as a 'micro-warehouse, controlled by customers' mobile phones and our algorithms' (which again raises the question of what a retailer is any more).[8] Hointer sells mostly branded jeans—about 150 styles—in a physical environment that is more warehouse than conventional store and notably devoid of staff, save for a security guard. Each product line has a QR code. Shoppers visiting the store download the Hointer app and scan the QR code of products they wish to try on—not something which can be done online of course. The app retains a list of all items selected and directs the shopper to a numbered changing room. A message is simultaneously sent to the store's automated stockroom and a robotics system delivers the items directly to the changing room. Unwanted items are dropped into a chute and deleted automatically from the virtual shopping cart. Shoppers can also use the app to request delivery of different sizes. If a purchase is made, the shopper taps the number of the changing room they used onto a touchscreen terminal and swipes a card or uses a digital wallet to make payment. Deliveries are free and guaranteed within forty-eight hours to all countries currently covered by the e-commerce site. Using the same app, staff have access to the customer's history, including everything they have tried on or returned, ensuring they receive service that is tailored and relevant. Frequent Hointer shoppers can leave the store without paying and be billed automatically by the app. The way that Hointer sees this version of a retail future is that store sizes can be smaller (there is less stock to display) but, most importantly, staff costs are far lower. In Hointer's view the customer gains a better experience than they can have online because they can try products on and also a better experience than they have in conventional stores because they do not have to engage with pushy sales staff.

Others may look to take the idea still further than Hointer. In early 2015, Amazon filed patent applications in the US for 'a system for automatically transitioning items from a materials handling facility without delaying a user as they exit the materials handling facility'.[9] It was reported at the time that the patent included using cameras, sensors, and RFID tags in-store, which would allow Amazon to identify customers and their purchases. The shopper leaves the location with their items and is automatically billed without having to queue to collect their items or to pay a cashier. All of the technology to enable such a system exists already. Interesting also is that the patent application talks of a system that could set an 'optional rental price or "borrow

---

[8] <http://www.theaustralian.com.au/business/no-clicks-but-online-ease-brought-to-stores/story-e6frg8zx-1226983490355>.

[9] <http://www.retailgazette.co.uk/blog/2015/04/amazons-revolutionary-idea-for-retail-stores>.

time" with the shopper'. This points to a move from outright ownership to hiring only at the point of need (something we discuss later in this chapter). Whether this is even a store or a customer accessible collection facility is a moot point that highlights the essential futility of trying to make the distinction.

Such an innovation will not be for everyone—retailer or shopper—and it may prove to be illogical to try to reinvent stores by taking away personal interaction rather than adding more in but it is, nevertheless, an interesting reinterpretation of what a retail store can be.

Stores Without Stock

We discuss in Chapter 8 the changing role of the physical store in an omni-channel world and the need for retailers to rethink how they continue to keep their stores relevant. One opportunity that can play to the relative advantage of a physical space is to conceive of the store as being less a selling space and more a place of brand immersion and product showcase. Rather than seeing 'showrooming' (viewing product in store and then ordering online—often from someone else) as a challenge to be resisted, an alternative view is to accept the reality that many shoppers want to use stores in this way, and facilitate the process by helping the shopper to order on the same business's website products that they have been inspired by in-store.

Naturally, product uniqueness is a prerequisite for this strategy to be effective. Desigual, the fashion clothing retailer of Spanish origins (there has to be something about Spain that the country produces so many fashion brands that grow to global pre-eminence), has taken a characteristically creative approach. Desigual has created a format—La Vida es Chula (Life is Cool)—which explicitly treats the store as a showcase for the product and the brand rather than a selling space. Shoppers who visit the store are encouraged to make their purchases online. Its designers, KikiLab, describe the store itself as 'a no-stock concept with the advantage being in the inventory cost savings it represents'.[10] The store—immersive showroom might be a better definition—displays only best-sellers from current and previous collections and guest collections.

Quite unlike Hointer, the key to this approach is skilled store staff who act as personal shoppers rather than sales assistants. Staff advise shoppers on the look they want to create and products can be tried on, but the purchase itself is then made online using in-store tablets. Joan Rouras, Expansion Director of Desigual, says that '"brick and mortar" retail should not fight against other

---

[10] <http://www.kikilab.it/eng/desigual-la-vida-es-chula-store>.

channels, it has to find the way to collaborate with them, finding the way to win'.[11]

Subscription Retailing

> The future of general merchandise is not big box, it's to be delivered in a cardboard box.
>> (Dalton Philips, Former CEO, Morrisons, UK grocery retailer)[12]

For many shoppers, much the biggest part of their retail spend is predictable and repetitive and does not change from one shop to the next. Much of grocery, health & wellness, and household basics retailing has this characteristic. In such low-involvement categories, there is obvious opportunity for enterprises to deliver more convenience to the shopper by removing the drudgery of making such purchases. The model of the shopper as a human picking and distribution agent—going to the store, picking the merchandise, and then bringing it home—is replaced by a model where these functions are performed by the enterprise, not by the shopper. All of the online grocery delivery services around the world follow this model in concept, even if the execution varies. It is worth noting that this can present very considerable challenges for brands that are not market leaders in their categories and for FMCG businesses seeking to introduce new products. There is a sizeable challenge in persuading shoppers to switch brands and trial new products when the ordering process is taking place entirely online and, very often, the shopper is not selecting specific items at all, rather they are simply pressing the button to confirm that their order will be the same as the one they placed before.

Subscription retailing, especially for commodity items, does not have to be conducted by traditional retailers. There is a clear opportunity for brands to deliver direct to the shopper, bypass the retailer entirely, and, in the process, capture for themselves the margin that the retailer would have earned and also eliminate the listing fees and promotional charges that FMCG businesses typically incur if they wish to have a presence on a retailer's shelves—real or virtual. Many are already exploiting this possibility. Two intriguingly niche examples are Dollar Shave Club in the US and Evian in France. Dollar Shave Club (dollarshaveclub.com) does what it says on the tin—delivers razors direct to the shopper's home for US$1 a month (or US$6 or US$9 if you want a better blade). In France in 2012, Evian launched their Evian Chez Vous bottled water home delivery service with a SmartDrop fridge magnet whereby the shopper

---

[11] <http://europe-re.com/an-interview-with-joan-rouras-desigual/41003>.
[12] A. Lawson, 'Analysis: Morrisons Boss Dalton Philips' "Killer Concept" ', *Retail Week*, 15 Mar. 2012.

at home enters the type and amount of bottled water they want and when they want it delivered. The SmartDrop fridge magnet then uses the shopper's home wifi network to send the order direct to Evian. This is just a small quirky (and, it should be said, marketing-led) innovation on the way to fully connected so-called smart home appliances where, for example, fridges will automatically replenish from preferred vendors items before they run out with no shopper involvement at all. (In 2015 at the hugely important Consumer Electronics Show, the CEO of Samsung Electronics announced that by 2020 every product they make will be connected to the internet.[13])

The automation of basic needs retailing in particular opens up significant opportunities but also raises challenges for enterprises fulfilling those orders as well as for vendors of the brands which are being purchased. Again, the point must be made that it cannot be assumed that traditional retailers will be either the best placed or the preferred enterprises to deliver this service.

Hiring, Not Buying

Ideas of consumption and attitudes to ownership are changing, especially amongst Millennials. Many shoppers are very used to and comfortable with the idea of hiring products at the point of need or desire, rather than outright ownership. (How sensible is to buy outright a power drill when the average drill is used for less than twenty minutes before being discarded?). Goldman Sachs surveyed their interns in 2013 and discovered that owning items ranging from cars to luxury bags and TVs were not primary goals for these individuals.[14] The automotive industry, for example, is having to address itself to the reality that many people—especially in high-density congested urban areas—do not want to own vehicles per se; rather, it is the mobility that vehicles provide which they want. As such, many manufacturers have developed schemes where customers can rent a vehicle appropriate to their needs at that time (van, people carrier, sports car, etc.) and for a specific time only—even just half an hour or so. Membership-based vehicle hire services that provide vehicle mobility without ownership have proliferated in many urban centres. Zipcar ('Wheels when you want them') is one of the largest such clubs with, at July 2015, over 900,000 members and 10,000 vehicles in North America and Europe[15]). In some ways more interesting is the Autolib' system in Paris which operates a fleet of identical electric cars designed for the scheme and which can be hired by members in thirty-minute units. An

---

[13] <http://mobilemarketingmagazine.com/samsung-iot-2020>.
[14] <http://www.goldmansachs.com/our-thinking/pages/millennials>.
[15] <http://en.wikipedia.org/wiki/Zipcar>.

annual membership costs €120 and the hire cost per thirty minutes is €5.50. In mid-2015, Autolib' had 3,500 vehicles and over 200,000 subscribers.[16]

There are compelling reasons to believe that consumers, especially in younger age groups, will continue to move away from outright ownership and towards hiring. The continued growth in urban populations globally, with the attendant challenges of living in small spaces, suggests that hiring, not owning, may be the best solution for many. Concerns for sustainability seem likely to strengthen the case for hiring at the point of need. Consumers may wish also to 'future proof' their purchases in categories subject to rapid change—consumer technology products being the most obvious example— by hiring products with a guaranteed upgrade when a new version of that product is launched. The smartphone market already works in just this way in many countries and it is not difficult to imagine the market for other consumer electronic and electrical products following suit. Retail enterprises— whatever form they take—have interesting opportunities to reframe at least part of their offer away from providing ownership across a product lifecycle and towards providing a hire service at the point of consumer need.

Peer-to-Peer (P2P) Sharing

As well as a future where some shoppers do not want to buy outright, we can also envisage a future where hiring and sharing takes place not just between an organization and an individual but rather directly between two individuals with an intermediary acting as facilitator. What eBay did for facilitating person-to-person ownership transactions, others are now aspiring to do for person-to-person sharing. Zilok is one example. Zilok began in France in 2007 and has subsequently expanded to other markets. In essence, Zilok is an online rental site that puts renters together with rentees—individuals and companies.

The idea of peer-to-peer sharing need not be limited to physical products alone. The French home improvement retailer, Castorama (part of the UK Kingfisher group), launched 'Les Troc Heures' (barter hours) in 2011.[17] The idea is that, through the Les Troc Heures website, people list the DIY skills that they have and the DIY skills that they need and an exchange of time and capabilities is made between two individuals. In its first five months of operation, 3,000 members signed up and 800 exchanges took place. Many enterprises will no doubt view this as something in which they would not wish to engage (consumer protection and liability issues would appear to loom

---

[16] <https://www.autolib.eu/en>.

[17] Press release, 2011, 'Castorama lance le troc des heures'. <http://www.aladom.fr/blog/castorama-lance-le-troc-des-heures-458.html>.

large). But it is nevertheless interesting to see a retail enterprise playing the role of facilitator in a peer-to-peer exchange and recognizing that the traditional linear model of selling products to shoppers may be only one of several ways in which a retailer can deliver value to a shopper. Biggest of all is Airbnb which connects people all over the world with a spare room with others who need a place to stay. At one level Airbnb is usurping the traditional hotel chains, but at another Airbnb is providing something more fundamental. Bill Carroll at Cornell University's School of Administration says: 'Airbnb is not a lodging brand. It's a virtual marketplace, like eBay. It's always going to be niche, constrained by how many people want to stay in an Airbnb type of experience.'[18]

Dynamic Pricing Models

There are interesting possibilities for retailers to move away from fixed pricing models with their implicit presumption that all shoppers must pay the same price at all times and offer instead dynamic pricing whereby shoppers are treated differently and where time of purchase also influences the pricing model. In many other sectors, notably travel and hospitality (hotel rooms especially), shoppers are well used to the notion that the price they pay will be different depending on when they are making a booking and whether they are, at a crude level, a Gold, Silver, or Bronze customer. Enabled by meaningful customer insights, it is very possible to conceive of retailers employing similar principles. Indeed, many already do. The US grocery retailer Safeway began trialling its 'Just for U' programme in mid-2010, which provides tailored price discounts of up to 20 per cent. By late 2014 the programme had around 5 million registered users out of around 9 million unique householders shopping with Safeway each week. Incremental spend by Just for U shoppers continued to exceed Safeway's original estimates by more than 50 per cent.[19] As Near Field Communication (NFC) devices in store become far more widespread, there is clear opportunity to personalize pricing much more closely to the point of purchase as well as to evolve this programme to one where the shopper nominates the products to which they want to have their personal discounts applied. Indeed, Waitrose, the grocery retailer in the UK, has done just this for members of its loyalty programme. At launch in mid-2015, customers could choose ten items out of nearly 1,000 products on

---

[18] <http://www.fastcompany.com/3027107/punk-meet-rock-airbnb-brian-chesky-chip-conley>.

[19] M. Johnson, 'Safeway's Just for U Loyalty Program Brings Great Customer Engagement'. <http://loyalty360.org/resources/article/safeways-just-for-u-loyalty-program-brings-great-customer-engagement#sthash.XmloGZSh.dpuf>.

which they could receive a regular 20 per cent discount for up to three months.[20]

Dynamic pricing can also be used to incentivize with lower prices not just those who are most loyal to a retailer, but also those whose opinions are most influential or have the greatest reach on social media. Spaaza, based in the Netherlands, is one amongst several innovative marketing businesses that provides this capability. Spaaza's MyPrice allows retailers to offer lower prices in store to individual customers according to their influence in social media. The retailer adds a MyPrice tag to price labels in store in addition to the regular price tag. Registered shoppers scan the QR code to gain access to their personal price which has been set by an algorithm which calculates the discount based on a shopper's influence in social media and their preferences and Likes on Facebook. Likewise, interesting opportunities exist to change prices by day part, perhaps especially for convenience-orientated food retailers.

Dynamic pricing is already very commonplace online (prominent examples include Uber and, of course, Amazon), but third-party price optimization businesses such as Boomerang Commerce with its Dynamic Price Optimizer, are successfully incorporating this capability into retail categories from office supplies to department stores—yet the principle is not without controversy.[21] Retailers considering deploying it need to think carefully and act with integrity. The online travel service, Orbitz, controversially tailored its prices based on the device users were employing to access its website when it found that Apple users would pay US$20 to US$30 more for a hotel room than other device users.[22] There can also be a suggestion that prices in-store become inflated artificially to fund discounts that are only available to those with a loyalty card. Multi-tiered programmes can be still more controversial. Dorothy Lane Market, an upscale grocery chain in Ohio, implemented customer-specific pricing through its DLM Club. Different prices were charged to a number of different customer groups, the effect of which was that the majority of all discounts available in store went only to the top 30 per cent of Dorothy Lane Market shoppers, to the considerable disenfranchisement of the other 70 per cent.

---

[20] <http://www.thedrum.com/news/2015/06/17/waitrose-rolls-out-game-changing-alternative-mass-discounting-pick-your-own-offers>.

[21] M. Carney, 'Democratizing Amazon: Boomerang Commerce raises $8.5M to deliver ecommerce intelligence to the rest of retail', Pando, 16 July 2014. <https://pando.com/2014/07/16/democratizing-amazon-boomerang-commerce-raises-8-5m-to-deliver-ecommerce-intelligence-to-the-rest-of-retail>.

[22] D. Mattioli, 'On Orbitz, Mac Users Steered to Pricier Hotels', Wall Street Journal, 23 Aug. 2012. <http://www.wsj.com/articles/SB10001424052702304458604577488822667325882>.

Case 5.2 XIAOMI AND THE NEW RETAIL

Xiaomi might just be the most important technology company that most people have never heard of. As with most things related to technology in China, the numbers are remarkable. Founded in April 2010, Xiaomi launched its first mobile phone in August 2011 and has subsequently launched a wide range of consumer electronics devices, including more smartphones, tablets, wearable tech, and smart home device ecosystems. Selling mobile phones is what Xiaomi is best known for and the business is exceptionally good at it. In 2014 (just three years after the launch of its first product), Xiaomi sold 60 million smartphones.[23] In 2015 the number is likely to exceed 100 million. Xiaomi is already the third largest smartphone maker in the world (Lenovo and LG being fourth and fifth respectively). It is growing outside China across Asia and growth into South America seems likely to closely follow. Some indication of Xiaomi's international ambitions came in April 2015 when the company launched its new premium smartphone, the Mi 4i, in India rather than China. At the end of 2014, Xiaomi secured US$1.1 billion in funding from investors, which valued the business at US$46 billion and made Xiaomi the world's most highly valued technology start-up business.[24]

The importance of Xiaomi extends far beyond its startling growth as a maker of smartphones and other consumer electronics products. Three main elements distinguish the Xiaomi business model:

(i) Hardly a hardware business at all

Xiaomi is quite unlike Samsung, Apple, and the other smartphone and consumer electronics makers. Xiaomi say that their products are sold at close to 'bill-of-material' prices.[25] This is achieved by keeping key products in market longer than the norm in consumer electronics—around eighteen months rather than six months in the case of a smartphone—in order to benefit from reductions in the price of key components over the lifecycle of the product. More importantly, for Xiaomi the hardware devices themselves serve as the entry point into the world of Xiaomi. As Hugo Barra, Xiaomi VP (and ex-Google), has been extensively quoted as saying, 'We are an internet and a software company much more than a hardware company.'[26] The objective is not to maximize profits from hardware sales, it is to build communities of Xiaomi users by keeping device costs low. The devices serve as platforms for entry into Xiaomi's content world of apps, games, and online video. (In late 2014, Xiaomi announced that it would spend around US$1 billion developing TV content.[27]) For Xiaomi the objective is to envelop its users into the total world of Xiaomi, which has at its heart its MIUI operating system that ties all of its devices together. In this respect, one could regard Xiaomi as bringing the 'internet of things' vision far more to reality than most others have been able to thus far.

---

[23] <http://techcrunch.com/2015/01/03/xiaomi-2014>.

[24] <http://www.marketwatch.com/story/xiaomi-raises-another-11-billion-to-become-most-valuable-tech-start-up-2014-12-29>.

[25] <http://www.telegraph.co.uk/technology/mobile-phones/10880495/How-can-Xiaomi-sell-its-phones-so-cheaply.html>.

[26] <https://gigaom.com/2014/10/28/xiaomis-hugo-barra-iphone-6-and-ios-8-design-have-been-inspired-by-htc-and-android>.

[27] <http://www.investing.com/news/technology-news/china's-xiaomi-says-to-invest-$1-billion-in-tv-content-building-315292>.

(ii) Selling to its fans

A second defining feature of the Xiaomi business is that the company seeks to build relationships with its users through their involvement in product co-creation. Software businesses typically launch new versions of software very quickly. But Xiaomi takes this to a further level by involving users in the co-creation of its operating system. Online forums capture customer feedback and new shipments of phones go out every week at midday Beijing time, incorporating customer feedback from the previous week. As well as co-creation, this is—by the conventional standards of the category—very short-run production that allows the opportunity for rapid and frequent product changes.[28] As the business says of the development of its latest MIUI operating system (v6 at the time of writing), 'Co-developed by millions of MIUI fans, well received by 100 million users.'[29]

(iii) Selling in a different way

We noted in Chapter 1 that the Millennial shopper in particular regards shopping as a 'digital first' activity which may, but very often will not, have a physical store component. Xiaomi has tapped into this reality. Xiaomi does not own any physical stores. Rather, it goes to market entirely online. Its own Mi.com website is its main channel to market and already the third biggest e-commerce website in China. (When Xiaomi bought the mi.com domain name for US$3.6 million in early 2014 it was the highest price ever paid in China for a domain name—certainly expensive for a domain name, but not for a flagship piece of retail real estate.) Hugely successful flash sales are a big part of how Xiaomi goes to market. In India, Xiaomi initially sold its Redmi note tablet only through flash sales on Flipkart ('The online megastore'), before it was made more widely available, but still only through online platforms. In the first flash sale of the Redmi note, the 50,000 units in stock were reportedly sold out in just six seconds.[30] On 6 April 2015, Xiaomi celebrated its fifth anniversary with its Mi Fan Festival. This included an online shopping day that broke the world record for most mobile phones sold on a single platform in twenty-four hours—a remarkable 2.1 million devices.[31]

Xiaomi also talks to its customers in a different way to many businesses. The business's extraordinary growth has been achieved without any investment in conventional advertising. Rather, word of mouth, digital, and social media are its main communication vehicles. Again, this points to a reality that Millennials in particular need to be engaged in a different way which, happily, is likely to come at significantly lower cost for a brand and be much more effective than traditional mass media.

As well as delivering extraordinary growth, Xiaomi is also achieving what it perhaps values most—deep reach into the lives of its target Millennials audience. Xiaomi users in China skew much more heavily towards 18–34 year olds than do other smartphone brands (Figure 5.1). These are the Millennials whose lives have been shaped by China's one-child policy and their concomitant desire to reach out and form connections with others, together with the enabling effects of extraordinarily rapid modernization and technology enablement.

(continued)

---

[28] <http://www.androidpolice.com/2013/10/23/hugo-barra-describes-how-xiaomi-pushes-out-weekly-hardware-updates-turning-user-feedback-into-shipped-product-in-a-matter-of-days>.

[29] <http://en.miui.com/default.php>.

[30] <http://tech.firstpost.com/news-analysis/redmi-note-sold-out-in-six-seconds-is-the-xiaomi-phablet-worth-rs-8999-243937.html>.

[31] <http://www.guinnessworldrecords.com/news/2015/4/mi-com-sells-2-million-smartphones-in-a-day-to-set-sales-world-record-376583>.

Case 5.2 Continued

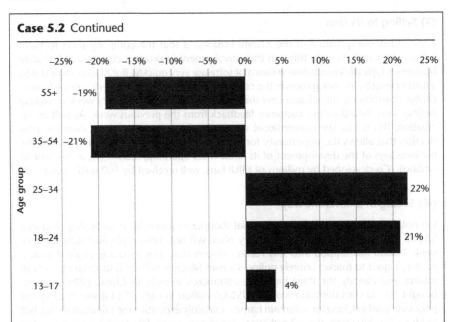

Figure 5.1 Xiaomi users indexed vs. age of all Chinese smartphone users

Source: http://flurrymobile.tumblr.com/post/115192342780/xiaomi-brings-apples-magic-to-chinas-young.

Some argue that Xiaomi has had a relatively easy run in its first five years—a huge domestic market with an apparently insatiable appetite for technology; addressing a young consumer of the one-child era who values making connections much more than most, and the absence of Google in China as a content competitor. The extent to which Xiaomi devices are truly innovative or simply very good facsimiles of Apple products in particular has also been raised by some.[32] What is undeniable, however, is that Xiaomi is very much a business created in the spirit of the new landscape of retail. It is part technology company, part retailer without stores, part co-developed content creator, and part user-centred 'internet of things' device developer and integrator. In the new landscape of retailing, the old conventions of what a retail enterprise is are no longer relevant. Xiaomi looks already like a formidable agent of change in, and increasingly beyond, China. It is a powerful example of what can be created when an enterprise is able to build a new type of business for the present and the future without being constrained by old thinking from the past.

The Changing Cost Model for Traditional Retailers

Most established retailers in mature markets will need to come to terms with a rather different operating cost model than the one they have been accustomed to in the pre-internet era when retailing was conducted entirely out

---

[32] <http://arstechnica.com/gadgets/2014/08/xiaomi-mi4-review-chinas-iphone-killer-is-unoriginal-but-amazing>.

of physical stores (with the exception of the mail order operators). In an omni-channel world where shoppers are, as we have discussed, showing much more appetite to shop online and across multiple touchpoints, the implications for the cost model of traditional retailers are considerable.

Table 5.1 Changes to main cost components for established, store-centric retailers: a generalized model

Change	Cost factor	Explanation of change
Increasing	IT	(a) Replacement & integration of legacy systems; (b) additional customer-centric capability requirements, offset by (c) growth in more automated decision-making.
	Distribution	Dominant model migrates from 'last mile' distribution costs being incurred by the shopper (visiting stores) to the retailer (delivering to multiple individual points).
	Inventory	Longer term upwards pressure on cost of goods for retailers sourcing from emerging markets moving from low cost manufacturing-led to more consumer-led economies.
No change	Labour	Decreases associated with exiting substantial store level personnel offset for many by growth in high cost, specialist roles elsewhere, such as data analytics and IT.
Decreasing	Store property	Ongoing costs will decrease for many as retailers exit substantial parts of their store portfolios. However, many will also incur one-off exit & transitional costs.
	Marketing	Material savings feasible for many moving advertising spend from high cost, broad reach conventional media to lower cost & more personally targeted & effective digital media.

Source: Authors.

Table 5.1 presents a general description of the major changes to key cost components to which many retailers will need to address themselves. For many, being relevant to their target audiences and competitive against other enterprises will require substantial additional ongoing spend in distribution and IT in particular as enterprises reorientate from a store-centric model to a truly customer-centric model with engagement across multiple touchpoints. Additional spend in these areas can, however, be offset partially or totally by reduced spend in physical store establishment and operating costs as retailers exit expensive retail space which is no longer needed and, with it, the associated staff costs to operate that space. It is, however, important to recognize that the one-off costs associated with exiting substantial amounts of real estate can be very considerable—as the UK's major food retailers will readily attest to (all of the 'Big 4' have had to take substantial write-downs on their portfolios of existing and pipeline stores). Nor is it always clear where demand is going to come from for the use of this space. Retailers with heavy real estate obligations are therefore very mindful of the timing of break clauses in leases and arrangements with landlords. For example, some 55 per cent of the leases entered into by UK retailer Argos were due to expire or have break points between 2015 and 2020, and 30 per cent by 2018.[33] For many, we would also expect enterprises to be able to realize savings in their advertising and marketing spend as those activities are reorientated out of expensive traditional media and into much lower cost digital communications. Of course, for almost all retailers cost of goods sold (COGS) is, by some considerable way, much the biggest cost of doing business. In this area it is not especially helpful to make generalizations but we suggest that for most retailers the pressure on cost of goods sold will be more likely to be upwards than downwards as input prices increase and the major centres of low-cost production, especially China, evolve away from manufacturing-led economies and towards more consumption-driven economies.

Quite where the new cost model for retailers nets out is difficult to say and, again, generalizations are not helpful. Some retailers—Argos in the UK being an obvious example—have found that, contrary to their early expectations, they have needed to open more stores as they migrated to an omni-channel operation, for example. And, as we note, the transitional costs—especially in real estate—of exiting a large proportion of the store portfolio can be truly alarming, not least for shareholders. For many, fulfilment costs will likely be a major area of concern. It is clear that for many omni-channel retailers around the world the fulfilment cost charged to the shopper is materially less than the actual cost incurred by the retailer. The solution to this issue might be to raise fees to the shopper to better reflect the actual cost of providing the service. But this will be by no means universally possible for obvious reasons of consumer acceptability and competitive realities. Rather better for many will be to seek efficiencies in the fulfilment process. However, driving out such efficiencies typically comes with a considerable price tag in the form of substantial capital investment in distribution architecture (notably automated warehousing). Nor is this challenge one exclusively faced by brick and mortar retailers. Amazon's warehouse building programme between 2010 and 2013 totalled US$13.9 billion to deliver fifty additional units in the US alone. These buildings are bigger than Amazon has historically operated and take advantage of efficiencies such as floor-to-ceiling racking and storage optimization techniques.[34] Squaring this particular circle for omni-channel retailers will be challenging. For many, the best opportunity may be to concentrate on growing sales and spreading a necessarily higher cost component across more sales

---

[33] <https://www.homeretailgroup.com/media/268370/investor_pack_may_2015.pdf>.

[34] D. Kucera, 'Why Amazon is on a Warehouse Building Spree', *Bloomberg Business*, 29 Aug. 2013. <http://www.bloomberg.com/bw/articles/2013-08-29/why-amazon-is-on-a-warehouse-building-spree>.

volume. In this respect, the experiences of many retailers that customers who shop with them across multiple channels spend considerably more in total than those that use one channel only, offers grounds for encouragement. We have talked in this chapter of the challenges that traditional retailers face from enterprises which see themselves as being in the business of retailing but do not have a heritage as retailers. But it is particularly difficult to compare the financial models of online-only, stores-only, and omni-channel businesses. Principally this is because of the difficulty of disaggregating specific cost components (rent, labour, distribution, and so on) from published accounts as well as different treatments of where in the P&L those costs are aggregated (often into a total cost of sales figure which includes cost of goods sold as well as employee, distribution, and other cost components). The challenge of making meaningful comparisons increases further for businesses which trade across a number of geographies and product categories (especially when that combines food and general merchandise) and which are subject to different accounting and tax regimes in different countries.

Table 5.2 illustrates rather more the nature of the challenge than it sheds clarity on the make-up of different cost components.

Table 5.2 Cost models of store and online grocery retailers: an example from the UK

	MORRISONS 52 weeks ended 1 Feb. 2014 Store:online sales = 100:0 % of sales	SAINSBURY 52 weeks to 15 Mar. 2014 Store:online sales = 95:5 % of sales	OCADO 52 weeks to 30 Nov. 2014 Store:online sales = 0:100 % of sales
Revenue	100	100	100
Cost of sales	93.9 (1)	94.2	67
Distribution costs			26.7 (2)
Employment costs	11.2	10.2	17.8
Depreciation charges—property, plant, equipment	1.9	2.2	4.2
Operating lease rentals			1
Administrative expenses	2.0 (3)	1.9	9.0 (4)
Operating profit before tax, JV & exceptional items			1.5

(1) Cost of sales consists of all costs to the point of sale including manufacturing, warehouse, and transportation costs. Store depreciation, store overheads, and store-based employee costs are also allocated to cost of sales.

(2) Distribution costs consist of all the costs incurred, excluding product costs, to the point of sale. In most cases, this is the customer's home. This includes the payroll-related expenses for the picking, dispatch, and delivery of products sold to the point of sale, the cost of making those deliveries, including fuel, tolls, maintenance of vehicles, the operating costs of the properties required for the picking, dispatch, and onward delivery operations, and all associated depreciation, amortization, and impairment charges, call centre costs, and payment processing charges.

(3) Excludes non-recurring exceptional charges: £903m in 2014.

(4) Administrative expenses consist of all IT costs, advertising and marketing expenditure (excluding vouchers), share-based payments costs, employment costs of all central functions, which include board, legal, finance, human resources, marketing and procurement, rent and other property-related costs for the head office, all fees for professional services and the depreciation, amortization, and impairment associated with IT equipment, software, fixtures and fittings. Additionally, this includes costs incurred on behalf of Morrisons that are subsequently recharged.

What insight can we gain from this table, or are we simply comparing apples and pears? (Ocado is an entirely online business. Morrisons had no online business for the period under review, and Sainsbury's online business was a relatively small proportion of group total sales—around 5 per cent—but nevertheless a reasonably large business in its own right at around £1 billion of sales or much the same as the total Ocado business.) Ocado's Cost of Sales is notably lower than that of Morrisons and Sainsbury. But this is much more to do with the treatment of distribution costs and employee costs than it is with any cost of goods advantage that Ocado enjoys. Employment costs as a percentage of sales appear to be higher for the online-only retailer than its competitors. While this may be the case—reflecting Ocado's need for a relatively greater proportion of staff in 'last mile' distribution functions—it is more likely to reflect the ability of the two much larger retailers to spread their employment costs over greater sales volumes. Administrative expenses as a percentage of sales are over four times higher in Ocado than the two other businesses. This may be a consequence of the treatment of specific cost components within this line item, but it seems likely also to reflect Ocado's substantially higher IT spend as a proportion of sales (IT costs being included in Ocado's total administrative expenses). All that can be said with certainty in this example is that a store-based retailer does not necessarily have an operating cost disadvantage, but it certainly has a very different cost structure to a pure online business.

What is of perhaps more interest in this example is that, irrespective of the cost model for the retailer, UK store-based retailers are already making significant adjustments to their balance sheets. During the period in this example, Morrison's wrote down the value of its existing stores by £379 million and the value of its pipeline of new stores by a further £319 million. In April 2015, Sainsbury announced that it planned to convert 6 per cent of its space (around 1.5 million sq.ft.) in UK grocery supermarkets into non-food as grocery sales continued to move online and into local convenience stores.[35]

Traditional retailers have to address themselves to the challenge of taking cost out of their store operations, revaluing their property assets and optimizing their store portfolios (which, for many, will involve making substantial reductions to store numbers and total trading areas). For internet retailers, the challenge is quite different. Here the issue is navigating a way out of what might be termed 'the profitless growth challenge'. The nature of this challenge is that efficiencies—especially in product picking and distribution—can only be achieved by making very substantial investments in warehousing, logistics, and IT as the necessary enabling business architecture components for an

[35] <http://www.telegraph.co.uk/finance/newsbysector/retailandconsumer/11539976/Sainsburys-to-convert-supermarkets-into-non-food-space.html>.

efficient online business. Amazon illustrates particularly well the problem of the profitless growth challenge. In the third quarter of 2014 Amazon reported a loss of US$437 million despite sales having increased by 20 per cent to US $20.6 billion. Jeff Bezos has always said that Amazon's priority is rapid growth and the profits will follow. To the non-believers this is an illusion: 'Add it all up, and Amazon's profits for its entire existence are still less than what ExxonMobil takes home every 2.5 weeks.'[36] For the believers, a share price multiple of well over 100 times (modest if any) earnings is justifiable if Amazon can reach so widely globally and so deeply into shoppers' lives that traditional brick and mortar retailers (trading on a multiple of perhaps five to twenty times earnings) are swept aside. The challenge of profitless growth is very familiar to many online retailers in many categories and geographies.

Our aim here is not to offer a prediction on which business model will win. Rather, it is to make the point that one of the most important defining features of the new landscape of retailing is the clash of business models and operating philosophies that is taking place. In markets of intense and disruptive competition, success and failure become very sharply polarized. We consider in Chapters 9 and 10 the attributes that are likely to be required of enterprises and business leaders if they are to be successful in these very changed times and environments.

The Need to Revisit Performance Metrics

As their go-to-market business models evolve, and possibly transform, retail enterprises will need to change their investment and return criteria. As we have shown, the investment and return model of an online business is almost entirely different to that of a store-based business. This changes the lens through which different parts of the enterprise need to be viewed and, therefore, the performance metrics that are employed. In any enterprise, what is measured naturally has a significant influence on what is done. It is critical, therefore, that the performance metrics that drive the business are aligned to the priorities and goals of the business. For most store-based retailers the key performance metrics are, understandably, focused on store performance, and space and staff productivity in particular. But it will be very difficult to persuade people to put their efforts into driving online sales if their personal rewards are determined by store sales, for example. Of course, conventional retail performance metrics are still relevant, not least to have visibility on the relative performance of different channels and shopper touch points.

---

[36] <http://www.investopedia.com/stock-analysis/031414/amazon-never-makes-money-no-one-cares-amzn-aapl-wag-azo.aspx>.

For many retail enterprises, it will probably be more helpful to employ more shopper-centric metrics as the key measures of overall business performance. For some retailers it may be most appropriate to focus on 'catchment sales' as the key metric while continuing to have visibility on the component parts of the total catchment sales number. For others, total sales per customer may be the better key metric (with the same caveat). As the chairman of a major European retailer told us (on condition of anonymity), 'Sales per square metre is not the right measurement any more. Sales per customer is what matters.'

The Shoppers' Contribution to the Retail Business Model

In the new retail landscape, the rhetoric is of a newly empowered shopper. Much discussion amongst commentators has been of the resultant structural disadvantage created for some retail enterprises.[37] The sector, it is suggested, has previously benefited from the lack of perfect information available to the shopper on prices, product attributes, and availability. As a result of this 'transfer of power', retailers' costs, particularly of IT and distribution, have increased (as Table 5.1 suggests). For example, the growth of home delivery has meant retailers taking on some of the shoppers' burden and absorbing many of the associated costs.

But the implications of cost transfers for established retail business models are not altogether negative. If we look at shopping as a total ecosystem (connecting suppliers, logistics companies, and retailers all the way through to shoppers) what we are indeed seeing are transfers of costs taking place as shoppers themselves acquire the wherewithal to undertake parts of the retailing process that have previously been undertaken by retailers. Writing critically of the ways in which efficiency and productivity are measured, noted UK economist John Kay suggested that 'the changes that have occurred in the past decade have, from an economic perspective, increased at virtually no cost the efficiency of household production'.[38] What he had in mind were the improvements in personal productivity for the individual consumer arising from activities ranging from newsgathering, ticket booking, and taxi hailing. Kay was writing to encourage new ways of collecting data on productivity, but there are important implications of this state of affairs for retailers, in that enterprises could actively promote more transfer of costs *to* shoppers

---

[37] e.g. B. Rezabakhsh et al., 'Consumer Power: A Comparison of the Old Economy and the Internet Economy', *Journal of Consumer Policy*, 29(1) (2006), 3–36.

[38] J. Kay, 'Miracles of Productivity Hidden in the Modern Home', *Financial Times*, 11 Aug. 2015. <http://www.ft.com/cms/s/0/a44d0a56-4009-11e5-b98b-87c7270955cf.html>.

(such as downloading, distribution, and information search). Paradoxically, the growth of home delivery is the precise opposite of this process. In a new retail landscape, a new trade-off would be the price that shoppers would have to pay to allow them to access, for example, more diverse engagement points and more convenient fulfilment opportunities. This process is, of course, no different in principle from the productivity gains that many retailers have historically achieved from a move to self-service—a situation in which shoppers picked up the burden (literally) of finding and carrying the physical product themselves.

Conclusion

Within the new landscape of retailing are to be found entirely new enterprises, which see themselves as legitimate players in the business of retailing, even given their very different starting points from established firms, with their historic merchandise focus. There is a strong sense that everyone is, or aspires to be, a retailer now, including technology companies, logistics enterprises, payment providers, and vendors. Shoppers on their own, or with their peers, are also taking up roles previously performed by retailers. 'New to retail' enterprises are in no sense less legitimate participants in the retail sector than are the conventional established retailers which, in earlier eras, built— literally—the landscape of store-based retailing and rose to national and, in some cases, international prominence.

What is taking place in the new landscape of retailing is not just a clash of business philosophies, operating cultures, and trading techniques but a clash, too, of business models. However, this debate has, we feel, become unhelpfully and simplistically polarized between those convinced that the business model of non-store retailing looks fundamentally better than that of store-based retailers and those convinced of the total opposite. When trading philosophies and business models collide, a willingness to contemplate and execute radical change may well prove to be necessary. For those retail enterprises with an established heritage in store-based retailing, this will almost certainly require a willingness to revisit fundamentally the ways in which the enterprise takes its offer to market. For many, this will suggest substantial change to the enterprise's operations and a very different business model in consequence. Savings made by closing large amounts of no longer needed real estate may be more than offset by investments needed in IT architecture, fulfilment systems, and people with more specialist skills than store-level staff have traditionally needed to have, for example. But equally it is far from clear that online retailers enjoy a built-in cost advantage over their store-led counterparts. The online retailers are going to have to prove the sustainability of their business models to anxious investors troubled by the spectre that the more they grow the bigger the losses seem to become.

Whatever the starting point, a large part of the answer for many enterprises will surely be to seek to extend their reach into more parts of their shoppers' worlds in order to drive greater sales volumes across a very different—and very possibly higher—cost base.

6

Bringing Order to the New World Order

The retail industry globally is in the early stages of a transformation that will, in our view, prove ultimately to be more profound in its impact on shoppers and retailers than any which has taken place before. Certainly, it will play out in different ways in different countries and locations and for different retail subsectors and individual enterprises. The landscape of retailing is not going to converge to a global norm. Rather, the forces of change which are reshaping the retail industry will have different expressions, reflecting the uniqueness of the locations and consumer environments where they are taking place as well as the very different starting points of those locations and consumer environments. But we should be in no doubt that the major forces of change reshaping the retail industry are global in nature. In the new landscape of retailing, it is legitimate—indeed necessary—to address questions which go to the very heart of what retailing is and what a retail business is.

All of the following questions can be answered with a definitive 'no'.

- Do you need shops to be in retailing?
- Will 'emerging' markets follow the same growth pathways as 'mature' markets?
- Are Western Europe and North America the exclusive sources of innovation in retailing?
- Do traditional retailers have an automatic right to 'own' the customer relationship?

And all of the following questions can be answered with a definitive 'yes'.

- Can tech companies, vendors, logistics, and payment companies be retailers?
- Can you be a retailer without selling products?
- Can a US$10,000 app sell more product than a US$10 million store?
- Can a blogger you've never heard of be more influential in shaping opinions on your business than a US$10 million advertising campaign?

While all of the following questions can be answered with a definitive 'maybe'.

- Will omni-channel be the dominant go-to-market model in the future?
- Will shoppers still value shops?
- Will traditional retailers be squeezed out of value chains as vendors and logistics businesses integrate forward to engage directly with the shopper?
- Will Alibaba be bigger than Walmart in ten years' time?

Technology is at the epicentre of the new landscape of retailing. In particular, technology in the hands of the shopper is changing profoundly the way that shoppers want to shop and the information to which they have access. In terms of access to information, what was once a relationship skewed overwhelmingly in favour of the retailer is now one skewed in favour of the shopper. As access to information has increased exponentially, so too has the access of shoppers to alternative opportunities to fulfil their needs and desires. For many already—and for very many more in the near-term future—shopping in many categories is becoming a global activity. While the choice criteria of shoppers are still based on their perceptions of quality, value, convenience, brand assurance, and fashionability—the relative emphasis varies by shopper and category—the sources of information that shape their opinions are radically different to those in an earlier era and so too are the range of fulfilment options, both domestically and internationally.

But technology in the hands of the shopper is not the only force of change in the new retail landscape. Technology is changing fundamentally the ways in which the business of retailing can be conducted. For established retailers, stores have to be constantly reinvented and store portfolios re-evaluated if they are to remain relevant and valued by a shopper who does not see retailing as a store-centric let alone a store-only activity. For major chains, reductions in store portfolio numbers of 50 per cent or more and radical reconfiguring of store formats is not difficult to envisage. Yet for others, increasing store numbers and reimagining stores as fulfilment points in an omni-channel landscape may be the right solution. Technology has a crucial role to play in the reinvention of established retail businesses. Technology in stores offers the opportunity to create more valued environments for the shopper, whether this comes from deeper experiences, more convenience, or both. Technology within the enterprise and across the value chain is an ever more crucial enabler of the ability of an enterprise to not only deliver the experience that the shopper desires but also to control what are becoming increasingly complex enterprises as retailers extend their reach geographically, by touchpoint, and across merchandise and service assortments. However, retailers, like all other enterprises, must act responsibly in their collection and use of customer information and, especially, in the security with which they treat it.

Technology is also bringing entirely new enterprises into the domain of retailing. To the question 'do you need to be a retailer to be in the business of retailing?' the answer is clearly no. Many enterprises with the potential to be amongst the most disruptive in the retail landscape do not self-identify with the notion that they are retail enterprises at all. Rather they are, at their core, technology companies applying their technology to build different types of retail enterprises.

While technology is at the heart of the new landscape of retailing, fundamental demographics are also reshaping the engagement environment between retailers and their shoppers. In particular, the Millennials are such an important and distinctive new cohort. Millennials have grown up in a world where digital is not an adjunct to their pre-existing lives; rather digital *is* their lives. It is the Millennials in particular who challenge time-honoured presumptions of what a retailer is and should be and what retailing is. The challenge for many retailers seeking to engage the Millennial shopper and secure the Millennial dollar is not to persuade them to keep coming into their stores, but to explain to them why stores are still relevant to them at all. For the Millennials, much of their shopping lives is a 'digital first, stores maybe' existence. It is, in particular, the combination of transformative technology and fundamental demographics that makes the new landscape of retailing so different from that which has gone before.

At a global scale, rapidly urbanizing populations are accelerators of retail modernization and transformation. In the new retail markets, most notably those in the Far East, this manifests itself in a highly digitally literate shopper, with disposable income, an awareness of and an appetite for modern forms of shopping. Here, the growth of e-commerce is concomitant with the enduring, even strengthening, appeal of modern shopping centres as places for both entertainment and shopping. Much of Western Europe and North America now looks over-spaced at both a category and a total sector level. This will not stop still more space being added, but it will be different in quality, location, and function to much of that which exists already. While better quality, better configured space is added in, poorer quality, poorer configured space will be removed. Tesco's announcement in early 2015 that it was abandoning the development of forty-nine superstore sites,[1] including several that had already been built and were ready to trade, seemed ominously indicative of a much wider trend. Furthermore, powerful forces of social change are radically altering the engagement environment for retailers (of whatever type) with their shoppers. Much of the physical landscape of modern retailing created in the Western markets since the early 1960s is predicated on a presumption of high levels of affordable car ownership. Neither high nor affordable can be

---

[1] <http://www.theguardian.com/business/2015/jan/29/tesco-towns-count-cost-retail-empire-retreat>.

presumed going forward. The nature of the engagement between many retailers and many of their shoppers has to change when these presumptions are no longer valid. Instead of the assumption embedded in the old retail paradigm that the shopper comes to the retailer, in the new paradigm that we are in the early stages of, the role of the retailer will be to come to the shopper with more convenient points of engagement—physical and/or digital.

As well as its disruptive nature, it is the speed of change which defines the new landscape of retailing. In the consumer landscape, trends and whims and opinions move around the world—physically and digitally—at speeds that would not have been possible or believable in the pre-internet era. Neither is the direction of travel linear and fairly predictable in the ways that it was when media was mass, not personal, and the message was controlled by the business, not the customer. As well as change being rapid, unpredictable, and difficult to anticipate in the consumer environment, the same is true in the competitive landscape. New brands, new competitors, and new business types are emerging—often to positions of great influence and prominence—with accelerating speed. One of the defining features of the new retail landscape is that businesses and brands can be created and destroyed at previously unimaginable speed.

The Ordering Change Framework

For business leaders, one of the main challenges in the new landscape of retailing is that change is happening so quickly that everything can seem urgent, immediate, and important. It is difficult to prioritize when everything seems to be a high priority. Figure 6.1 presents a framework for ordering the new world order of change in the retail industry.

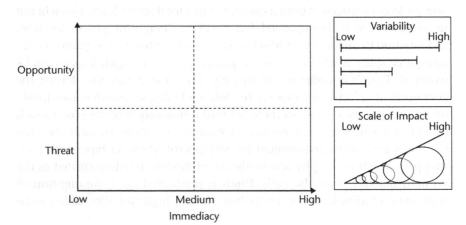

Figure 6.1 Ordering change framework
Source: Authors.

Our grid combines four dimensions for ordering change:

1. Whether change represents an opportunity or a threat
2. The level of immediacy of change (Low being long-term; High being immediate)
3. The anticipated scale of impact on the retail enterprise
4. The level of certainty or uncertainty (i.e. variability) that the change represents

Point 4 is especially important. We discuss in Chapter 10 the question of how certain an enterprise and a business leader can be on the nature of change in uncertain times. What appears to represent a strong business opportunity may in fact, when looked at from a different perspective or at a different point in time, represent a risk to the business. It is especially important to be able to accommodate the reality that absolute certainty is almost impossible to find in fast-changing and uncertain worlds.

Figure 6.2 populates our Change Framework with the major changes reshaping the retail landscape that we have discussed in Part 1, which is to say:

- Shopper-facing technology
- Consumer change: the Millennials
- Business technology change
- Urbanization
- Internationalization
- New business models

We begin with an important caveat. This is a very generalized positioning of the major change drivers reshaping the retail landscape. We are not suggesting that the positionings, the scale of impact we envisage, or the level of certainty (or uncertainty) that we suggest for each change dimension will be accurate reflections of the nature of retail change in all geographies, all retail sectors, or for all enterprises. In fact, to be rather more explicit, we are suggesting the precise opposite: that the positionings proposed very definitely do not reflect the actual nature of change in all geographies, subsectors, or enterprises. What is important is for different enterprises to conduct their own evaluations of the nature of change.

With this caveat in mind, there are a number of points of guidance that we are confident in making:

1. At the level of the retail industry overall, we suggest that the profound changes reshaping the retail landscape represent more opportunities than they pose threats for retail enterprises. But it must be acknowledged also that unrealized opportunities can quickly turn into threats and, equally, that threats successfully addressed become opportunities.

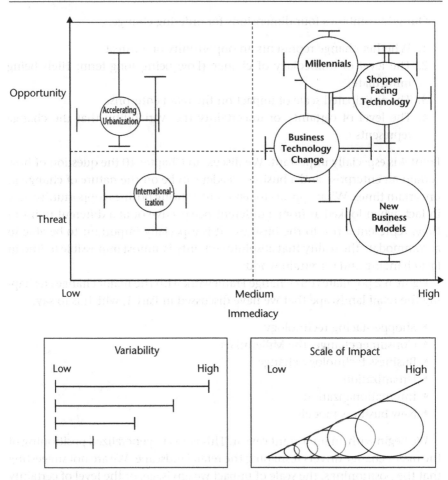

Figure 6.2 Change framework—the major change drivers
Source: Authors.

2. At the level of the retail industry as a whole, technology in the hands of shoppers and the rise of the Millennials as an ever-more powerful consumer group will likely be amongst the most important change drivers that most retailers face.

3. There is a high level of uncertainty around the level of importance that the Millennials in particular represent. It would be misleading to assign a higher level of certainty to the possible impact of Millennials as a consumer group (or tribe). This reflects in particular the extent to which Millennials are now and will in future be a significant part of any one retailers' target audience as well as the disruptive nature of new technology in the hands of this group.

4. The impact of technology within retail enterprises is both a major opportunity as well as a threat for many retailers. The opportunity, as discussed in Chapter 2, is for retail enterprises to enhance their technology architecture in order to better deliver an enhanced experience for the shopper. (Precisely how this is dimensionalized depends on the proposition a retailer is seeking to deliver.) The reason why technology change can represent also a considerable challenge is, again as we noted in Chapter 2, the problem that established retailers in particular have of needing constantly to update their technology architecture as well as integrate legacy systems.

5. The presence in the retail sector of new entrants with business models that are very different from those of traditional store-based retailers has the potential to be the most disruptive change of all. This is, however, also the territory where there is greatest variability surrounding the extent to which this change driver represents a threat or an opportunity. For 'non-traditional' retailers, notably the online-only or online-mostly enterprises, their entire operations are only possible because of the new business models they deploy. Similarly, that growing group of enterprises, including logistics businesses, payment providers, and technology companies, is aggressively exploiting the opportunity to bring their very different competencies and business models into the retail sector. The reason why we suggest that the entry into the retail sector of such 'new to retail' enterprises is likely to be an immediate threat is because of the disruptive challenge they represent to the interests of established retail enterprises in particular. But we are perfectly happy to accept that many established retailers will see the chance to engineer new capabilities into their own enterprises as a substantial opportunity.

6. In respect of industry internationalization, the extent to which this is a challenge or an opportunity will vary widely for different retailers. At a general level the challenge of internationalization is that it exposes a retailer to much more competition. Locally protected markets very quickly become globally accessible (as we discussed in Chapter 4 in the context of Australia). Nevertheless, the opposite is true also in that a retail enterprise now has access to, quite literally, a world of opportunities and consumers that it previously did not. Quite where the balance lies can only be addressed at the level of the individual business. We have suggested that internationalization lives more in the territory of a challenge than an opportunity because the globalization of markets is a *potential challenge* for almost all enterprises but a *realizable opportunity* for only some. We suggest also that for many retail enterprises, but certainly not for all, the challenges or opportunities associated with internationalization will be of less immediate priority than those of consumer and technology change.

7. Accelerating urbanization is, as we discussed in Chapter 3, a powerful force of long-term change in the retail landscape, particularly in countries that are currently less mature in a macro-economic if not a retailing sense. Clearly, the extent to which considerations of urbanization need to be on the agenda of retail enterprises and their leaders depends in particular on the extent to which they trade or seek to trade in countries and regions subject to this trend. In this respect, urbanization is the most geographically defined of the macro change drivers we identify. We do, however, caution that it is not just the scale but also the form of urbanization that is relevant to retailers. Even in those locations where the absolute scale of urbanization is not increasing, the form of urban living is nevertheless changing, often so significantly that this will have sizeable impacts on the shopper engagement needs and space requirements of retailers.

Retail enterprises will need to be much more granular in identifying and evaluating the key change impacts on their businesses. Figure 6.3 shows how this could be done, with a selection of examples.

We have chosen to cut to this finer level of detail for shopper-facing technology given the high order importance that this territory represents to almost all retailers. In evaluating the possible impacts of shopper-facing technology, we have identified some (but not all) of the key technologies and positioned them on the Change Framework. Again, there is no suggestion that this is definitive guidance and each retailer will need to go through a similar exercise reflecting its own particular circumstances and perspectives. There are, however, a number of useful general points that can be made.

1. Shopper-facing technologies represent much more an opportunity than a threat for most retailers. (Notwithstanding the fact that the general proposition that failure to realize opportunities can be the greatest threat of all holds true here as elsewhere.)
2. There is, in our view, very considerable uncertainty surrounding the likely impacts of many of the most important shopper-facing technologies. This is a territory is that is littered with over-hyped new pieces of technology that failed to come close to delivering on their promise to 'change everything'. Caution and a degree of scepticism seem prudent, especially where technology 'solutions' appear to be attempting to answer a question that nobody thought worth asking.
3. For retailers, mobile technology will likely be for many the highest order, highest impact change in the consumer landscape. We discussed in Chapter 3 the impact of mobile on shopping behaviours, especially amongst Millennials. The Internet of Things (IoT) certainly has the potential to be a true game changer. Here, our view is that the opportunity may,

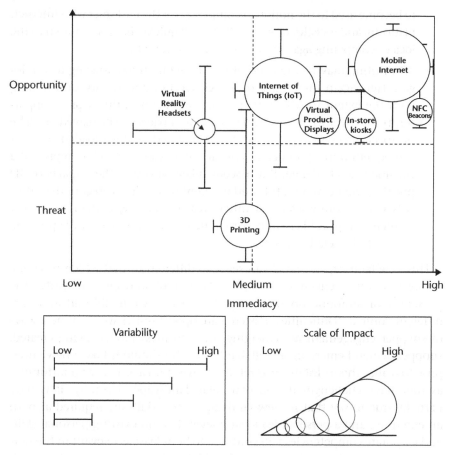

Figure 6.3 Possible impact of shopper-facing technologies
Source: Authors.

in fact, be both greater and more immediate than many anticipate. There is, though, a real risk to be alert to that IoT has the potential also to disintermediate retailers out the relationship between the shopper and their sources of supply. Management guru Michael Porter has spoken of a 'new era of competition' in which retailers and internet-enabled platform providers will increasingly find that they are competing for the customer relationship with the manufacturers of smart domestic devices.[2] A defining dimension of the narrative of the new retail landscape is that traditional retailers are no longer the automatic default or even the preferred custodians of the relationship with the customer. Retailers have had

---

[2] Michael Porter quoted in *The Economist*, 'Schumpeter. Smart Products, Smart Makers', 21 Nov. 2015, 73.

to become used to the notion of competing for the customer with internet, platform, and logistics providers. They will quickly have to get used to the idea of competing against device manufacturers also.

4. 3D printing may be the third of the three big shopper-facing technologies. Here again there must be a high level of uncertainty surrounding both the extent to which 3D printing represents a threat or an opportunity and over what timeframe its major impacts will be played out. The prospect of physical purchases being replaced by downloaded code for subsequent home production appears, at a headline level, to represent a considerable challenge. But it seems likely also that the impacts of 3D printing will be more subtle and different by product category than this. It is worth noting also that other areas of activity, perhaps especially medicine, appear likely to be very much more impacted by 3D printing than will the retail industry.

This new landscape of retail can seem so different to that which has gone before that calm reflection is needed. First, profound change creates the possibility of profound opportunities. As Winston Churchill said in a very different context, 'Difficulties mastered are opportunities won.'[3] If new ways of shopper engagement are emerging, new business models being created, shopper demand emerging at a global level, why should it take a new enterprise to realize them? Established retailers have at least as many opportunities as they have challenges in the new retail landscape. Secondly, it is only partially true to say that in new landscapes, new skills are required at both an enterprise and a personal leadership level. Certain existing personal skills and corporate competencies will continue to be at least as relevant in the new landscape of retailing as they were in the old. But their relative importance will almost certainly change and new skills *will* also be required.

---

[3] <http://www.ibiblio.org/pha/policy/1943/1943-03-21a.html>.

Part 2
Guidance for Business Leaders

Part 1 of this book explored the new landscape of retailing with the aim of analysing its nature and characteristics, now and into the future. It set out the main defining themes of the new world of retailing and shopper engagement. Part 2 moves on from describing this new landscape to exploring the attributes that retail enterprises and the leaders of those enterprises will need if they are to be relevant, valued, and successful in such an altered landscape.

As we have discussed, the forces of change are so powerful and interact in such complex ways that the new landscape of retail requires all enterprises operating within it to revisit—or perhaps visit for the first time—the very fundamentals of what the customer proposition is and how it is taken to market. It is difficult to imagine that a business that was fit for purpose even ten years ago, but has changed little since, will still be fit for purpose today—let alone in the near-term future.

One of the most important questions that traditional retail enterprises need to address is what is the role of the physical store in a world where retailing no longer needs to be conducted through physical stores and where shoppers—especially (but not only) the Millennials—live in a 'digital first, stores maybe' world. Chapter 7 considers this theme by discussing different ways that retailers can look to reinvent their stores such that they remain relevant and desired. For many, the absolute number of stores may be reduced sharply and the configuration of remaining physical points of presence will change from a network of largely similar stores to a far more diverse set of points of presence. This theme is developed further in Chapter 8—Delivering the Omni-Channel Experience. For established retailers, a key challenge in creating an enterprise relevant to the needs and expectations of contemporary shoppers is not just to reinvent the store but also to create networks of digital engagement within which to locate the stores that remain. For new to retail enterprises, the challenge is different and many internet-only enterprises are now discovering the value of physical points of engagement also. A multitude of hybrid models combining physical and digital engagement opportunities for the shopper have emerged already and many more seem likely to follow. (In mid-2015,

Alibaba made its first entry into bricks and mortar retailing when it paid US $4.6 billion for a 19.99 per cent stake in the Suning electronics stores retailer.[1]) This far greater complexity changes the capabilities that a retail enterprise needs in order to deliver effectively on its omni-channel ambitions. This is the theme of Chapter 8.

All retailers need to revisit the extent to which their skills and capabilities are aligned to the new needs of their enterprises in the very changed landscapes in which they are seeking to engage shoppers, realize new opportunities, and resist much more intense and diverse competitive challenges. This is the focus of Chapter 9, in which we suggest that there are four territories in particular that retailers will need to emphasize and focus on in the new landscape of retail. Organizational and even ownership structures may need to change also in order for the needs of the enterprise to be better aligned to the new operating landscape. This too is explored in Chapter 9. Chapter 10 is complementary to Chapter 9. Here we focus on the new needs of retail business leaders themselves. Certainly, some of what can considered 'conventional' retail-specific skills—such as merchandising and product sourcing—continue to be highly relevant in the new retail landscape. Other skill areas will become more important whilst others are, relatively if not absolutely, de-emphasized. More personal attributes that enterprise leaders will need if they are to be effective in the new landscape are discussed also. Prominent in this regard is the capacity of enterprise leaders to lead effectively in environments that are defined by uncertainty.

[1] <http://www.bloomberg.com/news/articles/2015-08-10/alibaba-to-buy-19-9-stake-in-suning-commerce-for-4-6-billion>.

7

Reimagining the Retail Store

New Engagement Options: New Roles for Physical Stores

There is a well-known, but probably apocryphal, story of an American tourist who goes into a bar in a remote part of rural Ireland and asks an elderly local for directions to Dublin. The local thinks for a while and then replies somewhat whimsically, 'Well sir, if it's Dublin you want to get to, you don't want to be starting from here'. Store-based retailing can feel rather similar—if it's the nirvana of a web of seamless shopper engagement across multiple touchpoints you want to get to, you don't want to be starting with stores. And yet the great majority of retailers are. We discussed in Chapter 5 the presence, growth, and impact of incursive new internet-enabled businesses on the retail landscape. While we believe that the new landscape of retailing is being reframed above all else by the impact of technology change, it is important to remember that in all countries the great majority of retail sales continue to be transacted in physical spaces: shopping centres, stores, markets, and street vendors.

The new landscape of retail is more fluid and complex than many retailers have been used to operating in, even in the recent past. In a digital world, the very notion of what a store even is has changed and whereas retailing used to be synonymous with physical stores, it no longer is. Furthermore, and as we have noted already, we anticipate that in the near-term future many shoppers will default to online as, at least, the starting point in many of their purchase journeys. In an environment where physical stores are no longer preferred or even needed at all, the questions for retailers with networks of stores are profound and go to the heart of the enterprise.

- What is the role of physical stores in the new landscape of retail?
- How can stores be kept relevant and desired by shoppers who no longer need them?
- What type of stores will be most effective?

The aim of this chapter is to provide insight and guidance on these questions.

How Much Space is the Right Amount?

Many physical store-based retailers have found already that the current amount of stores and space from which they operate substantially exceeds their present and future requirements. Here are some examples just from the UK.

- In supermarket retailing, all of the established 'Top 4'—Tesco, ASDA, Sainsbury's, and Morrisons (in order of market share)—announced between 2012 and 2015 their intention to close substantial amounts of their existing space in large-format supermarkets and hypermarkets and the discontinuation of much of their planned opening programmes of new large stores. All cited the same set of reasons for making these decisions: a shopper trend to purchase smaller amounts more frequently in locally convenient smaller stores; the accelerating migration of sales to online and the loss of market share to highly aggressive price-led competitors, most notably Aldi and Lidl. As the largest of the UK supermarket operators, Tesco has also been the most aggressive in rationalizing its large-store real estate in the UK. Tesco announced in January 2015 the closure of forty-three stores, of which 'over half' were large format, and freezing the planned development of forty-nine sites, all of which were large format and the construction of several of which had already been completed.[2]

- In home improvement, Homebase, the second largest home improvement retailer in the UK, announced in early 2015 that it planned to close approximately eighty of its 300 stores by the end of 2018 'as part of a strategy to cut costs and become more digitally focused'.[3] In the same category, Sir Ian Cheshire, former CEO of Kingfisher Group, Europe's largest home improvement retailer, has suggested that many of its core B&Q stores could be over-spaced by about 20 per cent as shoppers' buying behaviours change and they migrate increasingly to purchasing online in categories such as power tools and garden sheds.[4]

- Neither is the challenge of excess space confined to low-involvement, basic-needs categories. For example, Sir Philip Green, the charismatic head of the highly successful Topshop 'fast fashion' brand, has said that, whereas in a pre-internet era he felt Topshop needed around 200 stores to achieve national coverage in the UK, he now feels the number is around fifty.

---

[2] <http://www.tescoplc.com/files/pdf/results/2015/14-15_trading_statement/14-15_trading_presentation.pdf>.
[3] <http://www.ft.com/cms/s/0/38232d22-59c0-11e4-9787-00144feab7de.html#axzz3bnwhAvT6>.
[4] <http://www.ft.com/cms/s/0/11b87c56-7402-11e1-bcec-00144feab49a.html#axzz3bnwhAvT6>; <http://www.thisismoney.co.uk/money/markets/article-2474432/Ian-Cheshire-interview-B-Q-prof its-entente-France.html>.

Physical network and store rationalization is not limited to the UK. In the US, during 2015 alone, retail firms announced closures that would affect over 10,400 stores, compared to just over 4,000 in 2013.[5] In fifteen cases, store closures affected 200 branches or more of individual retail formats. These included office supplies retailers (such as Office Depot and Staples), booksellers (Barnes & Noble), and fast food outlets (McDonalds)—although no sectors were immune. Such is the appetite for a growing number of shoppers to buy online that it is difficult to foresee for many retailers in mature markets anything other than an acceleration of a now well-established trend of exiting a substantial proportion of their surplus real estate. For many, store portfolios are being reconfigured into a smaller number of stores in the best locations and the 'gaps' in between the catchment areas filled in by a stronger online transactional presence. Forecasting in this area is hazardous and discussion is often inevitably highly charged but the space race is clearly over for many. The average level of vacancies on UK high streets was 16 per cent in early 2013.[6] It is not difficult to envisage this substantially exceeding 25 per cent in the future as migration to online accelerates and leases expire over the next five years and beyond.

High and still increasing vacancy rates or store closures should not, however, be taken to imply that no new retail space is being added. Far from it. Research by global property developers Cushman & Wakefield suggested that for 2012 and 2013 alone, more than 1,650 new shopping centres comprising 63.9m m^2 of Gross Leasable Area (GLA) were brought to market globally, of which the great majority (891) were in the US (although only comprising a 2 per cent addition to stock) as that country continued to emerge strongly out of the depths of the 2008/9 recession.[7]

However, even stronger growth in new space, especially in shopping centres, continues to be a feature of emerging markets, particularly in Asia-Pacific but also in Latin America too. Between 2014 and 2016, 504 new shopping centres are forecast to be brought to market in China, 106 elsewhere in Asia-Pacific, and 115 in Latin America.[8] New shopping centres in Asia, especially China, tend also to be substantially bigger than the average for developments elsewhere—nearly five times larger in China than in the US, for example (Table 7.1).

[5] <http://retailindustry.about.com/od/USRetailStoreClosingInfoFAQs/fl/All-2015-Store-Closings-Stores-Closed-by-US-Retail-Industry-Chains_2.htm>.

[6] <http://policy.bcsc.org.uk/beyondretail/docs/BeyondRetail2013.pdf>.

[7] <http://www.cushmanwakefield.com/~/media/global-reports/Global-Shopping-Centers-Report_May2014-Update.pdf>.

[8] <http://www.cushmanwakefield.com/~/media/global-reports/Global-Shopping-Centers-Report_May2014-Update.pdf>.

Table 7.1 Number and average size of existing and forecast new shopping centre developments, 2014 and 2014–16

Country / Region	Total no. of shopping centres (2014) (m² GLA)	Total size of shopping centres (2014)	Average size, m²	Forecast no. of new shopping centres (2014–16)	% change on total no. of centres	Forecast average size of new centres, m² (2014–16)
USA	35,590	618,300,000	17,373	758	2	14,776
Canada	1,320	34,200,000	25,909	42	3	17,700
Latin America	1,167	34,300,000	29,392	115	10	29,200
Europe	7,178	153,800,000	21,427	306	4	21,400
China	621	53,200,000	85,668	504	81	85,625
Other Asia	970	30,700,000	31,649	106	11	52,700
Total	46,846	924,500,000	19,735	1,831	4	19,700

Source: <http://www.cushmanwakefield.com/~/media/global-reports/Global-Shopping-Centers-Report_May2014-Update.pdf>, 6 and 7.

What is happening is that retail space in both shopping centres and within the portfolios of retailers is bifurcating between, on the one hand, a smaller amount of better quality space and, on the other, the exiting of poorer, secondary space. A much sharper polarization in the quality of retail space is one of the defining features of the new landscape of retailing. This explains why, in the teeth of a deep recession in consumer spending in the UK, Westfield, the global shopping centre developer and owner, was able to bring to market in London two very large new centres, each with in excess of 150,000 m² GLA. Both have been highly successful despite the city in which they are located having an excess of total retail space per capita and, in consequence, overall vacancy levels of around 8 per cent.[9] There is no contradiction here. It is the high quality of new space that is being added which will further accelerate the exiting of poorer quality space.

Where Physical Stores Can (Still) Win

We have presented a picture of the landscape of retailing being transformed quickly by the disruptive impact of the internet. We have suggested also that this transformation will accelerate as younger shoppers enter their high spending years with a perspective that all of their shopping needs can be fulfilled online. Some categories of retail have already largely or wholly migrated to online and others will follow. Yet none of this should be taken to imply that we are anticipating the inevitable end of the physical store. Far from it.

[9] <http://www.theguardian.com/business/2014/feb/10/uk-retail-shop-vacancy-rates-fall>.

The challenge for retailers with a presence in physical retailing is two-fold. First, to identify how their customers—current and future—want to engage with their enterprise and, secondly, to be clear on the role of the store in delivering on shoppers' engagement expectations. Crucially, this needs to be done in ways that are different from, yet complementary to, the online alternative. Leaders of retail enterprises have to recognize and embrace the notion that their stores are just one part of increasingly complex webs of engagement within which their shoppers expect to be able to move freely and on their own terms.

There are, we suggest, five main territories physical stores can focus on and remain relevant and valued by shoppers. These are presented in Figure 7.1 and then discussed.

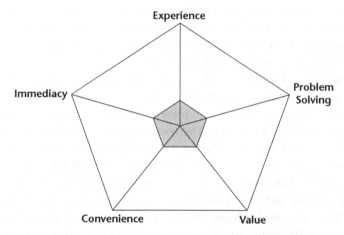

Figure 7.1 Territories where physical stores can achieve competitive advantage
Source: Authors.

Value Advantage

It might seem curious, in an increasingly online world, that we consider that physical stores can demonstrate a value advantage. Our starting point in this respect is that by value we mean more than just price. That said, there are some important general points to make on the subject of price in the new retail landscape. First, it is safest to assume that most shoppers in internet-enabled localities have total or near to total price transparency. For almost all retailers (super-premium luxury products are perhaps an exception) this means that they have to be price competitive because shoppers are able effortlessly to find out if they are not. Price comparison and aggregation sites around the world, such as mysupermarket.com, comparereja.in, and bond-faro.co.br to name but three amongst many, are ensuring that this becomes increasingly comprehensive and accessible. Second, and related to this first point, retailers must—if they have not already—become used to the reality that they are operating in environments of persistent downward pressure on prices rather than the reverse and, therefore, for margins to be squeezed (other things being equal). This is in part an economic consideration in markets where low inflation and in some cases deflation prevails and represents a global problem of weak demand, especially in advanced economies.[10] (In Japan, for example, it was regarded as a 'significant achievement' to raise inflation from −0.5 per cent in 2013 to 1.5 per cent in 2014—but the rate has since fallen back to 0.2% by the end of 2015.[11]) The consequence of low inflation generally is that price increases are more obvious to shoppers and it is even harder for retailers to raise prices and improve margins. But price transparency does not mean that all retailers have to aspire to be the price leader in their sector—clearly only one enterprise can occupy that position. What it does mean is that retailers have to be very clear and able to articulate in a very compelling way what their total value proposition is in order to justify any price premium they wish or need to charge.

Some store-based retailers could sustain price parity or better with online rivals because they have a cost advantage. This is by no means implausible. We discussed in Chapter 5 the different business models and cost components of online and store-based retailing. The cost model for an online retailer is not necessarily always lower than that of a store-based retailer: while the magnitude of the major cost components are obviously very different for both, it is far from clear that the *total* cost of doing business is necessarily lower for one model or another. Better buying, better inventory management, optimizing labour scheduling, and driving cross-selling are all areas where store-based retailers can realistically aspire to claw back some of the cost advantages enjoyed by online competitors. The domestic and international success of Aldi and Lidl, the limited assortment grocery retailers of German origin, also attests to this. So too does the enduring appeal and success of IKEA's huge home furniture and furnishings emporia, underpinned as they are by prodigious buying scale and a relentlessly efficient operating model. Also, exploiting break clauses in retail leases intelligently can allow a retailer to move progressively to a lower cost real estate base, through closures and/or strategic relocations. In this way, retailers have an opportunity to meet demand in a more locally targeted and potentially more profitable way than a regional or national warehouse-based online retailer. A proper understanding of the

---

[10] C. Coakley, 'The Elusive Pursuit of Inflation', IMF Survey, Apr. 2015. <http://www.imf.org/external/pubs/ft/survey/so/2015/new041715a.htm>.

[11] International Monetary Fund, World Economic Database, 2015. <https://www.imf.org/external/pubs/ft/weo/2015/01/weodata/index.aspx>.

evolution of the store-based enterprise's cost base at the local level is a prerequisite for the development of this model.

If absolute lowest price is not sustainable for most—and, by definition alone, it cannot be—then store-based retailers often have interesting opportunities to reframe shoppers' value expectations. The notion of 'value' can be a rather ambiguous and slippery concept. Too often, 'adding value' is used as an excuse by retailers to justify higher prices and disguise operational inefficiencies. Adding value should really be defined as truly delivering more attributes that the customer values, beyond just a low price. In this way, price becomes a consequence and a signal of the value that is being added. Not surprisingly, academics have mined the notion of consumer value extensively. Cutting to the chase, they agree that whilst the concept is a complex one, it is one rich in possibilities for firms. It is argued that value can be derived from three broad sets of factors: the shopping trip (including sensory stimulation and social interaction), the store itself (including the atmosphere, convenience, and service level), and the product itself (from which shoppers derive economic value and product performance).[12]

Framed like this, the opportunities for store-based retailers to add value—through the shopping trip and experience, from the store itself as well as, finally, from the product—are considerable and are present within all of the territories being discussed in this section.

Convenience Advantage

It may seem paradoxical to suggest that stores can be more convenient than online but it is not. There are two ways in particular that well configured stores can, in fact, deliver high levels of convenience to shoppers. First, they can more carefully edit merchandise assortments so that they address shoppers' specific needs in time and locationally relevant ways. We have discussed already (Chapter 1) the choice paradox whereby an excess of choice becomes problematic to shoppers and not helpful. Behavioural scientists confirm that, whilst the ability to choose is intuitively appealing, shoppers are willing to discount excessive choice and accept smaller rewards from fewer options because of the effort that would be involved in maximizing their search.[13] In plain English, this means that shoppers can be happy to have fewer things to choose from—and perhaps leave some of the hard work to others, particularly if they can learn to trust their judgements. There is, therefore, an

---

[12] L. Davis and N. Hodges, 'Consumer Shopping Value: An Investigation of Shopping Trip Value, In-Store Shopping Value and Retail Format', *Journal of Retailing and Consumer Services* 19 (2012), 229–39.

[13] D. D. Reed et al., 'Discounting the Freedom to Choose: Implications for the Paradox of Choice', *Behavioural Processes*, 90(3) (2012), 424–7.

interesting opportunity for physical store-based retailers to act as smart content curators, editing down broad assortments so that their stores deliver precisely to shoppers' requirements.

Secondly, stores that are carefully integrated into the fabric of shoppers' lives can be more convenient than the online alternative if engaging with them is seamlessly simple for the shopper. Reduction of consumer effort is a primary objective for marketers seeking repurchase in low-involvement categories through the encouragement of habitual behaviour by shoppers.[14] In FMCG marketing, Coca Cola is well known for its mantra that the whole world should never be more than an arm's reach away from a can or bottle of Coke. Store-based convenience orientated retailing needs to have much the same perspective. If the shopper has to do something—such as divert somewhere—that they would not normally do then the store cannot be said to be truly convenient. Often, the perception of convenience is very nuanced and site-specific. For example, a UK Sainsbury's convenience store traded at only 75 per cent of its predicted potential in one location because of a poorly perceived pitch in relation to a commuter rail station. It was a simple matter of being on the wrong side of the tracks.[15] — The notion of convenience in store-based retailing can be taken much further than purely locational convenience—to time-based convenience, for example. 7-Eleven in Tokyo has for many years in many of its outlets changed its food assortments by day part to align with customer needs.[16] Ahold's AH To Go format in the Netherlands and Germany, launched in 2012, is an interesting example of time of day merchandising where lighting patterns and music as well as the merchandise assortment itself changes at three different points in the day to maximize the relevance of the offer within a limited space. (The music 'gets livelier during the day to match shoppers' moods'.[17])

Value through convenience can be strengthened through collaboration— by means of retailers using their stores as hosts for others as, for example, in the partnership between Argos and eBay in the UK whereby over 650 Argos stores are used as collection points for products purchased on eBay. As shoppers purchase more online and as retailers look to intensify the use of their physical space, especially where they are over-spaced, there appears to be considerable opportunity to reframe convenience as fulfilment points for purchases made elsewhere. Furthermore, it is no longer the case that the

[14] D. Littler, 'Habitual Buying Behavior', *Wiley Encyclopedia of Management*. 9(1) (2015).

[15] S. Wood and A. Tasker, 'The Importance of Context in Store Forecasting: The Site Visit in Retail Location Decision-Making', *Journal of Targeting, Measurement and Analysis for Marketing*, 16(2) (2008), 139–55.

[16] <http://www.7andi.com/dbps_data/_template_/_user_/_SITE_/localhost/_res/ir/library/ar/pdf/2014_07.pdf>.

[17] IGD, 'AH To Go: New Concept Store Amsterdam', *Retail Analysis Store Visit Report*, Watford, UK: Institute for Grocery Distribution, 2012.

small physical size of locationally convenient stores need restrict merchandise choice. There are obvious opportunities to use technology in the form of kiosks, tablets, so-called 'endless aisles or shelves', and for such units to act as delivery points, to give shoppers access to wider product choice without the need for that product to be present in-store.

Immediacy Advantage

Physical stores can potentially fulfil shoppers' needs more quickly than the online alternative. But we caution that the immediacy advantage will narrow and may disappear as distribution businesses become more adept at delivering products ordered online to shorter timeframes, into narrower delivery windows, and more flexibly and ubiquitously in terms of locations. (The role of logistics in the new retail landscape is discussed in Chapter 8.)

The obvious immediacy advantage that physical stores have over online is in the ability of shoppers to go into a store and leave with what they came in to buy. Clearly, this relates closely to the convenience advantage that stores can also deliver. But immediacy is not just confined to the distress purchases of basic items that physical convenience makes possible. In many categories, the point of greatest influence is moving much closer to the point of purchase, especially for highly fashion influenced categories—and there are few discretionary spend categories which are not heavily fashion driven. So, for example, someone who has been motivated to buy a dress they saw an actor wearing in a movie might be persuaded to purchase a clone of that dress from a store on their way home to achieve the immediate gratification from consumption and ownership that online ordering does not fully permit (at present). US economists Ted O'Donoghue and Matthew Rabin observe that immediate gratification is linked to poor self-control, especially in the context of small day-to-day decisions, but is, they observe, behaviour that is 'simply part of being human'.[18] Technology that links the shopper to the store can also enable the delivery of an immediacy advantage. For example, shopping mall developers, such as Simon Malls in the US, already make widespread use of smartphone apps supported by beacon technology, which permit geo-fenced alerts and messages to promote a variety of mall tenants. This capability is not limited to managed malls: London's Regent Street has seen a similar implementation under the auspices of property owner the Crown Estate as part of its regeneration strategy for the street.[19]

[18] T. O'Donoghue and M. Rabin, 'The Economics of Immediate Gratification', *Journal of Behavioral Decision Making*, 13(2) (Apr./June 2000), 233– 50.
[19] 'Regent Street Becomes Europe's First Shopping Street to Pioneer a Personalised Mobile Phone App with Beacon Technology, 2014. <http://www.regentstreetlocal.info/regent-street-app.aspx>.

Problem-Solving Advantage

Store-based retailers offering well-executed store environments can play a highly effective role in helping shoppers meet their needs. Some context needs to be provided to this proposition, however. It is clear that today many consumers, especially in younger age groups, are less likely to trust information and advice from traditional sources of authority—government, church, business—and are more likely to be trusting of and influenced by advice and opinion from other sources, notably their personal networks and product reviews and advice given by other users (Figure 7.2). But store-based retailers and their advocates (whether paid or not) do nevertheless have interesting opportunities to play the role of trusted advisers in addressing shoppers' needs. In part this is a function of brand equity. While strong brand equity in retail is in no way solely the preserve of store-based retailers, there are many retailers in many countries that command very considerable trust with their shoppers because they are long-established and highly regarded brands. This is a complex territory which we discuss at greater length in Chapter 9 in the context of the attributes that retail enterprises need in order to be successful in the new landscapes of retailing and shopper engagement.

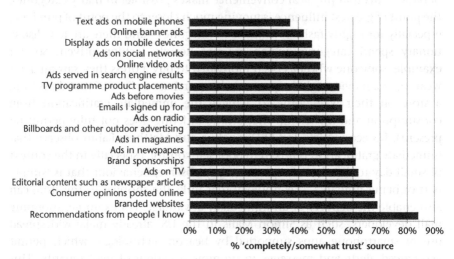

Figure 7.2 Global levels of trust in different forms of marketing and advertising, 2015

Source: © The Nielsen Company, 2015. Nielsen Global Trust in Advertising Survey, Q1 2015. http://www.nielsen.com/content/dam/nielsenglobal/apac/docs/reports/2015/nielsen-global-trust-in-advertising-report-september-2015.pdf. Based on over 30,000 respondents in 60 countries.

There are broadly three ways in which the store environment influences shoppers. First is store design, including layout to aid problem-solving convenience and level of shopfitting as a signal of merchandise quality. Second is store social elements, such as the presence and number of sales assistants on the shop floor, who can reduce search costs for the shopper. Third is store ambience, such as music, lighting, smells, temperature, visual merchandising, and informational messaging.[20] Exactly how retailers can help solve shoppers' problems through these means manifests itself in different ways for different retailers. There are, though, some specific territories that will be relevant for many retailers:

- editing choice and navigating shoppers through complex assortments;
- providing stimulation and information about new products;
- information about complex products, such as consumer electronics, and complex suites of products, such as home theatre systems;
- assistance in product personalization possibilities;
- reassurance towards the end of the purchase process and during post purchase.

Executing a problem-solving orientation at store level is similarly multi-dimensional. Most obviously, store staff need to be equipped to help shoppers. Here technology has an obvious role to play, especially in complex product categories, although simply equipping employees with tablets or headsets can often have a gimmicky quality, particularly if there is no reliable and well thought through sense of precisely how the technology can support shopper problem-solving. But the total store environment also plays an important part, including signage that informs, layouts that ease navigation, and technology that facilitates better information and decision-making on the part of the shopper. In the territory of the store as a problem-solving environment, retailers need to be clear that the role of the store is now to complement and enhance the other ways in which shoppers are gaining information, not to seek to replace them.

A further dimension to the use of stores to help solve problems for shoppers is the possibility of reimagining stores as much as service centres as spaces for displaying and selling physical products. The notion of firms reinventing themselves or extending their activities as service providers is not of itself a new idea in marketing. Enterprises ranging from motor vehicle manufacturers (who have redefined themselves as providers of personal transportation services) to soap manufacturers (who have repositioned themselves as skincare advice providers) have embraced a service-dominant logic to their business models. But in the new landscape of retailing it is clear—as we have already observed—that many traditional retail enterprises with large store networks are very substantially over-spaced, either with stores that are now too large, or with too many stores in their networks or both. There is therefore an added urgency. For many, 'right sizing' the stores and the network will be necessary and painful in light of the new realities of how shoppers want to shop. But

---

[20] J. Baker et al. 'The Influence of Multiple Store Environment Cues on Perceived Merchandise Value and Patronage Intentions', *Journal of Marketing*, 66(2) (2002), 120–41.

there are opportunities also to convert at least some of the no longer needed product selling space into a wide variety of service offerings that truly add value to the shopper. Examples are already legion: home improvement stores with learning studios; grocery stores with cooking class areas; cycling stores with maintenance areas; wine stores with tasting areas; and so on. Retailers with excess space can also act as hosts for other enterprises to use some of that space for complementary service-orientated offerings. The use of stores as collection points hosting kiosks for shoppers to collect orders that have been placed online is an obvious and increasingly visible example (and something we discuss more fully in Chapters 8 and 9).

Experience Advantage

For many shoppers in many categories and locations, stores have an important and valued role to play as a source of experience and entertainment. Stores can provide a physicality and sense of place, an opportunity for immersion, and a type of social engagement that cannot be created online. While the label can be debated—Retail Theatre, Experiential Retail, Retailtainment (hopefully not[21])—the proposition is the same: stores can bring retail experiences to life in ways which are presently impossible in virtual worlds. As Jerry Black, Chief Digital Officer of AEON Group, has observed, 'We have to make stores experiential, entertaining, inspiring and fun. Omni-channel does lead to repurposing stores.'[22] There are myriad examples globally of far-sighted retailers doing superb things with their store environments, which have worked to amaze and inspire shoppers. Amongst a plethora of store design awards globally, those of the World Retail Congress are amongst the most prestigious. A look across the more recent winners bears testament to the clarity of strategic intent and creativity of execution that makes the very best of store-based retailing so immersive, engaging, and—still—valued by shoppers (Figure 7.3). We might perhaps allow a special mention also for Burberry. When Burberry opened their London flagship store at 121 Regent Street back in late 2012, Christopher Bailey, Chief Creative Officer (and now CEO also), talked explicitly about the objective of the store being to bring to life in a physical space the experience of Burberry.com in a digital world.[23] Several years later, this store continues to be a standout example

---

[21] This term is sadly already in use, having been coined by sociologist George Ritzer, in 1999. He describes it as the 'use of ambience, emotion, sound and activity to get customers interested in the merchandise and in a mood to buy'.

[22] Jerry Black, speaking at World Retail Congress. Rome, Sept. 2015.

[23] <https://www.youtube.com/watch?v=CokbQWI_15U>.

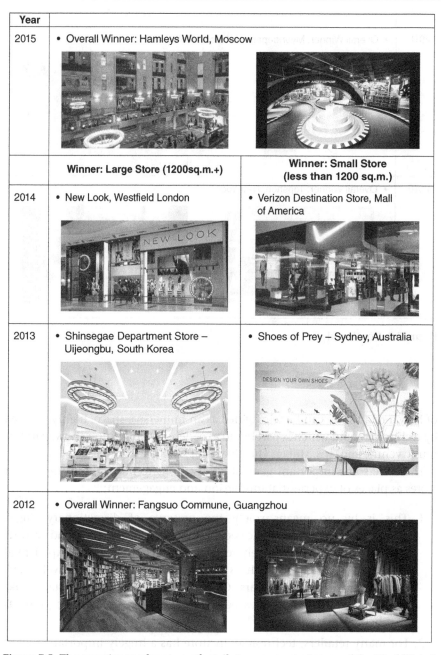

Year		
2015	• Overall Winner: Hamleys World, Moscow	
	Winner: Large Store (1200sq.m.+)	**Winner: Small Store (less than 1200 sq.m.)**
2014	• New Look, Westfield London	• Verizon Destination Store, Mall of America
2013	• Shinsegae Department Store – Uijeongbu, South Korea	• Shoes of Prey – Sydney, Australia
2012	• Overall Winner: Fangsuo Commune, Guangzhou	

Figure 7.3 The experience advantage of retail stores: recent winners of the World Retail Awards Store Design of the Year award

Sources: Hamleys LHS: © Fitch; Hamleys RHS: © Hamleys; New Look: © New Look; Verizon: © Anita Jader Photography (anitajader.com); Shinsegae: © JHP Design; Shoes of Prey: © Shoes of Prey Pty Ltd; Fangsuo LHS: © China Daily Asia; Fangsuo RHS: © Fangsuo Community; Myer LHS: © Mark Wilson Media; Myer RHS: © Marcus Wong; Topshop LHS: © Viviana Gonzalez De Marco; Topshop RHS: © EMAP Ltd.

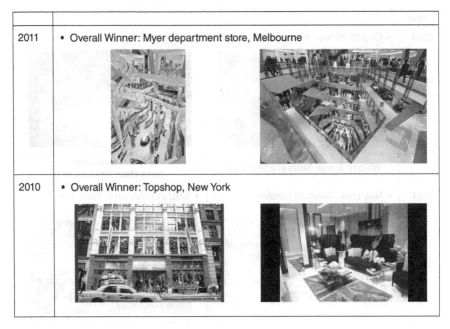

| 2011 | • Overall Winner: Myer department store, Melbourne |
| 2010 | • Overall Winner: Topshop, New York |

Figure 7.3 Continued

of how a retail store can be reimagined as an immersive space, highly enabled by technology, and which is part brand experience, part fashion show, part live music venue, and, yes, still an effective retail selling space.

There are some important general observations to make about the idea of stores as places of experiential immersion and engagement:

1. This is by no means solely the preserve of discretionary, high-involvement categories. Basic needs categories such as grocery and eyewear are quite able to be creatively reconceived to have a strong experiential dimension—as retailers such as Eataly and Luxottica respectively have demonstrated in recent years. Oscar Farinetti, founder of Eataly, talks passionately about his stores being a 'celebration of fantastic products that help people eat better'.[24]

2. For many retailers, technology in store has a hugely important role to play in the ability to deliver a heightened experience to the shopper.

---

[24] Oscar Farinetti, speaking at World Retail Congress. Rome, Sept. 2015.

We discussed in Chapter 2 territories in which technology can be applied in a customer-facing setting to enhance and even transform the experience.

3. There are interesting opportunities in store to create highly personalized experiences for shoppers, in both how they are engaged and the product that they purchase. Some current developments in automotive retailing illustrate the point. As this sector moves ever more quickly to allowing the customer to specify the product to their own personal desire—even amongst the mainstream brands—so the opportunity presents to move the personalization process beyond an online configurator and into an appealing retail setting where the process can be facilitated by a sales associate. Audi's Audi City format of highly technology-enabled stores (as opposed to dealerships) with just one or two vehicles in high-traffic high street locations is an impressive illustration of what is possible. So too is Tesla's approach to taking its highly innovative electric vehicles to market through stores in shopping malls rather than through traditional dealerships.

While we have spoken about retail stores as places of experience and engagement, the opportunity is at least as great for shopping centres too. Whereas historically the main rationale for shopping centres was as aggregators of retailers into one location, this role is far less relevant in a digital world. Today and in future the major rationale for shopping centres is to deliver to the shopper a stimulating, engaging, and participative experience. Kevin McKenzie, global chief digital officer at Westfield Labs (Westfield's digital innovation 'hot house' in Silicon Valley—profiled in Chapter 9), makes the point that 'the mall of the future is really a personalised experience . . . Not just by retailers, but by products, by events and by experiences for their own personal needs, which is much different from any experience that exists today. And the way that we are going to get to that is through technology. No question.'[25] The notion of shopping centres as places for personalized, immersive, and above all social engagement will, we feel sure, continue to be especially relevant in emerging markets where, for many, the relative lack of other social spaces means that shopping centres remain well placed to play the role of town square gathering place as much as transactional retail space.

[25] Kevin McKenzie, 'Reinventing the Shopping Mall'. <http://www.businessoffashion.com/2015/01/kevin-mckenzie-reinventing-shopping-mall.html>.

Case 7.1 REINVENTION OF THE DEPARTMENT STORE: HANKYU FLAGSHIP, OSAKA

One retail format whose future has been debated more often than most is the department store. With their origins in the late nineteenth century, as early as 1954 commentators were speculating on the competitive effects of specialty apparel retailers on the future of the format.[26] Department stores have been a traditional feature of Japanese retailing in particular. In many cases created by real estate or railway companies with little real understanding of contemporary consumer needs, Japanese department stores have often been seen as a legacy of an earlier age, slow to change, and in terminal decline. Hankyu Hanshin Department Stores in Osaka, owned by the H2O Retailing Corporation, operate fifteen department stores across the country. By the beginning of the twenty-first century the central Osaka flagship store Hankyu Umeda, founded in 1929 and operating in a highly competitive market, was in dire need of renovation. The business took the opportunity to 'reinvent' itself. 'We had to work out how to re-create the department store experience of old,' commented Hankyu business development division manager Hiroyuki Nakao. The company's solution was two-fold: to create a new physical experience and to change customers' focus from 'things' to lifestyles. The

Figure 7.4 'Lifestyle theatre' area in Hankyu's department store, Osaka
Source: © H2O Retailing Corporation, Inc.

---

[26] J. B. Jeffreys, *Retail Trading in Britain 1850–1950: A Study of Trends in Retailing with Special Reference to the Development of Co-operative, Multiple Shop and Department Store Methods of Trading.* Cambridge: Cambridge University Press, 1954. D. Knee, *European Department Stores.* London: Oxford Institute of Retail Management, Longman, 1988.

company set about rebuilding the fifteen-floor store, increasing selling floorspace by 20 per cent to 64,000 m² but more importantly increasing non-selling space by 130 per cent to 16,000 m². This increase took the form of a 'lifestyle theatre' on the ninth floor in the heart of the new building (Figure 7.4). A 'Festival Plaza' reaches up four storeys creating a central exhibition space designed to support adjacent trading areas. Country themed events (France, UK, USA) are complemented with seasonal activity (bridal, camping, and craft fairs) accompanying pop-up traders in adjacent selling areas. A lifestyle Umeda 'souk' intensifies innovative trading activity, with twelve-week contracts offered to local independent businesses.

The Hankyu main store was set a target of ¥213 billion (US$1.8 billion) for its first year of operation following the refurbishment, the equivalent of Isetan's Tokyo outlet—the largest department store by sales in the country. This target was comfortably exceeded.

Precisely where store-based retailers choose to focus their energies and resources across the five main territories of competitive advantage should be a decision driven by two considerations above all: what is most true to the brand and what is best aligned to the needs and desires of target shoppers. Irrespective of the precise resolution of these twin considerations, there are two points of guidance that we can offer:

1. ASPIRE TO SELECTIVE EXCELLENCE

Retail enterprises should aim to excel on no more than two territories, and to be industry competitive on the rest. This will be a minimum requirement to keeping stores competitive in the new landscape of retail. Figure 7.5 shows in illustrative form how this could play out for grocery convenience stores and department stores. For department stores, the principal opportunity to keep the physical store relevant and desired may be in creating unique experiences, in

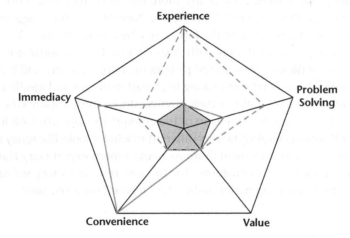

Figure 7.5 Where physical stores can still win: the example of Convenience Grocery (solid line) and Premium Department Stores (dashed line)
Source: Authors.

both the physicality of the space and the merchandise presentation within it. A further, secondary, opportunity for differentiation may be for the store to play the role of problem solver. Other territories will not be emphasized, but the store must nevertheless be industry competitive. Christopher Knee, Assistant General Secretary of the International Association of Department Stores based in Paris, suggests that one (of several) strategic options for department stores is to 'become a collection of stores, each unique, special and more flagship-like. This is the strategy of Rinascente in Italy as well as of the premium stores' breakaway from Karstadt in Germany—KaDeWe Berlin, Alsterhaus Hamburg, and Oberpollinger Munich. This is the store as icon with a concession-based business model. It can also be developed internationally.'[27] By contrast, for small-size food and beverage orientated convenience stores, focus will by definition be on emphasizing convenience attributes but reconfigured for a contemporary shopper—perhaps in particular leveraging technology to deliver broader and/or more tailored assortments than has historically been possible while also reassuring on value and with other attributes given less attention.

2. BE PREPARED TO BE RADICAL

Retailers must be prepared to push hard against the conventions that define their category and their stores as manifestations of these. As Doug Stephens noted about one of the most disruptive enterprises in the new retail landscape, 'Apple didn't just do things a little differently; it took a radical approach to defying retail industry paradigms and, in the process, established entirely new benchmarks for retailers everywhere.'[28] In grocery retailing, we are clearly now on the cusp of an era of major change, certainly in the UK, where the notion of what a large space store even is any more has to be reframed. Luke Jensen, Former Group Development Director for Sainsbury's, has suggested that the large-scale grocery store of the future may be part warehouse closed to the shopper and part delicatessen with 'experiential fresh assortments on the ground floor of dark stores with self-picking the boring grocery and household stuff above'.[29] For any retailer looking to at least maintain and ideally enhance the relevance and desirability of their physical stores, the question to be asked is what could the ultimate expression of the enterprise's objective look like? The answer will almost certainly be very different to what it looks like today and will be a departure from incrementalism. As management expert Gary Hamel has said of the present era of business: 'For the first time in history we can work backward from our imagination rather than forward from our past'.[30]

[27] Christopher Knee, International Association of Department Stores, personal correspondence.
[28] D. Stephens, *The Retail Revival*. Chichester: Wiley, 2013.
[29] Luke Jensen quoted in *Retail Week* (UK), 15 Aug. 2014.
[30] G. Hamel, *Leading the Revolution*. Cambridge, MA: Harvard Business School Press, 2000.

Stores as Part of an Engagement Ecosystem

In the new retail landscape, physical stores need to be conceived of as points of presence in a total ecosystem of engagement focused on the shopper. For some retailers, stores will be at the heart of that engagement ecosystem. So, for John Lewis, the iconic UK department store retailer, 'our beautiful stores are at the centre of our omni-channel strategy'.[31] For others, the physical store will play much more of a supporting role in a go-to-market strategy that takes place principally online. The relatively recent enthusiasm of eBay and Amazon for physical collection points, to supplement overwhelmingly online businesses, illustrates the point.

In this new landscape of shopper engagement, the role of the retailer is to make it as simple and as seamless as possible for the shopper to engage with the business howsoever they wish. This is leading to the rapid emergence of what can be thought of as hybrid models of engagement that are changing the geography as well as the landscape of retailing. Prominent developments in this regard include the following.

Stores as Order Fulfilment Points

The 'click and collect' model of ordering online and collecting in store has emerged quickly as a preferred model for many shoppers, especially but not exclusively in France. Some 20 per cent of the population used click and collect for grocery in 2013. A home delivery model has dominated in the UK, but here too there is enthusiasm from both shoppers and retailers for a shift to a click and collect approach, with a quarter of online shoppers interested in picking up online orders from a store.[32] Neither is this model limited to repeat orders of frequently purchased items. Already, around 6 million of John Lewis's online orders are click and collect, a growth from 350,000 in its first year.[33] For Argos, the highly distinctive UK general merchandise retailer (and which we profile in Chapter 8), the comparable figure was 34 per cent in 2014–15.[34]

The burgeoning appetite of shoppers to order online and collect from a store has led to the rapid reconfiguring of many stores into mini quasi

---

[31] Paul Cobi, CIO, John Lewis, quoted in *Retail Week* (UK), 24 Jan. 2014.

[32] Institute of Grocery Distribution, 'Developments in Click and Collect (Drive) for Groceries', 2013.

[33] R. Smithers, 'John Lewis to Charge for Click and Collect', *Guardian*, 1 July 2015. <http://www.theguardian.com/business/2015/jul/01/john-lewis-to-charge-for-click-and-collect>.

[34] Source: Home Retail Group, Annual Report and Financial Statements, 2015. <https://www.homeretailgroup.com/media/269233/home_retail_group_plc_annual_report_and_financial_statements_2015.pdf>. Multi-channel sales grew to 54% (or £2.2 billion) of Argos's sales in 2014–15. The internet represented 46% of Argos's sales; over two-thirds of this or 34% of Argos's total sales were shoppers using online Check&Reserve for store collection.

warehouses from which orders are collected by shoppers. In some instances this includes a drive-through capability—Leclerc had over 550 such outlets across its estate of grocery stores in France by the end of 2014, for example.[35] For others, stores act as host retailers from which shoppers can collect orders which have been placed online with other, often competitor, businesses. For example, UK logistics business DPD launched its PickUp service in 2015, allowing customers to pick up goods ordered from one retailer from the stores of another. Participating retailers include firms as diverse as car parts and bicycle retailer Halfords and Numark pharmacy.[36] There are also many examples of independent retailers opting into programmes that allow their stores to be used in a similar way, thereby potentially delivering additional footfall.

Order and Fulfilment Points in 'Non-Traditional' Locations

Several retailers are, at the time of writing, moving beyond the trial phase of putting so-called 'virtual stores' into high-traffic locations, often transport hubs. In these applications, shoppers typically use a smartphone to capture QR codes as a means to order from a display of virtual products. While Tesco was, arguably, first into this territory with its Homeplus subsidiary in Seoul, South Korea, in 2011, many others have now rolled the idea out elsewhere, including US footwear retailer Crocs, UK department store retailer Debenhams, and New Zealand's Warehouse general merchandise retailer. It is something of a moot point as to whether this can be called store-based retailing at all. Rather better is to think of this as a point of engagement with the connected shopper.

In the fulfilment part of the equation, it is not always especially convenient for shoppers to nominate a store to collect an order from or to wait at home for that order to arrive (or not) in its delivery window. To address this problem, several enterprises are rolling out collection points in the form of secure lockers located in places convenient to the shopper. In London, for example, Transport for London is strongly promoting the use of Tube stations for just this purpose.[37] Amongst others, ASDA, the third largest food retailer in the UK, has substantially increased its presence of secure lockers in these locations (in this case with ambient, chilled, and frozen compartments for obvious reasons).

Start-up enterprises have also realized the opportunity to use transport hubs as fulfilment points for products purchased online. One such is Doddle

---

[35] <http://fd6-www.leclercdrive.fr/default.aspx>.

[36] M. Chapman, 'Retailers Team up to Launch Click-and-Collect Alliance', *Retail Week*, 26 Mar. 2015. <http://www.retail-week.com/multichannel/retailers-team-up-to-launch-click-and-collect-alliance/5073348.article>.

[37] <https://www.tfl.gov.uk/info-for/media/press-releases/2014/september/tfl-expands-click-and-collect-services>.

(doddle.it) in the UK, which was established in 2014 by a business entrepreneur and Network Rail—the operator of the railway infrastructure in the UK (but not the trains themselves—it's a long story)—to put Doddle-branded collection points into train stations so that customers can 'commute and collect'. Numerous retailers have been signed up, including Amazon and ASOS. The aim of Doddle is to solve the 'last mile' delivery problem and reduce distribution costs for their retail partners. Charges to the shopper are, at the time of writing, set at £1.95 for parcel collections and £2.99 for parcel returns. Alternatively, shoppers can join Doddle Unlimited for £5 a month, which entitles them to free parcel collections and a 10 per cent discount on returns.[38]

The End of the Conforming Store

In an earlier era, it was common for retailers to talk of *conforming stores*: the idea being that each store conformed to a common footprint, layout, and merchandise assortment. No longer. In the era of customer-centric retailing, this is clearly inappropriate—if indeed it ever was. In consequence, the store portfolios of many retailers are quickly becoming much more diverse in size, assortment, location, and purpose. Consider Walmart for example. The world's largest retailer is strongly identified with its supercentre format of large-space, single-level stores combining general merchandise and food assortments (average size around 18,300 m^2 or around 2.5 football pitches to use the internationally recognized measure). But today Walmart is scaling back on large-store openings while it doubles smaller store openings to around 300 a year and trials self-service kiosks also. As the business said in its 2014/15 Annual Report, 'The future of retail is integrating stores and online together seamlessly. The company is investing globally to improve mobile capabilities and test alternative access points.'[39]

Case 7.2 CHILLI BEANS AND THE NEW RETAIL

There's a lot going on in Brazil—a stellar football World Cup in 2014 (unless you were supporting the national team in their painfully heavy semi-final defeat to the eventual champions) closely followed by the Olympic Games in 2016. And there's Chill Beans, one of the most innovative and certainly one of the most fun of the 'fast fashion' retailers to have proliferated globally in recent times. Still, a Brazilian sunglasses business founded by a 'Rock 'n' roller turned entrepreneur'[40] was always going to be lively.

On one level, Chilli Beans is a classically familiar story of a product-led entrepreneurial start-up. Caito Maia founded the business in 1997 and began by selling sunglasses to friends, then became a wholesaler before moving into retail. Sunglasses are still at the

---

(continued)

[38] Oliver Shah interview, *Sunday Times*, 31 May 2015, Business Section, 7.
[39] <http://news.walmart.com/news-archive/2015/04/22/walmart-releases-2015-annual-shareholders-meeting-materials>.
[40] <http://chillibeans.com.br/marca>.

Case 7.2 Continued

---

heart of what is now a wider merchandise assortment that extends also into related lifestyle categories, notably watches. Stores are franchised and there are over 600 throughout Brazil and, since 2005, an international store presence in, first, Portugal and now Colombia, Peru, Kuwait, and the US also. To date, the ultimate expression of the evolution of Chilli Beans into a fast fashion lifestyle retailer for the Millennial generation is the company's San Paolo flagship store which opened in 2013: 'The maximum expression of its concept' according to the company.[41] This 640 m^2 space is part retail store and part brand showroom, art gallery, music venue, and meeting space.

There are several features of Chilli Beans that distinguish this enterprise as one that is in the vanguard of 'the new retail':

- *Fast fashion; immediate buying.* Chilli Beans introduces ten new styles of sunglasses every week. Production runs are limited. 'It's important to buy what you like when you see it because chances are, they will be gone if you wait!'[42]

- *Collaborative design.* The world of fast fashion has many examples of retail fashion brands collaborating with celebrities and designers to create collections at affordable price points (H&M being amongst the most active). Chilli Beans embraces the same idea and has created many sunglass designs in collaboration with well-known celebrities and designers. This includes a partnership with Mattel, with which it produces co-branded Barbie® glasses through to a presumably rather edgier collaboration with Maia's fellow 'rock 'n' roller' Lenny Kravitz. Shoppers too can participate in the design process by, in some stores, custom designing their own sunglasses (the process takes around thirty minutes).

- *Technology in store to enhance the shopper experience.* Stores leverage technology to promote self-service and shopper engagement. Most stores have digital mirrors that take a picture of the shopper and superimpose selected frame styles judged best suited to the shape of their face. Shoppers can pay for their preferred frames by inserting a credit card in the slot below the digital mirror.

- *Not just stores—points of engagement.* Chilli Beans has embraced the idea that points of presence need to be flexible in a digital world. Physical points of presence range from the San Paolo flagship to vending machines, kiosks, pop-up and mobile stores.

- *Embracing digital.* Chilli Beans product can, naturally, be bought on its online store and shipped to most countries internationally. The company has perhaps been a little slow to embrace social media, more because of competing priorities than for any lack of enthusiasm. This is now changing. The business has a database of over 500,000 faces and email addresses that it uses to send personalized messages highlighting their latest fashions. For Maia this is not a selling tool, but rather a way to create a community. 'I'm not trying to sell you anything; I'm just trying to ask if you remember us.'[43]

---

[41] Quoted in <http://www.insideretail.com.au/blog/2014/01/15/rethinking-nature-retail>.

[42] Lilian Knighton, general manager at The LINQ's Chilli Beans quoted <http://blog.caesars.com/las-vegas/shopping/feeling-hot-hot-hot-chilli-beans-linq-completes-pool-time-look/?_ga=1.154419256.1224233583.1434009119>.

[43] <http://www.forbescustom.com/SectionPDFs/032612BrazilSection.pdf>.

- *Creating a branded community.* For its target audience extending the presence of the Chilli Beans brand into other, related, parts of their lives is key to keeping the brand visible and relevant. For Chilli Beans this means an active programme of supporting events such as 'parties, shows, sports and social actions'.[44]

Why the name Chilli Beans for a sunglasses and lifestyle accessories business? Because, according to Maia, 'Chillis are universal. Everyone knows what they are.'[45] Maia's goal is for Chilli Beans to be similarly universal and 'part of the portfolio of global brands in five years'.[46] Given what the business has achieved in its first fifteen years and the creativity and innovation with which it has embraced the opportunities in the new landscape of retail, you wouldn't bet against it.

Future-Proofing Physical Retail Space

Is it possible or even desirable to seek to physically future-proof retail space? One way of future-proofing is, somewhat ironically, through disposability. This is nothing new. The freeways and suburbs of the USA are littered with the cinder-block remains of former strip malls: retail real estate which has ceased to fulfil a market need, but cost relatively little to develop in the first place. Strip malls have always been what US writer on cities David Uberti has called 'retail's bottom feeders', able to thrive in rapidly changing and challenging environments.[47] Such malls represent small investments and are generally built, demolished, and rebuilt relatively quickly as circumstances change and largely thanks to low land costs. Of course, such centres do not have to be downscale in their positioning: Chapter 3 discussed the example of Box-park, the limited-life lifestyle mall in London's uber-trendy Shoreditch. The temporary mall's even more ephemeral store-based equivalents are the pop-up shops and stores that litter fashionable urban places and that stimulate shoppers' interests in the brands presented by marketing 'in the moment'. In the UK alone, there were just under 10,000 such outlets trading in mid-2014, ranging from temporary restaurants and shops to product trials by vendor brands.[48]

A second strategy lies in enhancing the longer term flexibility of retail real estate. For established retailers, flexibility can be achieved institutionally,

[44] <http://apps.fracta.com.br/beta/chillibeans/sitev2/thebrand?language=en#!thebrand>.

[45] <http://www.forbescustom.com/SectionPDFs/032612BrazilSection.pdf>.

[46] <http://www.forbescustom.com/SectionPDFs/032612BrazilSection.pdf>.

[47] D. Uberti, 'The Death of the American Mall', *Guardian*, 19 June 2014. <http://www.theguardian.com/cities/2014/jun/19/-sp-death-of-the-american-shopping-mall>.

[48] Centre for Economic & Business Research. 'EE & CEBR Study Identifies £2.1billion Pop-up Retail Contribution to UK Economy', 2014. <http://ee.co.uk/our-company/newsroom/2014/07/22/ee-and-cebr-study-identifies-2-1-billion-pounds-pop-up-retail-contribution-to-uk-economy>.

through shorter or more flexible leasing arrangements; by outsourcing real estate needs to third parties; or by means of imaginative design or refurbishment to overcome some of the physical obstacles to repurposing space. For example the Circulo Verde development in Quezon City, Philippines, uses a zoning approach which locates flexible space along a main road and in common areas. Architects RTKL describe a scheme in which 'an open market zone hosts specialty events and celebrity pop-up market kiosks; longer-lease zones tailored for international and boutique brands in a concentrated retail district are balanced with smaller, short-term leasable spaces for art galleries and the like; and a night market zone enlivens the complex after the main retail section has closed'.[49] Even for those relatively new participants in the retail industry that are reliant not perhaps on stores but on warehouses and specialized logistics, the extent of uncertainty over future physical space needs means that the development of space must be carefully phased to avoid costly over-expansion; but not so incrementally developed that potential longer term growth is inhibited.

Finally, future-proofing can be addressed through strategies of risk reduction through sharing or collaboration with others, either with forward-thinking landlords and developers, or with other retailers, as a way of reducing risk. 'In a faster paced market both parties [retailer and investors] should be able to decide whether a retailer's location is relevant in five or 10 years' time or whether their brand is still in keeping with consumer demand.'[50] Greater emphasis seems likely to be given to the need to 'curate' even hitherto unmanaged clusters of shops. This has implications for those tasked with developing policy for and designing and managing the urban realm, as well as for retailers themselves.

Conclusion

It is beguilingly easy to see the new landscape of retailing as one defined by the almost total migration of retailing from a store-based to an online activity. Easy, but wrong in our view. We discussed in Chapters 1 and 2 the powerful forces of shopper change and technology change which are indeed transforming many parts of retailing into an 'online first, stores maybe' activity. In addition, we talked in Chapter 3 of how the physical landscape of retailing is going to look very different in very many locations in the near-term future

[49] RTKL, 'Flexible Space and the Retail Revolution', 24 Mar. 2015. <http://www.rtkl.com/you-are-here/flexible-space-and-the-retail-revolution>.

[50] Lunson Mitchenall,.'Fit for the Future: How Shopping Centres are Adapting to Change', 1 Sept. 2014. <http://www.lunson-mitchenall.co.uk/fit-for-the-future-how-shopping-centres-are-adapting-to-change>.

as retailers radically review their store portfolios in the context of very changed technology and shopper engagement landscapes and with profound consequences for the fabric and vitality of urban areas in particular.

The reality for most established retailers is that they have built up, often over considerable time and at considerable expense, extensive networks of physical stores. Exiting significant amounts of space which is no longer 'fit for purpose' may very well be necessary for many operators. But it is also our belief that, in the new landscape of retailing, physical stores can and will continue to be valued by many shoppers in many territories. We discussed in this chapter five territories in particular which physical stores can emphasize in order to remain relevant and desired.

The transformation of physical retailing from inflexible networks of conforming stores to highly diverse networks of points of engagement, some of which would not traditionally be called stores at all, presents very interesting possibilities for retailers—both traditional enterprises and 'new to retail' businesses. Networks of engagement points become far more flexible, many are much lower cost and can be brought to market far more quickly and in far more diverse locations than was possible when retailing was synonymous with standard format physical stores only. Whatever the physical network of engagement points that is ultimately configured, it is clear that those points of engagement have to be connected seamlessly into the shoppers' digital life also. Physical stores of whatever form must be conceived of as related, complementary, and relevant to the shoppers' digital life such that one touchpoint supports another in a total web of physical and digital engagement with the shopper at the centre.

The effective delivery of an omni-channel experience is the theme of Chapter 8. It is sufficient here to observe that the best retailers always organize their businesses around what is best for the customer, not what is easiest for the enterprise. Never has this been more true or more necessary.

8

Delivering the Omni-Channel Experience

The Challenge of Delivering Seamless Engagement in a Complex Landscape

While the great majority of retailing activity globally is still conducted in physical retail stores, it is clear now that in the near-term future ever more shoppers in ever more categories and countries will expect to be able to engage with retailers howsoever they wish across a wide diversity of platforms, some physical, many digital. In the new landscape, retailing is no longer a store-only or even a store-mainly activity. Moreover, generations of younger shoppers in particular are moving into their high-spending years with a view that retailing is not primarily a store-based activity at all. The time is, we hope, not far away when the term omni-channel will disappear and we can call this new landscape of shopper engagement what it really is—retailing. Unfortunately, that day is not yet here.

In this chapter we discuss how presently store-centric retail enterprises can transition their businesses so as to be relevant to shoppers by effectively delivering on their engagement expectations for a seamless experience across multiple touchpoints—some physical, many digital. We focus in particular on the cultural, competency, and organizational attributes that retail enterprises will need.

Cultural Considerations

Many retailers that have made or are in the process of making the transition from store-only to omni-channel retailing will say that the biggest challenges they had to overcome were cultural rather than technical. Jose Gomez, at the time head of business development at the iconic global fashion retailer Mango, echoed the views of many when he said, 'When we started online in

1995 there was a lot of resistance in our company. The stores really didn't like it. We had to change the culture.'[1] For many retailers, the most important cultural changes are associated with transitioning the business from a store-centric to a shopper-centred culture and the attendant changes to corporate skills, competencies, and organizational structures needed to make this transition.

From Store-Only to Shopper-Centred

For most retailers with their origins in a pre-internet world, their stores are the centre of their universe. The enterprise and the efforts and skills within it are organized around delivering the best possible experience to the shopper in-store. In order to be an effective omni-channel retailer, this orientation must change. Retailers have to be able to view their stores as just one touchpoint in engaging the shopper and recognize also that for many shoppers this will not even be the most important and valued one. This alone is a difficult reorientation for many retail business leaders to make, particularly those who have spent their careers working their way up from the stores. But it goes further than this. We have suggested already that the very phrase omni-channel is not helpful because it puts the emphasis on the channel and not on the shopper. It is to be hoped that the time will soon come when we will not be talking omni-channel—we will simply be talking retail. But, for the time being, to truly transition into an effective omni-channel retailer, it is the shopper that needs to be at the centre of the retailer's world, not any one point or channel of engagement.

It is especially important to engage the stores in the programme of change that reorientates a retailer from store-only to shopper-centred. Store-level resistance will be a considerable impediment to change if the stores feel that the additional touchpoints with the shopper either do not support their interests or, still worse, undermine them. In the early era of internet retailing, many book retailers around the world faced just this issue. Given Amazon's hugely disruptive impact on this category in particular, book retailers had to develop their own online capabilities but often encountered great reluctance from within their own store networks faced with the risk of cannibalization. The learning from these experiences is surely that if a retailer is to lose sales from its stores to online it is far, far better that those sales are lost to its own online operation, rather than to a competitor's.

New Skills and People

Transitioning a retail business from store-only to shopper-centric requires new enterprise skills and probably introduces new people into the organization

---

[1] Jose Gomez, speaking at Retail Congress Asia Pacific, Singapore, Mar. 2015.

with those skills. The inevitable consequence of introducing new people and skills into an enterprise is that existing capability areas and the people in them are, relatively speaking, de-emphasized. We discuss in Chapter 9 quite how substantial changes to skillsets may need to be in retail enterprises. From a cultural perspective, enterprise leaders need to consider whether they want such change to be, on the one hand, as seamless as possible or, on the other hand, as disruptive as possible, or somewhere in between. There is no right answer. We present later in this chapter a case study of the UK general merchandise retailer Argos and their transition to an omni-channel retail leader. For this business, bringing in new people with new skills at senior level was done not just for obvious reasons of capability, but also to shake up other parts of the organization and impress across the business that substantial change needed to happen and happen quickly. It is often the case that the hotter the burning platform for change the more it serves the interests of the enterprise to make that change very visible and disruptive. For others, company culture and a desire for continuity and the relative absence of a need to respond to aggressive competitor challenges make the case for seeking continuity rather than disruption.

One important cultural issue for many retailers is the need to bring into the enterprise very different types of people as well as very different skills. We discuss in the next section of this chapter the need for many retailers to deepen the specialisms they have in many areas of their business, but especially in IT, logistics, and customer insights. This emphasizes skills which are less retail-sector-specific and more competency-specific. The last change of CEO at Tesco, the world's third largest retailer, illustrates this more general point. When Dave Lewis, the current incumbent and formerly at Unilever, was appointed to the role in 2014, Tesco's press release emphasized that, 'Dave Lewis brings a wealth of international consumer experience and expertise in change management, business strategy, brand management and customer development.' Clearly, these attributes were considered more relevant than a background in the grocery retail sector. Yet when Lewis's immediate predecessor, Philip Clarke, was appointed to the CEO role, several analysts noted approvingly that his entire career had been spent at Tesco since being a part-time shelf stacker aged 14.[2] This is not to suggest that one type of leader and background is better or worse than another. Rather, it is to suggest that different company circumstances and priorities make it likely that more retailers will face the challenge of integrating very different types of skills and cultures and may choose to prioritize on skills within specific competency areas rather than on more traditionally retail-sector-specific expertise.

---

[2] One analyst at Execution Noble, Caroline Gulliver, described Clarke as a 'Tesco man through and through'. Quoted in <http://www.europeanceo.com/profiles/phillip-clarke>.

It can be a source of friction if more traditionally valued skills are, relatively speaking, somewhat de-emphasized. Many of the great retail businesses have been built from and on cultures which emphasize traditional merchant skills—merchandising, sourcing, trading—and the sheer charisma of their founders and business leaders, however different those personalities might have been (Sam Walton and Gordon Selfridge are two examples amongst many). It can be notably difficult culturally to combine these traditional skills with the more scientific, granular, and customer-centric skills required in the new retail landscape.

Enterprise Capability Considerations

Effectively executing an omni-channel strategy changes fundamentally the basis of how a retail business needs to operate. Instead of the shopper being required to visit a single point of engagement—the store—the retailer is now expected to make it possible for the shopper to engage with the business in an almost infinite number of permutations. As such, capabilities that have been built and refined to serve one purpose are now being asked to perform very different functions. Figure 8.1 presents a generalized view of the importance of key business functions to the effective delivery of an omni-channel strategy.

At a headline level, we believe that four capability areas are of primary importance to retail enterprises with omni-channel ambitions. Merchandising is still at the heart of what it means to be a distinctive and valued retail enterprise. This much has not changed, although the capabilities required within the merchandise function have, as we will discuss. Marketing is a

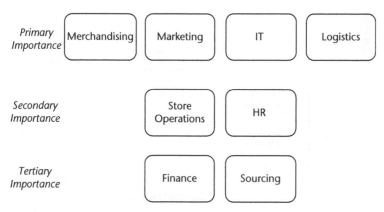

Figure 8.1 Capability areas required by retailers for effective delivery of an omni-channel strategy

Source: Authors.

179

capability area which we see as being, for many retailers, of higher order importance in an omni-channel world, given the far greater complexity today and in the future of effectively engaging with shoppers across an ever-growing plethora of contact points which are themselves interacting in much more complex and more personalized ways. IT and logistics are also of high order importance to retailers with omni-channel ambitions. This is unlikely to be a surprise to many readers.

For most retailers, capability areas of second-order importance will likely be store operations and human resources. The capability areas likely to be least important to the effective execution of an omni-channel strategy are finance and product sourcing. This is not at all to suggest that these functions are unimportant to the enterprise. Rather it is to say these functions will not, for most retailers, impact on their ability to execute their omni-channel ambitions.

Figure 8.2 maps the importance of each business function to the ability of an enterprise to execute its omni-channel ambitions and also the extent to which that function may need to change in order to be able to do so. Naturally, the amount of change required depends principally on the starting point of the enterprise in the first place. As such, this can only be a very generalized view. Our suggestion is that, for many historically store-centric retailers, it is the IT, logistics, and marketing functions that will need to change most if the enterprise is to execute its omni-channel plans effectively.

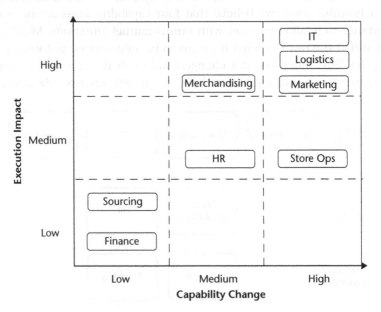

Figure 8.2 Execution impact and capability change requirements of key business functions
Source: Authors.

IT

For many retail enterprises, the role of the IT function has tended to be skewed towards bringing efficiency to and control over the enterprise and this will remain of high importance. But in an omni-channel world the requirement of the IT function changes considerably and becomes focused at least as much, and very possibly more, on enabling personalized shopper engagement across multiple touchpoints as it does on control of the enterprise. Moreover, IT is critical to the ability of a retail enterprise to be alert to and able to respond to opportunities to engage with new shoppers as well as to deepen relationships (and sales) with existing ones. We discussed in Chapter 2 the promise of so-called 'big data' initiatives in this regard.

We see tremendous opportunities for far-sighted retailers to change the focus of their IT function from that of a control orientated cost centre to a shopper orientated enterprise growth centre without losing the control function. The challenge that many retail enterprises have is how to get from where they are today to where they need to be—also today. When Sir Charlie Mayfield reflects on the changes that have taken place within the John Lewis Partnership to allow the execution of their omni-channel ambitions, he talks in particular of the 'enormous challenge' of continually upgrading legacy IT systems and ensuring that they integrate with new systems. And all this has to take place live in an environment where the shopper is ever less tolerant of service underperformance against their higher expectations.[3] Moreover, for most retailers a relatively small proportion of shoppers account for a large proportion of sales and profits so that, as one CEO said (anonymously) 'investing in understanding the customer becomes more and more important'.

For some, perhaps many retailers, the right solution to the changed requirements of the IT practice may be to at least partially dismantle it. This is especially relevant where IT has been biased historically towards a highly centralized and control orientated function that is no longer consistent with the needs of the enterprise for far greater agility, flexibility, and personalized shopper engagement. As one retailer told us (anonymously), 'we have largely dismantled the monolithic bureaucracy of the central IT department. They now run the core systems architecture and facilitate API [Application Programming Interface] interfaces to allow frontline managers to write their own applications. The resultant agility and customer orientation fits the new landscape that we're operating in.'

For some, it may be appropriate to outsource at least part of the IT function in order to migrate both the capabilities and the culture from where it is

---

[3] Personal conversation, Sir Charlie Mayfield, 2015.

currently to where it needs to be. There is no right or wrong answer to the decision to outsource or not. Considerations on levels of risk, investment, and the required speed of change all inform this decision (and not just for the IT function). For Argos, the UK general merchandise retailer, outsourcing the delivery of the IT function was seen as essential to achieving the business objective of a truly omni-channel operation within a very ambitious time-frame. For others, outsourcing is not seen as the right answer because IT is considered to be so much at the heart of the enterprise and as such too much risk is associated with outsourcing the function. For still others, outsourcing is the right approach in one period, but the function is then taken back in-house, typically once the big transformations have been made.

Logistics

Traditionally, distribution has been regarded as something akin to the retail equivalent of drain cleaning—necessary, grubby, distinctly unglamorous, but 'someone's got to do it'. No more. Myriad new fulfilment options are emerging quickly—all with the primary objective of getting product to shoppers more quickly and/or more conveniently. We discussed in Chapter 1 the need for retailers to create webs of engagement with the shopper at the centre. The same principle is true in the fulfilment domain where the range of options available to retailers will become still more diverse. Click and collect has emerged very strongly as a preferred fulfilment model for UK shoppers especially. (Consultants OC&C forecast that, by 2017, click and collect parcels will account for 30 per cent of non-food deliveries in the UK, equivalent to growth of 60 per cent per year between 2012 and 2017.[4]) But the point of collection has also changed and no longer needs to be the store.

- Many grocery retailers are using secure lockers with chilled, frozen, and ambient temperature compartments located in drive-through areas of their parking lots.

- Others are locating secure lockers in transport hubs such as train and underground stations for shoppers to collect orders on their way to or from offices.

- Australia Post offers 24/7 Parcel Locker addresses in 180 locations, explicitly designed for more convenient parcel tracking and collection when shopping online.

- Office buildings are becoming collection points where secure lockers are located.

[4] <http://www.telegraph.co.uk/news/shopping-and-consumer-news/11324611/Click-and-collect-overtakes-home-delivery-at-John-Lewis.html>.

- Small, often independently owned, shops are being used as order collection points by distribution businesses such as Hermes and Collect Plus (UK) and Point Relais (France). Hermes is especially interesting. Hermes began in Germany in 1972 as the in-house delivery business for the Otto group of mail order businesses. Otto has now become one of Europe's largest online retailers and Hermes has been transformed into a fulfilment partner for a large number of other businesses while also extending its reach into other European countries.[5]

Case 8.1 PACKSTATION, GERMANY

In Europe, one of the most developed networks of secure kiosks for parcel collection and sending is Packstation, operated by DHL Germany, part of Deutsche Post. Packstation is a network of around 2,650 secure automated kiosks with around 250,000 compartments located in 1,600 cities and towns across Germany (at mid-2014); 90 per cent of people in Germany live within ten minutes' drive of a Packstation[6] (Figure 8.3). Use of Packstations is free for both personal and business users. However, users need to sign up

Figure 8.3 One of over 2,600 DHL Packstations across Germany
Source: Deutsche Post AG, 2015. http://www.dpdhl.com/content/dam/dpdhl/presse/mediathek/bilder/dhl_packstation_2014/dhl-packstation-2014-zusteller-anlieferung-668.jpg

(*continued*)

---

[5] <http://www.ottogroup.com/en/die-otto-group/konzernfirmen/hermes-europe.php>.
[6] <http://postandparcel.info/61068/uncategorized/dhl-to-expand-packstation-network-inside-and-outside-of-germany>.

Case 8.1 Continued

---

in order to obtain the magnetic stripe Goldcard and mTan (Mobile Transaction Authentication Number) needed to access the secure Packstation locker. At mid-2014 there were approximately 5 million registered users in Germany.

The Packstation network also helps address the challenge of what to do with orders that cannot be received at home because the recipient is out. In this case, the parcel is automatically redirected to the closest Packstation and the customer informed via a green card with a bar code and the address of the Packstation. The barcode is scanned to open the compartment. The initial pilot of Packstation in 2001 preceded the internet age and was launched to make parcel collection and sending possible outside normal Post Office opening hours. Growth has been rapid since then, and Packstations are now used widely as collection points for orders placed online. More Packstations will be added to the network in Germany and Deutsche Post plans also to develop the network in other European countries, starting with the Netherlands and Italy.[7]

Case 8.2 KIALA/UPS ACCESS POINTS

Kiala is a logistics company, established in Belgium in 2001. Kiala combines 6,700 package collection points located in retail stores and 1,000 Click & Collect secure kiosks in five European markets (France, Belgium, Luxembourg, the Netherlands, and Spain). Since early 2012, Kiala has been part of UPS and the collection points and kiosks have been rebranded as UPS Access Points. The combined UPS/Kiala network now comprises over 13,000 collection points in nine European countries. In October 2014, Access Point kiosks were set up in Chicago and New York City. The business expected to grow its network to 20,000 locations across Europe and the Americas by the end of 2015.[8] Kiala has more than 350 B2C business customers across its European markets, including many of the best-known online retailers. As with Packstation, when UPS cannot deliver a package to a customer's home, delivery defaults to the nearest Kiala pick-up point.

More radical fulfilment options are also being trialled. Two in particular have received much attention.

DRONES

Small drones have achieved the seemingly impossible of making logistics sexy and of interest to the mainstream media. When Amazon began its pilot (pun irresistible) of pilotless small drones in 2014 it said that, 'The goal of this new delivery system is to get packages into customers' hands in 30 minutes or less using unmanned aerial vehicles.'[9] Google's drone trials in

---

[7] <http://www.dpdhl.com/en/media_relations/press_releases/2014/dhl_packstation_success_story_continues.html>.

[8] <https://www.kiala.com/facts-figures>.

[9] <http://www.marketingmagazine.co.uk/article/1223302/amazon-plans-30-minute-delivery-drones-prime-air-service>.

Australia even prompted an editorial in the UK *Times* newspaper which noted that 'It took the Pentagon 20 years to get from drawing board to training flights with a fixed-wing propeller plane that could take off and land vertically. It has taken Google two.'[10]

The possibilities for deploying drones will likely depend to a large extent on the view that regulators take, especially those with responsibility for air traffic movement and safety. The early signs are mixed. At the start of 2015, the US FAA (Federal Aviation Authority) issued its first draft guidelines on drone movements that, if implemented, would make it effectively impossible for Amazon to operate its proposed Prime Air drone fulfilment system. But in April 2015 the same authority announced that Amazon would be one of 128 exemptions allowed to trial drones for commercial purposes.[11] Amazon has filed a patent for an unmanned aerial vehicle delivery system (UAV) that includes dynamically updateable origin and destination planning, coordination between drones, return to 'trusted' locations, and a 'Bring it to Me' option tuned to the customer's mobile phone GPS location.[12] In mid-2015, Amazon proposed that a separate airspace zone be created at a height of between 200 and 400 feet (61 to 122 metres) as a 'high speed transit space' for commercial drones.[13] What is clear is that this issue will not be solved quickly as regulators seek to catch up with technology and with the commercial goals of those seeking to deploy it.

ROBOTS

Ground-based robot technologies may be another part of the answer. Amazon and Google have both made substantial investments in robotics companies in recent years (not just, it should be said, with the objective of using robots to address the fulfilment challenge). In 2014 EU legislators started to address the notion that autonomous intelligent systems (AIS) may need to be granted rights and protections similar to those of humans if they are performing tasks conducted by humans.[14] The discussion was given a particular urgency in part by the development in Pisa, Italy, of a robot that could be employed to collect groceries from stores. As one of the researchers in that project, Andrea Bertolini, observed: 'In Pisa, they

---

[10] <http://www.thetimes.co.uk/tto/opinion/leaders/article4191425.ece>.

[11] <http://www.usatoday.com/story/money/2015/04/09/faa-amazon-drone-approval-prime-air/25534485>.

[12] <http://appft.uspto.gov/netacgi/nph-Parser?Sect1=PTO1&Sect2=HITOFF&d=PG01&p=1&u=%2Fnetahtml%2FPTO%2Fsrchnum.html&r=1&f=G&l=50&s1=%2220150120094%22.PGNR.&OS=DN/20150120094&RS=DN/20150120094>.

[13] <http://www.bbc.co.uk/news/business-33698812>.

[14] M. de Cock Buning et al., *Mapping the Legal Framework for the Introduction into Society of Robots as Autonomous Intelligent Systems*. Centre for Access to and Acceptance of Autonomous Intelligence, 2014. <http://www.caaai.eu/wp-content/uploads/2012/08/Mapping-L_N-fw-for-AIS.pdf>.

are developing a robot that is capable of travelling from your home to the grocery store and paying for goods that it needs. In cases like this you may want to consider the robot as a legal person that is able to enter into a contract.'[15] The European Commission is currently exploring the ways in which robotic and human enhancement technologies could be safely and successfully introduced into society.

Case 8.3 DELIV—CROWDSOURCED SAME DAY FULFILMENT

Deliv (deliv.co, 'Delivery. Shortened'), based in California, aims to solve the so-called last mile delivery challenge with a crowdsourced model by which it connects retailers to self-employed local drivers that act as same day delivery drivers for purchases made in-store or online (then delivered to store) with a wide and growing range of highly credible non-food retailers. Retailers using Deliv include Bloomingdales, Brooks Brothers, Crate & Barrel, Macy's, Nordstrom, Staples, Williams Sonoma, and Walgreens. Deliv drivers only need to have 'a vehicle, a smart phone, and a friendly, professional work ethic'.[16] Deliv began operating in 2012 in the San Francisco Bay Area and has subsequently expanded into other major metro areas across the US, including Chicago, New York, Seattle, Miami, and Los Angeles.[17] In mid-2014, Deliv joined IBM's Smarter Commerce ecosystem of, at the time, '41 certified pre-built partner solutions with integrated cloud, mobile and social capabilities'.[18] Several major shopping centre owners, including Simon and Westfield, partner with Deliv so that the service is available to traders in their centres. The Deliv operation is 'white labelled' so that the delivery service does not intrude into the relationship between the retailer and the shopper.

This is not a model that will be for everyone, as some will have concerns about the quality of the delivery experience that the shopper receives from a self-employed delivery driver using an unbranded vehicle that is up to fifteen years old. (Vehicles have to be newer than the year 2000.) But it is an interesting and fast growing example of using close to ubiquitous technology—a smartphone—and an under-utilized asset—a vehicle—to create a very lean enterprise which is primarily a technology company providing a logistics service to connect shoppers to stores, both physical and digital. (Interestingly, Uber has for a long time seen huge opportunity to extend beyond being primarily a cab hailing service and into an on-demand delivery fulfilment enterprise. In late 2015, the UberRush delivery service launched in San Francisco and Chicago following trials in New York. As the *Financial Times* reported, 'Travis Kalanick, Uber chief executive, has often talked about expanding beyond ride-hailing to create a logistics network that will be "as reliable as running water." '[19])

Not only is the role of the logistics function becoming substantially more important within retail enterprises, so too is the role of logistics and logistics businesses within entire value chains. It used often to be said that Walmart is

---

[15] H. Devlin, 'Grasp Future and Give Robots Legal Status, EU is Told', *The Times*, 2 Oct. 2014. <http://www.thetimes.co.uk/tto/law/article4223866.ece>.

[16] <http://www.deliv.co/drivers>.

[17] <http://recode.net/2014/06/10/with-amazon-in-mind-ibm-begins-giving-retail-clients-same-day-delivery-tool>.

[18] <http://www.retailingtoday.com/article/same-day-delivery-looking-smarter-ibm>.

[19] <http://www.ft.com/cms/s/0/8a6f1084-7295-11e5-a129-3fcc4f641d98.html#axzz3sgXzzB4A>.

as much a warehousing and distribution business as it is a retail business (in that it built the distribution centre in a new territory and only later built the stores around the DC). Today, Amazon, eBay, Alibaba, ASOS, and other online trading communities are surely at least as much logistics businesses as they are retail businesses. In a previous era (around the 1980s in Western Europe and North America), wholesale businesses were being squeezed out of value chains because they were felt to be adding little value and too much cost to the process of moving product through supply chains. Whilst wholesaling is still a significant activity in many European markets (there were 1.8 million wholesale firms generating €593 billion in added value in Europe in 2013[20]) the distinction between manufacturing, wholesaling, and retailing has become increasingly blurred.

Today, it is established retail enterprises which face the very real challenge of being bypassed by logistics businesses, or logistics-focused businesses. In several sectors and several countries, enterprises are being established and brought quickly to market with the specific objective of using a technology and logistics competency in order to connect suppliers directly to end users without the need for a traditional retailer intermediary. This is not the actions of vendors 'going direct'—although that is clearly happening too. The grocery market is a case in point. Most of the world's largest retailers are grocery businesses either wholly or partially. Yet in the new retail landscape, a number of enterprises—perhaps platform providers is the most appropriate descriptor—are being brought to market with the specific objective of connecting vendors directly to shoppers without using established retailers as intermediaries. As well as the behemoths, notably Alibaba and Amazon, others are country and/or grocery specific such as Jumia (Nigeria) and Redmart (Singapore). Their rationale for seeking to bypass retail intermediaries is conceptually the same rationale that led grocery (and other) retailers in an earlier era to seek to bypass traditional wholesalers—capture more profit by taking a cost element out of the value chain. What retailers did to wholesalers in an earlier era, new kinds of logistics businesses are now seeking to do to retailers. As well as allowing for the rather ironic observation that 'what goes around comes around', there is a more useful insight here also: retail enterprises—however mature, large, and established they may be—do not have an automatic right to maintain their position in the value chain. It is a right that has to be earned by adding more value than you cost and by delivering a more valued experience to the shopper than they could gain without the retailer being present.

We suggest in Figure 8.1 that there are four capability areas within a retail enterprise that will have a substantial impact on the ability of a retailer to

[20] J. Reynolds and R. Cuthbertson, *Retail and Wholesale: Key Sectors for the European Economy*. Brussels: Eurocommerce, 2014. <http://www.eurocommerce.eu/media/87967/eurocommerce_study_v2_hd.pdf>.

successfully execute their omni-channel plans. These are Merchandising, HR, Marketing, and Store Operations. In the case of Marketing and Store Operations it seems likely that many retailers will need to make substantial changes to how these functions operate and the skills within them if they are to be fit for purpose in an omni-channel world, depending on where their starting point is.

Marketing

For many retailers the essential objectives of the marketing function are unlikely to change—build preference, drive traffic, increase average transaction values, and so on—but the *ways* in which those objectives are delivered may change very considerably. Marketing is an area where there is real opportunity for smart retailers to simultaneously remove cost while adding effectiveness. This is made possible because of the interaction of two factors: the desire of consumers for more personalized communications relevant to them, together with the growing importance of social media and the relatively declining importance of paid traditional media as digital media grows in relevance and share of voice.

Communication spend can be considered to have three component parts:

- *Paid*—both traditional media and digital media
- *Owned*—that which is owned by the retailer (their website, stores, in company magazines, opt-in databases, and so on)
- *Earned*—that which is earned in the sense of earning the right to have positive messages about the business in social media.

It is not a big leap from where many retailers (and vendor brands also) are today to suggest that the proportion of paid for media will decline as the proportion of owned and earned media continues to increase as enterprises seek to engage with audiences in far more personal ways, with more targeted messages and in much less expensive and, for many, more impactful social media. This is shown in concept form in Figure 8.4. The writer and social observer, Laurence Scott, talks of the 'Four-Dimensional Human' where the fourth dimension is our digital selves—'a world of ceaseless communication, instant information and global connection'. As Scott says, 'Fully fledged young 4D Adults find it natural and efficient for ads to be (in the cosy language of marketing) "targeted at you". How crude it must seem to them now, this idea that television commercials used to come at us, in comparison, like grapeshot, rather than lined up through a sniper's site.'[21] It seems certain that competency in digital media will become still more important in many marketing functions. Moreover, the need for IT to support the marketing

[21] Laurence Scott, *The Four-Dimensional Human. Ways of Being in a Digital World*. London: William Heinemann, 2015.

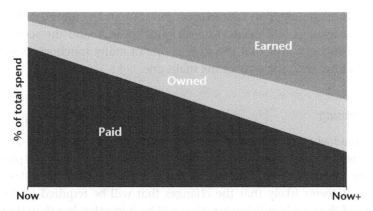

Figure 8.4 Illustrative changed composition of communication media
Source: Authors.

function will increase for many as retailers mine for still more granular insights into their shoppers' behaviours and preferences.

Store Operations

Store operations is a capability area that is not only important to the effective delivery of an omni-channel strategy but is also likely to require considerable change in scope and activity for many retailers. This is a consequence in particular of the need to reframe the role of the store in an omni-channel world. We discussed fully in Chapter 7 how stores may need to change in order to retain their relevance. For many retailers, we anticipate that changes to the store environment will involve substantial reformatting that goes well beyond the normal incremental changes that are part and parcel of keeping retail real estate fresh. For some this will involve reconfiguring stores to facilitate their roles as collection points for orders placed online. Radical change, especially in food retailing, could take the form of reformatting large stores into dark store picking areas for orders placed online (and closed to the shopper) and the remainder of the space used for highly experiential fresh food presentations.

Across most categories, especially but not exclusively high-involvement discretionary spend categories, it seems very likely that retailers will need to emphasize presentation, theatre, and service as meaningful differentiators to the value-driven and/or online alternatives. Here again, the implication is that considerable change to operational requirements will be needed. This will be especially in the areas of store presentation, space allocations, technology provisioning, shopper engagement, and staff service. Technology has long been a hugely important part of operational requirements at a store level, of course, and this will only accelerate in the near-term future. If we see the property function as a part of store operations (many retailers do) then, here too, many retailers will need to revisit both the role and the scope of the property function, now that the store is one of many touchpoints with the shopper rather than the only or the main one.

Merchandising

The requirements of the merchandising function are changed in an omni-channel world. Here we are distinguishing merchandising—product planning, selection, display—from, but related to, the sourcing function. For many retailers, it seems likely that the changes that will be required to the skills and role of the merchandising function will be somewhat less than those that are required in other parts of the enterprise (Figure 8.2). But again, this will vary widely by retailer, depending on both their starting point and on where they aim to get to.

Two dimensions of the new retail landscape have particular relevance for the merchandising function—the speed of change in consumer buying behav-iours, together with the far wider range of choice available to most shoppers in most locations. This means that the merchandise function will need to be still more adept at forward trend spotting as well as at interpreting historic sales data (pointing also to the great importance of the IT function across the enterprise to provide such insights). As the leader of one highly regarded general merchandise retailer told us, 'we take a much more agile approach to merchandising and ranging than we used to'.

For many retailers, especially the general merchants with large assortments across multiple categories, we would expect to see a trend towards editing assortments and exiting categories rather than the reverse. For such retailers, much of the last twenty-five years or more has been about adding items, lines, categories, and broadening as well as deepening assortments. In the internet age, we suggest that, for many, the more important skill will be to edit assortments and to act as a choice curator for the shopper. If the role of the internet is to provide almost infinite choice, the role of the store will—for many—be to curate, edit, recommend, and stimulate. Great merchandising is all about flair and boldness and, in some senses, giving customers things that they did not realize they wanted. (In a different context, Steve Jobs was once asked how much market research went into Apple's designs. 'None', he remarked, 'it's not the consumer's job to know what they want.'[22]) While this is not changed in the new retail landscape, what is required is more science in the form of trend and shopper insights to match the flair.

---

[22] Steve Jobs, cited in S. Lohr, 'The Yin and the Yang of Corporate Innovation', *New York Times*, 26 Jan. 2012. <http://www.nytimes.com/2012/01/27/technology>.

HR

Servicing the changing talent needs of the new retail enterprise is the responsibility of the human resources function. We have already made it clear that the evolving omni-channel business has to recruit employees with new skill-sets, as well as train and develop existing staff to accommodate new capability requirements. Although we have suggested that HR is of secondary importance to such enterprises in terms of both capability change required and execution impact by comparison with—say—IT and logistics, this is only relative. It by no means implies business as usual. Not least, this is because much of the kind of talent required is in significantly short supply. Consultants PwC, in their annual global survey of CEOs, reported that 73 per cent ranked skill shortage as the biggest threat to their business—a proportion that has been rising since 2009.[23] European policy-makers worry that there could be over 800,000 unfilled vacancies for ICT professionals by 2020.[24] Moreover the search is not just for those with technology skills but, more importantly, those with a successful track record in implementing change.

Some firms have made responding to this challenge a priority. Writing in the *New York Times* in 2015, Jodi Kantor and David Streitfield note that 'Amazon's legions of recruiters identify thousands of job prospects each year, who face extra screening by "bar raisers," star employees and part-time interviewers charged with ensuring that only the best are hired.'[25] But not all retail brands have the allure of new economy enterprises like Amazon and they may, therefore, find it harder to attract talent and will have to resort to other means. These more inventive strategies will range from more imaginative identification of recruits, selective outsourcing, freelance service agreements, through to collaboration with other firms and even enterprise acquisition to obtain the requisite skills. Some firms have created innovation accelerators as a way not just to explore new ideas for the enterprise, but also to attract new talent. In Chapter 9, we discuss the example of Walmart Labs, which at the time of writing had acquired fifteen companies since its inception in 2010.[26]

It may prove to be the case also that retail enterprises operating in omni-channel worlds, be it their own or those of their competitors, will need to put more emphasis and resources into enhancing the capabilities of their store-level staff. For many this may seem counter-intuitive if not impossibly expensive in

[23] PwC, 'People Strategy for the Digital Age', 2015. <http://www.pwc.com/gx/en/hr-management-services/publications/people-strategy.jhtml>.

[24] European Commission, *Grand Coalition for Digital Jobs.* 4 July 2015. <http://ec.europa.eu/digital-agenda/en/grand-coalition-digital-jobs-0>.

[25] J. Kantor and D. Streitfield, 'Inside Amazon: Wrestling Big Ideas in a Bruising Workplace', *New York Times*, 15 Aug. 2015. <http://www.nytimes.com/2015/08/16/technology/inside-amazon-wrestling-big-ideas-in-a-bruising-workplace.html>.

[26] <http://www.walmartlabs.com/about/acquisitions>.

the context of falling foot traffic in physical stores as shoppers migrate online. But for at least some retailers it is probable that as foot traffic declines, the quality and profit potential of that traffic which remains does, in fact, increase. Kip Tindell, the widely admired co-founder and CEO of The Container Store, observes that in his business, 'because of their phones, they [shoppers] are making more purposeful visits when they do come to the store. It's hard not to have higher ticket sales with declining traffic. Better training, less bottom feeding of who we hire is the answer. Get better people, pay them more, train them more.'[27]

We identify product sourcing and finance as the functions likely to have least impact on the ability of an enterprise to deliver its omni-channel plans and also as likely to require least change to their scope and capability in an omni-channel world.

Sourcing

The principal role of the sourcing function is, of course, to identify, develop, and maintain supplier relationships appropriate to the product needs of the enterprise. As the impact of omni-channel is so concentrated on the relationship between the retailer and the shopper, there is less sense in which the distribution and engagement options available to the two affect the downstream sourcing requirements of the enterprise. There is an important caveat to this general proposition which is that the online world opens up more potential product sourcing opportunities, perhaps especially through web platforms hosting vendor communities. So, here again, the point should be made that awareness and responsiveness to new sourcing possibilities become still more important in an environment where the choice of merchandise and suppliers available to the retailer becomes wider—just as it has for the shopper.

Finance

In terms of capability requirements the finance function is, we suggest, likely to be little changed by the new needs of retail enterprises in the delivery of their omni-channel ambitions. Again, we emphasize that this does not mean that the finance function is not important. Rather it means that the scope of the tasks and the skills that are needed are largely unchanged. Finance remains mostly an asset allocation, control, and reporting function. It is just that the suite of areas over which it needs to allocate assets, control, and report has

---

[27] Kip Tindell, speaking at World Retail Congress, Rome, Sept. 2015.

changed. In particular, a new suite of performance reporting metrics will be required that are aligned to a customer-centric omni-channel enterprise rather than to a store-only or store-centric enterprise. Focusing on, say, sales per customer becomes very much more relevant than, say, sales per square metre. (We discussed in Chapter 5 the new performance metric requirements of retail enterprises.)

Organizational Structure Considerations

Not only does the move from store-only to omni-channel retailing change the capability requirements of key parts of a retail enterprise, it also has significant implications for the organizational structure. Within key functional areas, skillsets need to become deeper in ways we have noted. In essence, specialists become still more specialized. As such, it becomes much harder for people to move between functions. One retailer of considerable scale talks of the borders between functional areas of the business that he leads being 'far less porous' than they were even ten years ago as a consequence of specialisms deepening within each capability area. In this environment, it is important to ensure effective integration across capability areas so that specialisms do not inadvertently become autonomous silos.

There are a number of ways to promote the connectedness that is needed between specialisms. For many retailers, the IT function may be the glue that connects functional areas together since there is unlikely to be any part of an omni-channel enterprise that does not rely heavily on the IT function. Important also is to both have and communicate across the enterprise a common view of what the retail business stands for, who its target audience(s) are, and what it is aspiring to deliver to those audiences. The point can be made that any retailer—omni-channel or otherwise—needs to have this. This is certainly true, but it becomes especially important when the 'natural' gravitational forces within an enterprise are towards being introverted and specialized, rather than outward-looking and integrated. For all enterprises, the leadership at the top has the key role to play in setting both the goals for the business and the ways, direction, and tone by which the goals will be realized.

For some retailers starting from a presence in store-based retailing, it will be desirable to give explicit focus to their non-store channels, especially in the early stages of their development. Establishing the role of Director of Omni-Channel as a senior role and reporting to the CEO (rather than into the head of stores, for example) can give the focus that is needed. It also allows the emergent non-store operations to operate in a way that connects to but lives a little outside the well-established store operations, and thereby institutionalizes the need for a start-up venture to operate to a somewhat different set of rules—especially with regard to resource allocation—than the rest of the enterprise. Over time, and especially when the non-store part of the enterprise grows more quickly than the store-based part (which is the experience of many retailers), the case for integration will exceed the case for separation. A further important consideration in this regard is that separating out one channel can lead to wasteful duplication of resources as well as making it more difficult to deliver a truly seamless proposition to the shopper.

Many aspiring and current omni-channel retailers define themselves as being 'channel neutral' in the ways they seek to engage the shopper. This is to say, the retailer—at least in principle—professes no preference over how the shopper engages with the business and sees their role as being solely to provide all of the points of engagement desired by the shopper and then to make it as easy as possible for the shopper to move across those points howsoever they wish. There has in recent years been something of a tendency to see this as the highest order and the purest expression of the omni-channel promise to the shopper. But for some retailers there are entirely appropriate reasons to want to direct a shopper to one engagement point over another at different stages in their shopping journey. This is for both shopper experience and commercial reasons. If a retailer has organized their omni-channel offer such that different touchpoints are optimized to fulfil different functions for the shopper then logically one would want to orientate the shopper to those touchpoints at the appropriate stage in their purchase journey. A website may have been optimized to present the merchandise range story, the stores may have been optimized to present the brand experience story, and the secure kiosks are optimized for collection (obviously). There is nothing intrinsically wrong or anti-customer in the notion of seeking to orientate the customer to those touchpoints that will best deliver on the shopper's needs at different stages in their purchase 'journey'. Equally, there will likely be good commercial reasons to be at the very least mindful of the implications for the business of which touchpoints the shopper wishes to use. If the real cost to serve a customer in one channel is materially higher than in another (as it often is), then it may be appropriate to seek to navigate the customer to one touchpoint over another.

It is important to be clear that we are in no way making a case for forcing the shopper to engage in ways that suit the business but not the shopper. Not only is this entirely incompatible with the notion of true customer centricity, it is also commercial folly. If you do not allow the shopper to engage with your business in the ways that they want to, you can be certain that there will be many competitors who will.

Case 8.4 ARGOS: A TURBULENT JOURNEY TOWARDS OMNI-CHANNEL SUCCESS

Argos has been a staple part of the UK general merchandise retail scene since the early 1970s. By 2012, Argos had over 700 stores and an estimated 96 per cent of the UK population lived within 10 miles of an Argos branch.[28] Since 2006, Argos has been part of Home Retail Group, which also includes Homebase, the home improvement retailer, Habitat, and Financial Services.

Given that almost all of Argos's product mix is essentially discretionary (well over one-third of sales are in consumer electronics) and it skews to a slightly younger and less affluent demographic, it was not surprising that the business was particularly badly affected by the severe recession in UK consumer spending that began in 2009. From a high of £376.2 million in 2008, operating profits collapsed to just £94.2 million in 2012 (Figure 8.5). But for Argos there was an additional factor contributing to its trading difficulties—the entry and aggressive growth of Amazon into the UK. Katy Gotch, Head of Group Strategy at Home Retail Group, talks of a business that was at 'crisis point', having lost its leadership position on price and service to a competitor that offered both lower prices and broader assortments than Argos.

The business had a burning platform to change. This was recognized by Terry Duddy, CEO of HRG (and Argos before that) until his retirement in mid-2014. Duddy also recognized that HRG needed a new leader to create and drive the execution of the transformation programme that Argos needed. John Walden from the US was appointed CEO of HRG in March 2014, following two years as Managing Director of Argos and with a background in customer-facing strategy roles for service businesses and retailers, most notably Best Buy. Walden had both a mandate to make radical change to Argos and a trading imperative to do so.

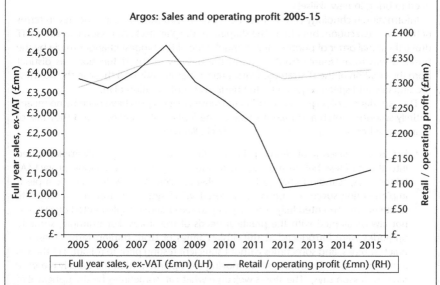

Figure 8.5 Argos sales and operating profit, 2005–15

Source: Data from Home Retail Group, 2015. https://www.homeretailgroup.com/investor-centre/.

(continued)

[28] <http://www.theguardian.com/business/2013/aug/25/argos-40-years-catalogue-shopping>.

Case 8.4 Continued

The guiding architecture of the change programme at Argos is a transformation plan announced in October 2012 to 'reinvent Argos as a digital retail leader'. The plan has four foundational elements:

- Reposition channels for a digital future
- More choice available faster
- Universal customer appeal
- Lean and flexible cost base

A major strength for Argos was that the business had already been a multi-channel retailer for many years. Indeed, as a business where products are browsed in a catalogue—usually at home—and then ordered and picked up in a store, one could say that Argos has always been a multi-channel business. As Katy Gotch says, 'There was a strong start point for transforming into a truly omni-channel business.' The company's first transactional website was launched in 1997 and Argos can lay claim also to being the pioneer in the UK of the 'click and collect' model of ordering online and taking delivery in store (launched in 2001). By January 2016, internet originated sales represented 53 per cent of total sales and, within that, mobile commerce sales were 31 per cent of total internet sales.[29]

Integral to driving the transformation programme was the appointment of a large number of new individuals to senior roles across the business. Several new roles were created also, including that of Head of Transformation. Jonathan Inkson, who occupied that role for three years, describes the need to bring a lot of external talent into the business in order to create a culture of urgency to change, as well as the more obvious need to bring in new skillsets.

Information technology is central to the Argos transformation plan, not only in terms of the plan's execution, but also in the shaping of the plan itself. As Inkson explains it, 'IT drove the initial order of priorities for change'. One of the biggest changes made by the business was to outsource (to Accenture) the delivery of the IT function—as distinct from the creation of the IT strategy. Outsourcing IT emphasized to those in the business the urgency and speed required by the business transformation plan.

The experiences of Argos in executing its transformation plan have been by no means entirely smooth. Gotch and Inkson speak of the 'upheaval of change' and they talk of four areas where change has been especially challenging.

- First is the challenge of 'landing change': i.e. getting a change fully implemented into the business before moving on to the next part of the change project. As Inkson says, 'Landing change has not always been done well.' One example is implementing successive updates of store-level IT systems before the first update has been implemented fully. The urgency to see changes implemented quickly has not always aligned with the practical needs of the stores. For example, some IT upgrades were introduced at the busiest times of store trading rather than the quietest times, and sometimes without sufficient testing prior to rollout. Yet there is a strong sense in this business that moving to implementation too quickly is a *good* fault. As Inkson says, 'The stores welcome what can sometimes be the upheaval of

---

[29] <https://www.homeretailgroup.com/media/284529/home_retail_group_q3_15-16.pdf>.

change, within reason, as long as this is on the way to things getting better in the long term.'

- Second is the need to engage the rest of the organization in the change programme. Some important internal functions were not integrated fully into the transformation plan. One example is the trading function which, according to Katy Gotch, remains driven principally by the two main 'big book' product catalogues that Argos launches in January and July, 'even though it's well understood now that the business is far less dependent on the new catalogue drops than it used to be'. There is also the issue that, after three years of relentless change, 'some of the change agents themselves might also be feeling a little burned out'.

- Third is the challenge of prioritizing in an environment where everything can seem to be important, urgent, and immediate. (The importance of effectively setting priorities is discussed in Chapter 10.) According to Inkson, setting priorities was 'relatively straightforward when there was a burning platform necessitating radical change and it was obvious what had to be done quickly'. Today it's less immediately obvious what the priorities are 'now that the lowest hanging fruit has been picked'. The process of establishing priorities is through 'robust discussion' amongst a twelve-strong Executive Team, with the CEO having the casting vote.

- Fourth, the Argos transformation programme has been largely internally driven, especially by the much-changed IT requirements needed to execute the business goal to 'reinvent Argos as a digital retail leader'. By early 2015—year three of the transformation programme—relatively little attention had yet to be given to explicitly considering and incorporating the needs of the shopper into the transformation programme. According to Katy Gotch, only now is 'more attention starting to be given to inputting "the voice of the shopper" into what we do going forward'. This expresses itself in the establishment in 2014 of a customer experience team and more research being conducted into shopper experiences and expectations. In 2015 CEO John Walden explicitly referenced the need for the business to be more customer focused when he said that, 'it is important that we achieve an appropriate balance between the implementation of these new capabilities [in the transformation plan] and ensuring good customer experiences'.[30]

For Argos, the transformation plan created in 2012 remains the key template driving the direction of change for the business. The fundamentals of the strategy have not altered, but the ways in which the strategy is delivered have—often considerably. The purpose of the plan is to set an overall direction for the business, not to be excessively prescriptive on the detail of how to get there. For example, whereas the plan originally called for a reduction in the number of Argos stores, the business is, in fact, opening more now that, as Katy Gotch says, 'by the time we defined the transformation plan it was acknowledged that we should maintain the number of stores but move to shortening our leases to give us greater flexibility'. In practice, the business is actually opening *more* stores, specifically more small-format concessions in Homebase and Sainsbury's. A partnership has been established with eBay whereby almost all Argos stores now serve as collection points for products ordered on eBay (an interesting example of two competitors collaborating for mutual benefit). A Digital Concept Store format is also being rolled out where the old printed big book catalogues are replaced with digital

(continued)

---

[30] <http://www.retail-week.com/newsletter/5072893.article?WT.tsrc=email&WT.mc_id= Newsletter200>.

Case 8.4 Continued

tablets and the total design of the store is aligned to their role as collection points as well as ordering points (Figure 8.6). As John Walden sees it, 'The Argos national store network, with 734 stores that are smaller and more efficient than traditional stores, is

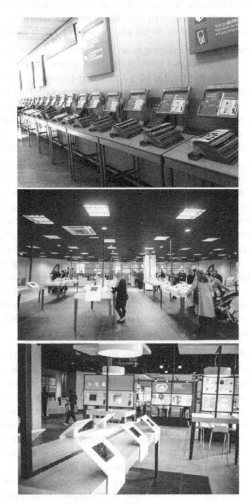

Figure 8.6 Old and new format Argos stores

Sources: http://d.ibtimes.co.uk/en/full/431832/argos-stores.jpg (top). Argos store, Sheffield. http://homeretailgroup.pressarea.com/image/details/8564 (middle). http://i1.manchestereveningnews.co.uk/incoming/article7006408.ece/alternates/s615/JS35154265.jpg (bottom).

a potential strategic advantage in a digital future. Increasingly customers will seek local product collection, and will appreciate face-to-face customer service.'[31]

Argos is a business that is driven more by action than planning. Many other retailers share a similar bias. Argos regards its transformation plans as far from complete and is self-effacing about the distance it still has to go. As at January 2016, only 20 per cent of its 840 stores had been refurbished into the digital format.[32] Notable areas that still need work are embedding 'the voice of the shopper' into its business; giving the shopper a totally seamless 'joined up' engagement experience across Argos's multiple platforms; and executing the change programme in a way that engages the whole of the business. Moreover, the business is still vulnerable to short-term adverse changes in its trading performance. Same store sales declined 2.2 per cent in the key Christmas 2015 trading quarter (following a 3.4 per cent decline in like for like sales in the first half of FY2015/16), leading John Walden to remind investors that the Transformation Plan is 'building for a business that anticipates a digital future . . . [it is a] long-term investment and we might have to work through short-term variations in quarterly results'.[33]

A very significant coda to the story of Argos's journey towards excellence in omni-channel retailing occurred at the start of 2016 when Sainsbury's, number two by volume in UK grocery retailing, announced successive bids to acquire the business at a substantial premium to the then share price.[34] Sainsbury's pursuit of Argos is significant for two reasons in particular. First, central to its rationale is Sainsbury's desire to acquire Argos's online and same-day delivery capabilities so that the combined group can, if successful, 'bring together multi-channel capabilities including digital, store and delivery networks to provide fast, flexible and reliable product fulfilment to store or to home across a wide range of food and non-food products'.[35] In other words, to address the reality that omni-channel shopping has, for many shoppers already and for very many more in the near future, become—simply—shopping. Secondly, a substantial number of Argos stand-alone stores—between 150 and 200 has been suggested[36]—would be closed and replaced with order and collection counters in Sainsbury supermarkets. This points to the need for large store retailers—not just Sainsbury's and not just supermarket operators—to find productive uses for the excess space that many of them are now carrying. (At the time of writing it was not known whether Sainsbury's bid was successful.)

As recently as 2012, some were seriously questioning the very future of Argos, whereas today the business looks ever more like a model omni-channel retailer. The experience of Argos provides a compelling example of how starting with an extensive store network and reimagining the role of those stores—as both pur-chase _and_ fulfilment points in a network of connections for the shopper (some digital, some physical)—can be a powerfully engaging model for shoppers as well as an effective model with which to compete against the pure-play internet retailing giants.

---

[31] <http://www.homeretailgroup.com/media/198098/2014_home_retail_group_annual_report.pdf>.

[32] <http://www.telegraph.co.uk/finance/newsbysector/retailandconsumer/12097885/argos-homebase-christmas-sales-home-retail-group.html>.

[33] O. Shah, 'Argos Boss: We Can Live Without Sainsbury's', _Sunday Times_, 17 Jan. 2016), Business Section, p. 1.

[34] <http://www.bbc.co.uk/news/business-35232254>. <http://www.telegraph.co.uk/finance/newsbysector/retailandconsumer/12135292/sainsburys-home-retail-group-argos-1.1bn-second-bid.html>.

[35] <http://www.j-sainsbury.co.uk/media/2776023/HRG%20Offer%20-%20RNS%20020216.pdf>.

[36] <http://www.bbc.co.uk/news/business-35290161>.

Conclusion

As we discussed in Part 1 of this book, ever more shoppers expect to be able to engage with retailers howsoever they wish in complex webs of digital and physical connection and to use and combine those points of connection in ways which are specific to their particular needs at a particular point in time. Shopping journeys and, therefore, engagement with retailers are no longer linear, straightforward, and easy to predict, with the shopper forced to engage with a retailer on the retailer's terms. Already, shopping journeys are non-linear, complex, difficult to predict, and shoppers will only engage with retailers on the shoppers' terms. This trend will only accelerate as more shoppers globally embrace more fully digital lives; as shopping becomes a still more digitally led activity and, crucially, as more shoppers enter their high-spending years with a perspective that the role of the retailer is to organize themselves around the needs of the shopper and not the other way round. These changed realities are as true for the new to retail, web-enabled enterprises as they are for long-established store-centric traditional retail enterprises. However, it is for the latter in particular that the challenges of migrating the enterprise from a store-only to a truly connected, seamlessly integrated omni-channel retailer are at their greatest.

Very different engagement landscapes call for very different thinking. We have suggested in this chapter that enterprises and their leaders will have to be prepared at least to consider making substantial changes to their enterprises if they are to deliver on their omni-channel ambitions and remain relevant to the shopper let alone secure competitive advantage over others. Some enterprise capability areas will, we suggest, need to be given much more importance and the types of competencies as well as the scope of activities within those areas changed, perhaps very fundamentally. We have suggested that this will be the case for IT, logistics, and marketing functions in particular. Other capabilities that, historically, have been at the very heart of many retailers' operations will be de-emphasized, at least in relative terms and very probably in the absolute also. Prominent in this respect will, for many, be the store operations function. As the competencies within and the relative importance of different functional areas changes, so organizational structures will likely need to change radically also. When this happens, cultural considerations are likely be at least as important as capability and structural considerations.

For most, we are tempted to suggest for all established retail enterprises the journey to omni-channel excellence will be very challenging. Our Argos case study showed as much—and this an enterprise that, in several important respects, had a considerable head start over many others. This is not just because there is simply no single roadmap of how to move an enterprise from where it is today to where it needs to be—also today—but because neither can there be any crystal-clear view of where one is seeking to get to either. If shoppers are (as we discussed in Chapter 2) very uncertain about how technology will impact on their behaviours, then how can retailers be any more certain? How is it possible to chart a path to 'True North'—the nirvana of omni-channel excellence—when we don't know where True North is and there isn't a map of how to get there anyway. But there are, in fact, practical points of guidance. We discuss in the following chapter the new needs of retail enterprises and in the related Chapter 10 the new needs of retail business leaders.

9

The New Needs of the Retail Enterprise

Changed Landscapes—Changed Competencies Needed

> *When the wind blows even a turkey can fly. But it's still a turkey.*
> (Wall Street saying)

It is broadly true to say that retail enterprises have traditionally been either process orientated or experience orientated. Characteristically, retailers catering for more functional needs have emphasized process efficiency over experience, whereas high touch retailers, especially in discretionary categories, have emphasized experience over process. (This is not an entirely clear-cut distinction, nor is it necessarily mutually exclusive.) In the new landscape of retail, enterprises will need to revisit their process/experience trade-offs and consider the new needs and capabilities required in their enterprises. We anticipate and advocate much greater convergence. Process-driven enterprises will need to become more experience orientated if they are to retain (or develop at all) meaningful and enduring engagement with their shoppers, especially across a growing multitude of touchpoints, and if they are to avoid creeping commoditization. Likewise, experience-driven enterprises will need to become more capable and efficient at execution if they are to deliver on shoppers' expectations of a seamless engagement experience across what is becoming an increasingly complex set of platforms and touchpoints.

The truly ground-breaking enterprises will be those that transform shoppers' expectations of what is possible through a combination of outstanding experiences *and* delivery through flawless execution. In transforming shoppers' expectations, they transform and transcend their category also. Others will not seek to be so ambitious. This will likely be appropriate when it is a considered decision created out of a complete understanding of the potential risks and rewards associated with a more cautious approach. Such a transformation also presupposes an ambitious agenda for experimentation and innovation within the enterprise, and a pragmatic approach to the commercial exploitation of new ideas. It also requires the ability to change the organizational and cultural capabilities of the firm. These considerations provide the main focus for this chapter.

Functional Enterprise Capabilities

The ability to combine in the same enterprise high order process capability with experience excellence challenges all enterprises and business leaders. What retail enterprises now need is the ability to combine the heavy engineering science with the softer arts of retail. We suggest that four building blocks in particular—two derived from heavy engineering and two from soft arts—will be crucial to the ability of retailers to compete successfully in the new retail landscape:

Heavy engineering:	Soft arts:
• *Technology for 20/20 visibility*	• *A strong, differentiated brand*
• *Distribution excellence*	• *Appetite for innovation*

Some retailers have historically regarded all of these areas as necessary costs of doing business on which they spend only reluctantly. This perspective needs to change: each territory has the potential to build substantial and enduring competitive advantage to a retail enterprise as well as making the enterprise far more resilient to competitive challenges—challenges which may come from enterprises that do not currently even exist.

Technology for 20/20 Visibility

We have discussed already the impacts of technology on the customer engagement landscape and in delivering richer experiences to shoppers in-store and online. Here, our focus is on the opportunities for retailers to employ technology in order to have greater insight into their shoppers and visibility across their organizations. An essential prerequisite for effectively engaging with shoppers in an omni-channel world is to have a single view of the shopper and of the merchandise across their multiple touchpoints with the retail enterprise.[1]

In the old landscape, retailers typically confined their ambitions and capabilities to the relatively straightforward task of knowing what their shoppers had purchased from them (Figure 9.1). In the new landscape of retailing, this

---

[1] The notion of the 'touchpoint' refers to an 'episode of direct or indirect contact' between a customer and a retailer. P. C. Verhoef et al., 'From Multi-Channel Retailing to Omni-Channel Retailing', *Journal of Retailing*, 91(2) (June 2015). doi:10.1016/j.jretai.2015.02.005.

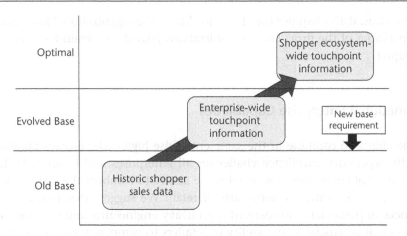

Figure 9.1 The evolving nature of a single view of the shopper
Source: Authors.

is nothing close to the minimum base requirement needed to have a useful (i.e. actionable) single view of the shopper. The new base requirement for a retailer is to have visibility of how, where, and when a shopper is engaging with all possible retail enterprise-related touchpoints—online, by mobile, by tablet, in-store, at secure kiosks, and so on. As the network of possible points of engagement with the shopper becomes more complex, so the need for visibility of that engagement across all customer-facing aspects of the business becomes more important—yet also harder to realize. Research undertaken by the Economist Intelligence Unit amongst fifty senior retail executives in North America and Europe in 2013 suggested that only 16 per cent of them believed that data analysis 'had yielded a 360-degree view of the customer'.[2] Furthermore, it is being able to 'see' the shopper across *all* points of engagement relevant to the enterprise that matters, rather than just those engagements that actually lead to a purchase. Only through such insight is it possible to engage with the shopper in more relevant and personalized ways: ways that have the most potential to change behaviours and, ultimately, drive a purchase.

If this is the new base requirement for a single view of the shopper, a higher order and more evolved requirement is to have visibility of how the shopper is behaving not just when s/he engages with the retailer's own enterprise, but also across the shopper's personal engagement ecosystem. This will include other enterprises, online and offline and across social media. An ecosystem-wide view of how a shopper is behaving clearly offers the best possibilities to

---

[2] Economist Intelligence Unit, *The Data Storm: Retail and the Big Data Revolution*. Research commissioned by Wipro Retail, 2013. <http://www.economistinsights.com/sites/default/files/The_Data_Storm_Web_1.pdf>.

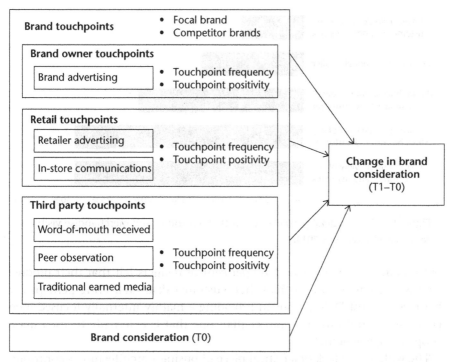

Figure 9.2 One view of the consumer touchpoint ecosystem

Source: Baxendale, S., McDonald, E.K. & Wilson, H.N., 2015, 'The Impact of Different Touchpoints on Brand Consideration', Journal of Retailing, 91(2), June, pp. 235–253. doi:10.1016/j.jretai.2014. 12.008. Creative Commons Attribution License (CC, BY).

engage with the shopper at their most important touchpoints: those with the biggest potential to alter behaviours with highly targeted messages. Figure 9.2 shows one possible visualization of this ecosystem, distinguishing between brand owner touchpoints, retail touchpoints, and, most elusively, third-party touchpoints where peer-to-peer engagement takes place.

Likewise with physical merchandise. It is not possible to deliver a consistent, seamless experience to the shopper without having visibility on where product is throughout the supply chain and across the enterprise. Even in the UK, an already highly evolved omni-channel market, most retail enterprises still have a long way to go to get to this base level of capability. Research commissioned by LCP Consulting in 2014 indicated that, while over 85 per cent of UK retailers identify themselves as operating in more than one channel, less than three in ten (27 per cent) say that they have a single view of both their customers and their stock (Figure 9.3).[3] In another survey by process

[3] LCP Consulting, *The Omni-Channel Dilemma*, 2014. <http://www.lcpconsulting.com/ 2014-omni-channel-study>.

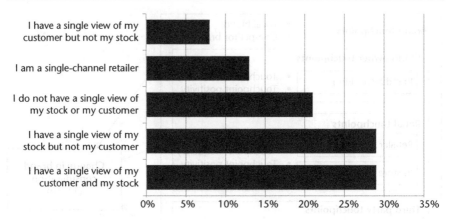

Figure 9.3 UK retailers' perspectives on their customer and merchandise visibility
Source: Retail Week, May 2014.

outsourcing company eClerx, 80 per cent of retailers felt that their product data were more advanced than their customer data—reflecting perhaps the heritage of most IT functions in providing a mainly internally focused merchandise control function, rather than one that is externally focused upon shopper engagement.[4]

The widespread lack of a critical piece of business architecture is contributing to significantly high levels of shopper dissatisfaction with the reality of their omni-channel experiences. Take the example of click and collect. In the 2014 fifth annual RIS/Cognizant Shopper Experience Study of 5,300 shoppers in the UK, US, Germany, and China, fully 49 per cent of shoppers experienced service failures in their click and collect experience. Reasons included long wait times (27 per cent), the order not being ready for collection (14 per cent), and the order not being found (10 per cent) (Figure 9.4).[5]

Consider also the base requirement of presenting to the shopper consistent prices across multiple platforms: in a 2015 global survey of over 13,000 shoppers conducted by OXIRM/Planet Retail, fully one in five shoppers had recently experienced a situation in which the price on a retailer's website did not match the price in-store.[6] The message for retail enterprises is this: in an omni-channel world, not only are there many more opportunities to engage the shopper across multiple points of contact, but so too are there many more

[4] *Retail Week*, 'Data management. Re-engineering retail structures, skills and Strategies for a Data Culture, eClerx', 2014. <http://www.retail-week.com/technology/report-re-engineering-retail-structures-skills-and-strategies-for-a-data-culture/5059208.article>.

[5] Retail Info Systems News, 2014. '2014 Shopper Experience Study'. <http://www.slideshare.net/cognizant/fifth-annual-2014-shopper-experience-study-why-omni-channel-success-starts-with-customer-empathy>.

[6] Planet Retail/Oxford Institute of Retail Management, 'The Retail Business Model of the Future', white paper for the World Retail Congress, Rome, Sept. 2015.

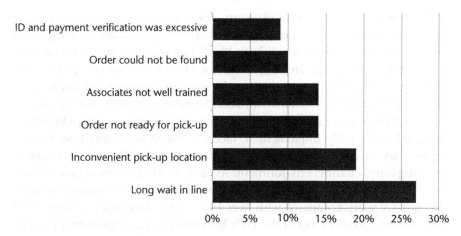

Figure 9.4 Reasons for service failures during pick up in store of online orders

Source: RIS. 2014. 2014 Shopper Experience Study. Retail Info System News. http://www.cognizant.com/InsightsWhitepapers/2014-Shopper-Experience-Study.pdf

opportunities to disappoint them—both at each engagement point, as the shopper seeks to move between those engagement points, and as shopper expectations rise.

One of the main problems that retailers have in realizing their omni-channel ambitions and those of their shoppers is in effectively integrating customer and product data from multiple sources—the challenge of multiple legacy systems. Such systems are either failing to meet business needs, represent a risk to the business (for reasons of data security, for example), or introduce growing costs to the business through the need for expensive integration programmes, upgrading, and maintenance as they age. Such systems are often poorly documented and have been developed incrementally over time to meet changing needs. But what should be the priorities? Janet Schalk, at the time CIO of US general merchandise retailer Kohl's, makes one suggestion: 'we started with some of the basics, like purchase orders and pricing, which are important if we want to be able to support more flexible pricing strategies than we could with our old set of systems. The other piece will be—and we're not finished with this yet—supporting localized assortments, to be more locally relevant.'[7] UK department store retailer John Lewis has also made the decision to make significant investments in this area. Their IT Director, Paul Coby, comments: 'we are building a technology infrastructure that will link the different systems. We're not there yet. We are rolling

---

[7] Janet Schalk, quoted in L. Heller, 'Kohl's CIO Janet Schalk: Out with the Legacy Systems and in with the New. Fierce Retail IT blog, 4 Mar. 2015. <http://www.fierceretail.com/retailit/story/kohls-cio-janet-schalk-out-legacy-systems-and-new/2015-03-04>.

out a new epos, a new web platform, and we're starting on a new order management system. We are fundamentally engaged in architecting what an omni-channel business will look like.'[8] Judgements over IT investment for established retailers are, however, not always as clear-cut as for John Lewis or Kohl's, and may need also to be more pragmatic. As Marks & Spencer's then IT Director, Darrell Stein, said: 'Sometimes it's not cost effective to rip out and replace legacy systems.'[9] Similarly, new systems, perhaps inflexibly designed and rapidly implemented, face the risk of becoming new legacies faster than an enterprise expects. This is particularly the case in a rapidly evolving omni-channel environment. As early as 2010, business process consultants Martec Investment found that the average life of e-commerce systems was just 4.9 years, compared with over 10 years for store-based systems.[10] Sir Ian Cheshire, former CEO of the UK's Kingfisher home improvement group, makes the point that legacy systems are a challenge not just to the ability of a retailer to keep pace with their online competitors but also to keep pace with customer change: 'You've got to move faster than your customers and that's getting more difficult. We've got legacy systems, they've got an iWatch.'[11]

In seeking a better understanding of evolving customer needs, retailers need also to go beyond the immediate data that they themselves collect from customer transactions. UK retailer Tesco has won awards and admiration for its twenty-year-old Clubcard loyalty card scheme. The (possibly apocryphal) story has it that the then Chairman commented at the project trial: 'you know more about my customers after three months than I know after 30 years'.[12] It has, however, been estimated that tracking the buying behaviour of the 15 million Clubcard customers in the UK alone costs Tesco £500 million annually.[13] It should, however, be recognized that the retailer—Tesco or otherwise—has numerous opportunities to recover some or all of the costs of its loyalty programme by selling data and additional promotional opportunities to its suppliers. As well as being expensive to administer, loyalty programme-derived data only tell the retailer about the actual historic buying behaviours of its own shoppers. It tells the firm nothing about the changing attitudes of existing shoppers (although these might be inferred), about the behaviours

[8] Quoted in: <http://www.retail-week.com/technology/john-lewis-redeveloping-legacy-systems-to-build-omni-channel-infrastructure/5053398.article>.

[9] Quoted in: <http://www.retail-week.com/technology/analysis-marks-spencer-technology-boss-darrell-stein-on-the-retailers-evolution/5056397.article>.

[10] Martec International, 'IT in Retail UK 2009/10', 2010. Quoted in <http://www.retail-week.com/technology/retail-it-investment-back-to-the-future/5013411.article>.

[11] Sir Ian Cheshire, speaking at World Retail Congress, Rome, Sept. 2015.

[12] C. Humby et al., *Scoring Points: How Tesco Continues to Win Customer Loyalty*. London: Kogan Page, 2008.

[13] Dave McCarthy, analyst HSBC, quoted in: <http://www.telegraph.co.uk/finance/newsbysector/retailandconsumer/10577685/Clubcard-built-the-Tesco-of-today-but-it-could-be-time-to-ditch-it.html>.

of non-cardholders, the behaviours of cardholders in other retailers, or about non-shoppers of the brand. These considerations have led some retailers to explore what insights can be gained from other, less conventional, sources of data. For example, in a project with data scientists from University College London, the UK general merchandise retailer Argos is undertaking sentiment analysis of 500,000 product reviews on its website. Gaining effective insight from product reviews has the potential for Argos to cut operating costs, in particular by reducing the volume of product returns.[14]

It is in the area of technology in particular that established retailers face especially serious challenges from new entrants unencumbered with either legacy systems or a pre-existing heritage of how they engage with shoppers. For example, Singapore's online-only grocery business Redmart is making strong inroads into the grocery sector, from its beginnings in late 2011. As the founders say of themselves: 'we're not retailers, we're a bunch of tech guys who are applying our technology to retail'.[15] This perspective is mirrored in many other enterprises that have entered the retail sector in the last ten years or so and of many more who will do so in the near-term future. Online retailers have, in some important respects, an inbuilt advantage over their store-based peers in that they have access to far more granular customer data, not just about what customers have bought from them, but where else they have been online, what other brands they have considered, and where else they have made purchases.

Distribution Excellence

We discussed in Chapter 8 the prime importance of the distribution function in the context of successfully delivering a seamless omni-channel engagement experience for the shopper. Steve Agg, CEO of the UK Chartered Institute of Logistics and Transport, says that, 'e-commerce has completely revolutionised logistics companies. . . . It is a re-orchestration of supply chains to service individual customers . . . the consumer is now in control of the supply chain.'[16] We will not reprise here the discussion in Chapter 8. Suffice to reaffirm that distribution excellence has become a crucial territory for securing competitive advantage and differentiation in environments where many shoppers are showing a clear preference to engage with retailers through multiple touchpoints—many of them digital—where shoppers have ever-more demanding fulfilment expectations, and where those expectations are too often still not being met.

---

[14] R. Kowalski, 'Optimising Sentiment Analysis in Commercial Context', paper presented at GISRUK UK, Leeds. <http://leeds.gisruk.org/abstracts/GISRUK2015_submission_76.pdf>.

[15] Todd Kurie, speaking at Singapore Retail Association Convention, Singapore, Oct. 2014.

[16] J. Wild, 'Logistics Companies Race to Keep up with Consumer Shopping Habits', *Financial Times*, 7 May 2014. <http://www.ft.com/cms/s/0/7d36250e-d5fe-11e3-a239-00144feabdc0.html>.

The distribution function is no longer just supporting the business—it is supporting the business *and* serving the shopper. For many, this will involve putting greater focus on and resources into the distribution function. For some it may mean creating new senior leadership roles. Online fashion retailer ASOS, for example, created the role of Director of Delivery Solutions in 2013. For others, acquisitions to enhance capabilities will be needed. In mid-2014, Chinese e-commerce company Alibaba acquired 10.4 per cent of Singapore Post for US$249 million, in order to enhance its logistics capabilities in SE Asia.[17]

Durable, Desired Brands for Competitive Advantage

Creating and maintaining strong affinity to the retail enterprise as a brand is the third enabler and the first 'soft art' that we identify as critical to the ability of retail enterprises to at least maintain competitiveness and shopper appeal in the new retail landscape. Seeing the retailer as the brand and building strong affinity of shoppers to that brand matters more now than ever before. There are three, related, reasons why we take this view:

1. Retailers need their brands to stand out, be noticed, and desired in environments of intense and diverse competition. Now that the competitor set and choice set has internationalized so rapidly for so many shoppers, strong brands play a crucial role in helping retailers to resist those more intense competitive challenges as well as to exploit the greater range of opportunities that are emerging. Retail intelligence analysis firm Planet Retail's Shopology research amongst 13,500 global consumers in 2015 revealed that fully six out of ten shoppers felt that being a trusted brand would have a lot of influence on their choice of a retailer.[18]

2. Strong brands deepen the relationship between retailers and shoppers, giving retailers a legitimate platform from which to extend their reach into other parts of shoppers' lives, in new product-oriented and geographical territories, as well as to engage with new shopper cohorts. This is a still more important consideration in online environments where (especially for the 'pureplay' online-only retailers) the willingness that the majority of shoppers still have to engage with a retailer, especially for the first time, can be influenced strongly by the confidence that they have in their brand. The same Planet Retail survey nevertheless found a significant minority of one in three shoppers suggesting that

---

[17] <http://www.ft.com/cms/s/0/8993b654-e62f-11e3-bbf5-00144feabdc0.html>.
[18] Planet Retail/Oxford Institute of Retail Management, 'The Retail Business Model of the Future'. White Paper, World Retail Congress, Rome, 2015.

they'd be entirely comfortable in shopping from online retail brands that they didn't know well.

3. For many retailers and many retail categories, meaningful differenti-ation through product alone is very difficult if not impossible to achieve (think books, music), especially in categories where vendor brands dominate (consumer electronics, health & wellness, packaged grocery in many markets). In such environments, brand strength for the retailer is critically important both to strengthen the relationship with shoppers who have a range of fulfilment alternatives for the same products as well as to reduce the tyranny of having to compete solely or largely on the basis of having the lowest price or the deepest promotions.

The enabling role of technology has broken the historic nexus between the longevity of a brand and its strength. No longer is it the case that brand longevity is a prerequisite of brand strength. Table 9.1 shows the Top 25 brands by value according to Interbrand's 2015 ranking. Any listing—and there are many—of the world's most valued brands has a number of defining features.

Table 9.1 The world's most valued brands, 2015

Rank 2015	Brand	Sector	Brand value ($mn)	% change
1	Apple	Technology	170,276	+43
2	Google	Technology	120,314	+12
3	Coca Cola	Beverages	78,423	−4
4	Microsoft	Technology	67,670	+11
5	IBM	Business Services	65,095	−10
6	Toyota	Automotive	49,048	+16
7	Samsung	Technology	45,297	0
8	GE	Diversified	42,267	−7
9	Macdonalds	Restaurants	39,809	−6
10	Amazon	Retail	37,948	+29
11	BMW	Automotive	37,212	+9
12	Mercedes Benz	Automotive	36,711	+7
13	Disney	Media	36,514	+13
14	Intel	Technology	35,415	+4
15	Cisco	Technology	29,854	−3
16	Oracle	Technology	27,283	+5
17	Nike	Sporting goods	23,070	+16
18	HP	Technology	23,056	−3
19	Honda	Automotive	22,975	+6
20	Louis Vuitton	Luxury	22,250	−1
21	H&M	Apparel	22,222	+5
22	Gillette	FMCG	22,218	−3
23	Facebook	Technology	22,029	+54
24	Pepsi	Beverages	19,622	+3
25	American Express	Financial Services	18,922	−3

© Interbrand.
Source: <http://interbrand.com/best-brands/best-global-brands/2015/ranking/>.

1. Several of the most highly valued (and, we might add, influential) brands were only created within the lifespan of the current cohort of Gen Y shoppers—Amazon, Facebook, Google, eBay, Alibaba, Paypal, and so on.

2. Traditional retailers are conspicuous by their absence at the top of such listings. It is consumer products and technology brands that tend to dominate.

3. The fact that Amazon often appears as the most highly valued retail brand is indicative of this new world order.

For any enterprise, retail or otherwise, it is important not to confuse brand ubiquity and visibility with brand affinity and desirability. It is worth restating that brands—perhaps especially retailers' brands—can be very visible and very much a part of a shopper's life while, in fact, being little if at all *desired* by the shopper. Many retailers have made the mistake of either failing to understand the difference between ubiquity and affinity or else assuming that, because a shopper has engaged with a brand, they must like it. UK grocery retailing is one example amongst many. In a previous era, engagement with supermarket brands was exceptionally high at a local level, not because those brands were loved by shoppers, but rather because shoppers had no realistic choice other than to engage with them in the absence of online alternatives in a pre-internet era and of any other store-based supermarket option due to local planning rules. It was a case of what we might call 'monopoly loyalty'. It was only when the competitive landscape changed that several operators realized, in rather stark terms, why shoppers were engaging with their brands—not because they were especially desired but because of the sheer absence of choice. It is in particular the ubiquity of choice, being played out now at a global level, which makes real brand equity, based on provable criteria, so important to create, nurture, grow, and sustain in the new retail landscape.

Strong brand equity is also fundamental to the ability of retailers to realize growth opportunities as well as to defend their existing businesses. This is especially true in discretionary spend categories particularly, but certainly not exclusively, in more premium market positions. We have suggested already (Chapter 1) that affluent shoppers in the world's major urban centres have, in some important attitudinal, lifestyle, and behavioural respects, far more in common with their counterparts in other urban centres globally than they do with fellow citizens outside those major urban centres. The world of premium brands benefits from this phenomenon, a so-called 'sprinkler strategy' of market entry, where international expansion takes the form of establishing a presence in multiple key global cities rather than building scale in a few territories only.[19] The very considerable success globally of brands such as

[19] S. Kalish, V. Mahajan, and E. Muller. 1995. Waterfall and Sprinkler New-Product Strategies in Competitive Global Markets', *International Journal of Research in Marketing*, 12 (1995), 105–19.

Burberry and those within the LVMH stable demonstrates the reach, appeal, and desirability of such brands across geographies. In the case of LVMH, this seventy-brand business generated €30.6 billion in revenue in 2014 with a selectively located retail network of 3,700 stores in over fifty countries. In less elevated positions, many other retail brands have shown themselves also to have international if not truly global appeal. We have noted already (Chapter 4) how geographically mobile and internationally desired are many of the fast-fashion brands, such as Zara, Mango, H&M, Uniqlo, and Topshop.

Appetite for Innovation

Most business leaders agree that encouraging innovation is 'a good thing' and a desirable capability for the enterprise to have. In a 2013 Accenture study of over 500 companies across twelve sectors in the UK, France, and the US, fully 93 per cent of those interviewed said that the long-term success of their organization relied on their ability to innovate and 18 per cent put it as their top priority.[20] Today, whilst we consider innovation in retailing to be mandatory, the external perception by many of the sector 'is that firms of all sizes are poor innovators by comparison with other sectors, and are poorly represented in terms of traditional markers of innovation intensity'.[21] This perception largely arises because retailers innovate differently by comparison with manufacturing or technology firms. Certainly, leading retail enterprises can be both product and process innovators as well as innovative in their use of technology. Many larger retail enterprises also engage in non-technological innovation, in marketing and operational terms. The best of the largest firms are also open innovators, coordinating across the value networks in which they operate. Moreover, the history of retail innovation is essentially incremental rather than radical, in part because of the nature of competitive retail markets. Retail competition takes place, as we mentioned in Chapter 4, in what strategist David Teece has called conditions of 'low appropriability': that is to say, the barriers to the copying of ideas by competitors are low compared to other sectors. Innovation has therefore tended to be fast, cheap, and more incremental than radical. Can it safely remain incremental? We suggest not. The question is not whether to promote innovation but where, how, and how much.

One growing area of commitment to innovation amongst retail enterprises has been the establishment of 'innovation laboratories', either through acquisition

---

[20] W. Koetzier and A. Alon, *Why 'Low Risk' Innovation is Costly: Overcoming the Perils of Renovation and Invention*. Boston: Accenture, 2013.

[21] European Commission, *Retail Sector Innovation: Final Report from the Expert Group, DG Research & Innovation*, 2014. <http://ec.europa.eu/research/innovation-union/pdf/Report_from_EG_on_Retail_Sector_Innovation_A4_FINAL_2.pdf>.

or by organic growth. Such initiatives are a recognition that innovation does not just happen—it has to be nurtured (or, more fashionably, incubated)—and also that innovation often benefits from the stimulus of external thinking that sits somewhat outside of the day-to-day business. (Accenture's innovation study suggested that almost a third (31 per cent) of the 500 enterprises surveyed had a formal system in place to promote innovation.) Typically, in retail enterprises these innovation groups focus on near-term innovation that is expected to lead to initiatives capable of being commercialized in relatively short order. Three such innovation initiatives are profiled in Case 9.1. We have chosen to profile Westfield as one of the world's largest mall developers challenged with the task of keeping physical environments relevant in the digital age. Secondly, we discuss Walmart which, as well as being the world's largest retailer, is a retailer associated more than most with a single operating model as well as a very singular business culture. Our third example is the UK's John Lewis, which has been quietly but radically transforming itself from a rather traditional department store business into a much admired omni-channel retailer.

Case 9.1 INITIATIVES IN INCUBATING INNOVATION

(i) Westfield Labs

As one of the world's largest shopping centre developers and operators, Westfield has a keen interest in promoting the continued vitality and appeal of shopping in physical locations. In a previous era, for many retailers and property businesses, this goal manifested itself in a reluctance to acknowledge the growth of online shopping. (It is easy to forget that it was not King Canute who believed he could stop the tides—it was his fawning courtiers. Canute was simply demonstrating that rising tides are no respecter of royal personages. A lesson for retail leaders as well as for fawning courtiers perhaps?) This has been replaced by a realization that the best way to maintain the relevance of physical retailing is to see stores and shopping centres as nodes in a connected web of shopper engagement that does, inevitably, have a strong and growing focus on digital for many shoppers.

One expression of Westfield's recognition of this reality has been the establishment of Westfield Labs in San Francisco in 2012 with a mission to develop shopper-facing innovation in social, mobile, and digital media that 'converge the digital shopper with the physical world'.[22] There are around seventy people in Westfield Labs as well as satellite innovation centres in the UK and Australia. Innovation in the labs is focused on the near-term application of technologies that both deliver more engaging and personalized experiences within the mall environment—such as personalized product and brand wayfinding—as well as connecting the shopper to the mall before and after a visit—such as delivery of products bought in the mall.

---

[22] <http://www.westfieldlabs.com/about>.

For Kevin McKenzie, global Chief Digital Officer at Westfield Labs, keeping malls relevant and desired by technology-enabled shoppers is about reinventing the mall experience so that: 'Our shopping centres, especially Westfield London and Westfield Stratford, are more than just shopping. They are a whole experience with entertainment, leisure, food, and shopping . . . and now we're at a point when we are beginning to layer on digital and technology to become very complementary with that experience.' An objective also is that innovation that has been incubated in Westfield Labs comes to market quickly. For example, within two years of establishing the initiative, Westfield began piloting digital storefronts comprising large screens displaying in ultra-high definition curated products from retailers within its centres that shoppers can scroll through interactively.[23]

(ii) @WalmartLabs

As befits the world's largest retailer, @WalmartLabs (www.walmartlabs.com) is an initiative in incubating innovation on a very substantial scale. The self-defined objective of @WalmartLabs is to act as 'an accelerator in the effort to meet the needs of our customers wherever they are—shopping in a store, browsing our web site, or out and about with their mobile devices'.[24] Walmart bought Kosmix, a shopping search engine, in 2011 to form the nucleus from which to develop @WalmartLabs. The centre is based in San Bruno, San Francisco. Since 2011, substantial scale has been added to @WalmartLabs, including hiring over 1,000 people in 2014 alone, to a total of around 3,500 people by the end of that year. Additionally, Walmart operates five R&D centres—three in California, one in Oregon, and one in Bangalore.[25] Fourteen technology start-up businesses have also been acquired.[26] The work of @WalmartLabs is focused in two main areas:

(1) Developing mobile applications to enhance the shoppers' experience, especially around easing the shoppers' journey through stores (such as mobile payment platforms), navigation in-store, and reinforcing price credibility and credentials. One of many initiatives is the Savings Catcher app that scans a receipt to find prices at competing stores. If the app finds a cheaper price, shoppers get the difference refunded in the form of a gift card.

(2) Acquiring, incubating, and bringing quickly to market open source platform providers that facilitate Walmart's wider e-commerce ambitions. Characteristically, Walmart seeks to derive a strong commercial benefit from its investment in innovation. One dimension of this has been the creation of Walmart Exchange, or WMX. WMX is a platform available to product suppliers to Walmart, whereby vendors (and their media agencies) can deliver tailored online advertising messages in real-time and based on shoppers' actual purchase behaviours. The effectiveness of such advertising can also be tracked at an individual item level.

(continued)

---

[23] <http://www.retailingtoday.com/article/westfield-labs-displays-digital-physical-vision>.
[24] <http://www.walmartlabs.com/about>.
[25] K. Deighton, 'The Rise of Retail Research and Development Labs', *Retail Week*, 28 Feb. 2014, 32–3.
[26] <http://www.adweek.com/news/technology/473-billion-retailer-wants-be-next-ad-tech-star-161471>.

Case 9.1 Continued

(iii) John Lewis JLab

The John Lewis department store business in the UK is widely regarded as being in the vanguard of clicks and mortar retailing. The extent and speed with which the Partnership has transformed its business from a stores-only operation is indeed impressive and receives considerable attention. There is a strong and tangible commitment to innovation from the top of the business. JLP's Chairman, Sir Charlie Mayfield, said in an influential speech in 2012 that 'Technology has always been the driver of major changes in human behaviour, with occasionally massive implications for markets, industries and businesses. . . . I believe we're in the middle of one of those major transitions. Such times are never easy—they challenge the vested interests, but they also offer great opportunities for those that adapt.'[27]

In March 2014, John Lewis announced its JLab initiative. JLab is an incubator of innovation in small, start-up enterprises, with the hope that the initiatives they support will have a commercial application in John Lewis department stores and across retailing more generally. The digital workshop launched in June 2014. Businesses were encouraged to apply for support and the top five were given lab space as well as mentoring from technology entrepreneurs for four months to develop their ideas. This approach of nurturing innovation in small enterprises points to the importance of looking outside the enterprise for initiatives capable of being developed. Andrew Murphy, at the time John Lewis's Retail Director (and now Group Productivity Director), defined the scope of the initiative in this way: 'What I'm looking for from the successful JLab applicants is deliverable but stretching innovation which offers real benefit for customers in both our bricks and clicks businesses.'

At the end of the incubation period the winner was given £100,000 funding to further develop their innovation with a view to it being trialled and then rolled out across John Lewis as well as more widely. In September 2014 the winner was announced as Localz, a start-up business that developed micro-location positioning technology using a combination of Apple iBeacons and other positioning technologies (notably near-field communication) to allow retailers to send highly personalized and targeted messages to the phones of shoppers at very precise locations in store.[28]

These initiatives, and others like them, serve to institutionalize and provide a focus for innovation, especially into businesses that have, historically, pursued approaches defined much more by improving the existing business rather than contemplating or initiating radical change to it. But we caution that such initiatives are unlikely to have significant or sufficient impact in isolation. Writing in *Harvard Business Review*, innovation consultant Scott Anthony and his colleagues observe:

> Practically every company innovates. But few do so in an orderly, reliable way. In far too many organizations, the big breakthroughs happen despite the company. Successful innovations typically follow invisible development paths and require

---

[27] <http://www.johnlewispartnership.co.uk/media/speeches/retail-new-rules-for-a-new-era.html>.
[28] <http://www.telegraph.co.uk/technology/news/11127958/John-Lewis-crowns-iBeacon-startup-Localz-the-winner-of-JLAB.html>.

acts of individual heroism or a heavy dose of serendipity. Successive efforts to jump-start innovation through, say, hack-a-thons, cash prizes for inventive concepts, and on-again, off-again task forces frequently prove fruitless.[29]

Instead, Anthony talks of a 'minimum viable innovation system' (MVIS), which makes possible a leaner, and arguably more responsive, innovation function. Fortunately, this turns out not to be rocket science. To achieve an effective MVIS, the firm is urged to differentiate between core innovation, which is about doing existing things better, and non-core innovation, which is about doing wholly new things for the firm (and where innovation lab-type initiatives have the best opportunity to bear fruit); and then focus quickly on just a few areas, using customers and staff to help in this process. Dedicated teams are then set up to develop the innovation. Finally, firms should take a venture capital-type approach to the aggressive shepherding of new ideas (and also be willing to kill off so-called zombie projects, that is, 'projects that, for any number of reasons, fail to fulfil their promise and yet keep shuffling along, sucking up resources without any real hope of having a meaningful impact on the company's strategy or revenue prospects'[30]).

The Need to Change Organizational Structures

For many retail enterprises, organizational structures as well as skill requirements will have to change to accommodate an enterprise transformation that recognizes new operating realities—both positive and negative. Addressing this question goes to the heart of what a retail enterprise is today and will become in the future and, in consequence, what skills that enterprise needs. The resolution to this question depends on the nature of the retail enterprise, its starting point, and where it aspires to be in the future, but we feel able to put down a marker at least to serve as a starting point:

> The essence of a retail enterprise is the ability to select and offer merchandise that shoppers want to buy. Everything else is executional and non-core and therefore able in principle to be outsourced.

Doubtless this will be contentious (unless you happen to be a retail buyer). Many readers will likely disagree with us. Our position is this: without great merchandise that shoppers want to buy, nothing else matters. Everything else that a retail enterprise does—all the complexity, all the energy, all the investment—is only there to support the single-minded idea that getting great

---

[29] S. D. Anthony et al., 'Build an Innovation Engine in 90 Days', *Harvard Business Review*, Dec. 2014. <https://hbr.org/2014/12/build-an-innovation-engine-in-90-days>.

[30] <https://hbr.org/2015/03/zombie-projects-how-to-find-them-and-kill-them?cm_sp=Nav%20Landing-_-Modules-_-Big%20Ideas>.

merchandise to shoppers is the raison d'être, the reason for being, of a retail enterprise. As Marketing Professor Rosemary Varley has stated: 'product management has always been at the centre of the healthy retail business. In the past, traders and merchants who thrived did so because they gave their customers a better product offer than their contemporaries; intuitively knowing what the consumer market will judge to be a superior product offer is the prowess of the retail entrepreneur.'[31] Naturally, different retail enterprises take different positions. Some see themselves as product curators, others as choice editors, others as limitless choice providers, still others as product developers. Many also augment their merchandise offers with a wide, and growing, range of consumer services. And so it goes on; all positions are valid. But whatever the merchandise strategy, the role of the enterprise is to support the delivery of great merchandise to the shopper. Stores—physical and virtual—are not there as an end in themselves, they are there to engage shoppers with merchandise. So too are all the other shopper touchpoints and all the other functions across the retail enterprise.

Appropriate competences and skills are critical to the delivery of an organizational capability and culture that is fit for purpose and able to deliver both innovation and growth in productivity and performance in the much more competitive arena that so defines the new landscape of retailing. Interviews with retailers undertaken by the Oxford Institute of Retail Management into the link between skills and productivity nevertheless showed that the majority continue to wrestle with squaring the circle on gaining efficiency without sacrificing customer focus.[32] One non-food retailer commented: 'It felt like alchemy to me ... at the same time as we've taken out 20% of our headcount in stores—so a huge proportion of the stores are on minimum manning levels, the customer satisfaction measures have continued to improve. Most of our KPIs have continued to improve, whether that's cost to sales or stock ratios.'

We often hear about a skills 'shortage' in many economic sectors, not least retailing. But this headline is not helpful and a more considered view is needed. Enterprises need to distinguish between those competencies that are business critical, those that are business important, and those that are hygiene skills of lesser importance to the enterprise. It is important also to distinguish between skills *shortages* (where recruitment must address the fact that there are not enough people to fill the number of jobs available of a particular specification), a skills *gap* (where a competence shortfall amongst existing staff can be overcome by training), and a skills *mismatch* (where a difference exists

[31] R. Varley, *Retail Product Management: Buying and Merchandising*. Abingdon: Routledge, 2014.
[32] Oxford Institute of Retail Management, *Productivity and Skills in Retailing*, report for Skillsmart Retail. Oxford: OIRM, 2010.

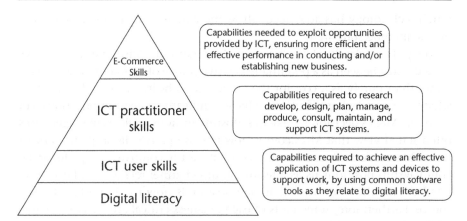

Figure 9.5 Competences for collaboration and knowledge sharing in digital society
Source: Messias, I. & Loureiro, A., 2014. http://www.slideshare.net/accloureiro/competences-for-collaboration-and-knowledge-sharingin-digital-society.

between what educational and training institutions are producing and what employers need).

One particular area of skills shortage for retail firms is in the area of digital skills. Such skills are often thought of as being equivalent to those found within the field of information, communication, and technology (ICT). This is not correct. Most commentators are agreed that digital business skills go beyond the purely technical and extend, at the highest or most evolved level, to digital skills needed to create and deliver e-commerce enterprises. Figure 9.5 charts this skills hierarchy. As has been suggested: 'E-business skills can be seen as strategic in nature, in that they address longer-term developmental needs of firms, rather than providing solutions to more immediate technical or tactical questions.... They are a subset of more general business skills and comprise the mixed set of competences which are required to exploit business opportunities provided by ICTs.'[33]

Given the proliferation and evolution of particular skillsets, what capabilities and skills to own and what to outsource will be related to the perceived importance to the organization of each competency area. Information technology provision in relation to internet platforms in the early days of multi-channel retailing was often a target for finance directors seeking to cut costs. Neither were retail finance directors alone in their cynicism of the claims made by IT professionals. As one frustrated CEO said in the mid-1990s, 'all you do is increase costs, year after year, and I am sick of it. All I get are these esoteric benefits and a bunch of baloney on how

[33] J. Reynolds, *EBusiness: A Management Perspective*. Oxford: Oxford University Press, 2010.

much technology has advanced. Show me where you put one more dollar on the income statement.'[34]

Today, IT is clearly at the heart of the retail enterprise and, as we have argued, must be seen as a potentially decisive source of competitive advantage rather than purely as a cost for the enterprise to bear. As such, decisions on what to own and what to outsource have significant strategic implications. For example, M&S's decision to take web hosting in-house reflects management's often stated view that M&S.com is now the company's flagship, and not its iconic Marble Arch store in central London. As the company says, 'Our M&S.com flagship positions us as a leading multi-channel retailer.'[35] Many other retailers take the same view that web hosting is now too important to outsource. Furthermore, some parts of each business-critical area may be owned while other parts of the same area are outsourced. Logistics is likely one such area. For some enterprises, the most appropriate structure will be to own all of the logistics function, while for others it will be to own some parts (such as warehousing) and outsource others (such as fulfilment). Andy Clarke, CEO of ASDA, Walmart's grocery and general merchandise business in the UK, says that, 'We've taken the decision to own fulfilment because we believe that the point of fulfilment is going to be ever-more important to the customer.'[36] Whatever the corporate priorities and the ownership model, the most important consideration is to engineer robustness and resilience into the enterprise so that failure or underperformance in one area does not critically undermine the ability of the total enterprise to deliver to its customer promise.

In even the near-term future it is perfectly possible to envisage very different organizational structures to those traditionally found in retail enterprises. The logical corollary to putting more emphasis and resources into the more important competency areas is that, other things being equal, less focus and attention (at least relatively and possibly in absolute terms) will be given to others. It is certainly possible to envisage retail enterprises where the property function is much reduced or perhaps subsumed entirely into let us call it the 'Shopper engagement function' or reports into the Director of Omni-channel. As little as fifteen years ago, most of the largest grocery retailers in the UK thought it essential to own their store real estate and to acquire huge amounts of new sites for future development. No one in that sector believes this to be the case today. Property functions are being scaled back and huge write-downs are being incurred as property 'assets' are reviewed. (For financial year 2014/15, Tesco took an 'impairment' charge of £3.8 billion against its currently

---

[34] US CEO quoted in M. C. Lacity et al., 'The Value of Selective IT Sourcing', *MIT Sloan Management Review*, Spring 1996. <http://sloanreview.mit.edu/article/the-value-of-selective-it-sourcing>.

[35] <http://annualreport.marksandspencer.com>.

[36] Andy Clarke, speaking at World Retail Congress, Rome, Sept. 2015.

trading stores and a further £900 million against its pipeline of new stores.[37])
Asking the CEO of a retail business fifteen or so years ago 'do you need
physical stores to be in retail?' would have been a very short conversation. It
still is today—but the answer is usually very different.

Mark Price, Managing Director of Waitrose (but due to retire from that role
in April 2016), the grocery business of the John Lewis Partnership, has referred
to the impact of the internet on consumer behaviour and on the business he
leads as 'the kind of model change that happens once every 50 years or so—it's
as fundamental as the advent of the self-service supermarket in the 1950s'.[38]
The case is similar in relation to both logistics and information technology.
Doubtless for some the right answer is to invest more and to see one or both as
a core competency that the enterprise must own and operate. But for others,
exactly the same rationale—the growing centrality of logistics and IT—will
take an enterprise in quite the opposite direction and suggest outsourcing to
experts as the best model.

What to retain and invest more in and what to reduce spend in and,
possibly, outsource requires constant reappraisal. University of Maryland Professor Jie Zhang and her colleagues conducted a wide-ranging review of the
operations of multi-channel retailers.[39] They suggest that, in the early stages
of the development of multiple channels for shopper engagement, many
retailers ran their internet channel as largely separate from their store-based
operations. The rationale for doing so was partly functional—especially the
different fulfilment and logistics requirements of supporting stores versus
online—and partly cultural—in particular a desire to create an environment
that promotes rapid growth in online. They note also that, over time, the case
for integration tends to be stronger than the case for separation. In particular,
the need to drive efficiency synergies across store and online operations and,
for many still more importantly, put greater focus on creating a seamless
experience for the shopper across multiple touchpoints makes integration a
better operating model for many than keeping online and store operations
separate. When Neiman Marcus, the US department store retailer, merged
their store and online merchandise and planning teams in 2014 their rationale for doing so reflected that of many other retail enterprises which had
made the same change, often several years earlier. CEO Karen Katz explained
the change thus: 'We are one brand to our customers. Our customers do not

---

[37] <http://www.tescoplc.com/files/pdf/results/2015/prelim/prelim_2014-2015_results_
statement.pdf>.

[38] M. Price, 'Grocers Must Remember that in Retailing, Bigger is Not Always Better', *The Times*,
5 June 2015.

[39] Jie Zhang et al., 'Crafting Integrated Multi-Channel Retailing Strategies', *Journal of Interactive
Marketing*, 24(2) (2010), 168–80.

differentiate between channels, and now neither will we.'[40] Concomitant to this it has become very usual for enterprises to designate a role as 'Head/ Director of Omni-channel' and for this position to report directly to the CEO and be part of the enterprise's leadership team.

The transformation in the operations of many retailers from store-focused single-channel enterprises to omni-channel businesses engaging with shoppers across multiple touchpoints (some physical, others virtual), impacts also on skill requirements at an outlet level. ASDA, the UK's third largest food retailer (and owned by Walmart), substantially restructured the roles of its store management in 2014.[41] Partly this was done for 'trading reasons' (for which read weak sales) but also it was a consequence of up-weighting the importance of e-commerce at store level such that store managers needed a different set of skills. Some 4,000 roles were affected.

This points to the need for retail enterprises to be prepared to make very substantial changes to the structures of their businesses as well as to the skillsets within them such that they are far better aligned to the realities of the new retail and consumer landscapes, in order to be both resistant to new challenges and equipped to realize emerging opportunities. For many, this will very likely mean being much leaner organizations, with far more outsourcing and very much lower capital commitments than has defined the conventional operating models of retail enterprises hitherto. The challenges of successfully making what, for many, will be substantial changes to an enterprise are considerable, both for the enterprise itself and for the business leader. Three related issues are especially important.

1. Transitioning Challenges

The scale of the transformation may be such that enterprise leaders may feel that they have to make more changes to the business than the ownership structure would allow and that stakeholders (both internal and external to the firm) would find acceptable. Sir Terry Leahy, former CEO of Tesco, once referred to this as 'changing the engine while in the middle of a race'.[42] This is especially challenging when change needs to be both radical and quick. Moreover the ability of an enterprise to absorb radical change is also an important consideration during significant periods of change, as our case study of Argos in Chapter 8 makes clear. Operating within the framework of

[40] <http://www.kurtsalmon.com/uploads/Dont%20Call%20It%20Omni-channel_final_UK%20eng.pdf>.
[41] <http://www.thegrocer.co.uk/channels/supermarkets/asda/asda-confirms-1360-management-redundancies-in-stores/359233.article>.
[42] Quoted in J. Reynolds et al., 'Perspectives on Retail Format Innovation: Relating Theory and Practice', *International Journal of Retail and Distribution Management*, 35(8) (2007), 647–60.

what is realistically achievable may be very suboptimal for the enterprise, especially where the amount of change that can be tolerated is largely incremental tweaking of an existing model when what is required is a very different model.

2. Educating Stakeholders

Investors in particular need to understand that the business model for many retailers has changed so profoundly that the old ways of evaluating a retail enterprise and the old benchmarks of what level of returns to expect may no longer be relevant. Expectations will need to be reset—often downwards. For some, this may mean that the retail sector will have little if any appeal as an asset class. (In 2012, former Panmure Gordon analyst Philip Dorgan famously described the UK supermarket sector as 'uninvestable'.[43]) Furthermore, investors appear often to have very different criteria for evaluating and indeed valuing 'new model' retailers—especially the online operators—than they do for traditional retailers attempting to manage the challenges of transitioning their enterprises so as to be fit for the new retail age. It may not seem fair or even rational that Amazon stock—with still modest earnings relative to income—traded at a rather remarkable average p/e (price/earnings) ratio of 625 for the five years to November 2015 (and a scarcely believable peak of 3,659), —while Walmart—with still huge dollar earnings—traded at an average of 14 and always within a range of 10 to 19 over the same period. More rationally, real estate investors have noted future requirements for and present shortage of logistics and warehousing space. European logistics property investment volumes increased by over 30 per cent in the year to September 2014, with this property class generating an 8 per cent total return on investment in that period, compared to 5.6 per cent for retail.[44]

3. Ownership Structures

In very changed landscapes it is appropriate to review the suitability of the ownership structures of enterprises. If the needs of the enterprise are no longer aligned to the expectations of its investors, then a change in ownership structure may be required. Sir Charlie Mayfield has made the point often that much of the change that John Lewis has been able to make to its business would not have been possible if the business was in public ownership rather

---

[43] *Retail Week*, 'Sainsbury's: What the Analysts Say', 3 Oct. 2012. <http://www.retail-week.com/sectors/food/sainsburys-what-the-analysts-say/5041388.article>.

[44] K. Allan, 'Retail Revolution Sparks Change in Logistics Sites', *Financial Times*, 23 Dec. 2014. <http://www.ft.com/cms/s/0/60ce1b3a-85ec-11e4-a105-00144feabdc0.html>.

than owned by its employees and not, therefore, subject to shareholder pressure.[45] Between 2009 and 2013, the John Lewis department store business in the UK spent 15 per cent of its investment on IT, and forecast that this would rise to 37 per cent for the period 2014 to 2019, reflecting in particular the continued growth of online sales relative to store-based sales.[46]

This is not to suggest that 'going private' is necessarily the answer, although for some it could be, especially where management's view of the scale and timeline for restructuring is inimical to the expectations, and indeed to the interests, of shareholders. Ownership by private equity interests has often been seen as a way to take the necessary urgent decisions about a business out of the public gaze, whilst extracting value for PE investors out of the enterprise when it is taken public again at a suitable moment. An interesting example of this is Restoration Hardware, a seller of nostalgic discovery items in the US home furnishings marketplace. Founded in 1980, the business had lost its way in a highly competitive market by 2008 and was taken private. Over the space of four years, the store portfolio was reduced by over a quarter and repositioned into larger experiential gallery stores, with Source Books and websites 'serving as virtual extensions and compelling tours of the brand', leading to the business, rechristened RH, as 'a curator of the finest historical design the world has to offer'.[47] The business was successfully taken public in 2012 and has since produced record results.[48]

The Fundamental Value of Fundamental Values

In a world where everything is changing in the engagement landscape for retailers, it can be instinctive to assume that everything must also change within the enterprise. To believe so would be a mistake. In fact, in times of abrupt, discontinuous, and difficult to anticipate change, the fundamental values of an enterprise are actually more, not less important. How those values are articulated and communicated to the shopper will likely change very considerably, but the values themselves should not.

This is important territory for enterprises and enterprise leaders. If, for example, a retail enterprise defines itself as being in the business of 'delivering exceptional convenience to shoppers', every element of how this proposition is dimensionalized and delivered needs to be questioned constantly and, almost certainly, reframed, but the fundamental raison d'être of the enterprise

---

[45] <http://www.director.co.uk/sir-charlie-mayfield>.
[46] M. Chapman, 'John Lewis Increases Spend on IT to Two-Fifths of Capital Expenditure', *Retail Week*, 3 Mar. 2015.
[47] <http://ir.restorationhardware.com/phoenix.zhtml?c=79100&p=irol-irhome>.
[48] <http://ir.restorationhardware.com/phoenix.zhtml?c=79100&p=irol-newsArticle&ID=2121829>.

should not change. This reframing might turn a chain of, say, 10,000 conventional convenience stores into a business with perhaps 1,000 physical stores, 20,000 collection points, innumerable digital points of engagement and merchandise assortments, and prices that change by day part. It may also change the way in which the enterprise is organized to deliver on these much-changed executional requirements, but what should not change is the fundamental reason for being of the enterprise.

Case 9.2 FABINDIA: CHANGING THE ENTERPRISE, RETAINING THE VALUES

Fabindia could well be one of the retail world's most admirable businesses. Its history is a story of radical change and strong growth while maintaining the principles upon which the business was founded in 1960 by a remarkable American, John Bissell—principles that continue to be upheld by his son and current Managing Director, William.[49]

John Bissell started Fabindia because of his passion for the Indian fabrics produced by small artisan producers. As such, Bissell can rightly take his place amongst the great retail entrepreneurs to have created their businesses out of a huge passion for merchandise. Originally, Fabindia's business was sourcing fabrics for export to retailers around the world. Today Fabindia is not in the export business; rather it is a retail business with around 190 stores across India and a small number internationally. Traditional Indian clothing made from beautiful fabrics is still at the heart of the business, with homewares and furniture as important additional categories. (Fabindia is not short for Fabulous India, as some assume, but is a reference to fabrics of India.) Yet John Bissell established the business not just out of his passion for fabrics but also because of his equally strongly held passion for the business to be a force of good in improving the lives of artisan producers and their communities across India. Today Fabindia sells around 200,000 SKUs (Stock Keeping Units) sourced from a remarkable 40,000 small artisan producers.

Despite all the growth and transformation, John Bissell's original vision is still at the very heart of how Fabindia sees and conducts itself. As Sunil Chainani, Senior Director and one of the principal architects of the business's growth over the last fifteen years, puts it: 'Our values are part of the DNA of our business. It's the only way we know.'

For its community of small artisan producers, Fabindia does much more than merely provide a regular buyer for their output at a fair price. Fabindia helps its suppliers to work as groups in order to make collective investments in improving their businesses by, for example, buying new looms. In the past Fabindia has itself acted as an investor in the creation of such groups. However, in recent years these investments have had to be unwound largely because of India's laws on related-party transactions. Fabindia also encourages its suppliers to develop relationships and sales with other companies so that they are not over-dependent on Fabindia alone. Conventionally, this could be interpreted as Fabindia ultimately helping their competitors by improving the quality of their supplier base. But from Fabindia's perspective this is not an act of misguided altruism, rather it is the logical consequence of a fundamental commitment to

(continued)

---

[49] For an insightful and hugely enjoyable account of the first fifty years of Fabindia, we encourage readers to read Radhika Singh's book, *The Fabric of our Lives: The Story of Fabindia*. Delhi: Viking by Penguin India, 2010.

Case 9.2 Continued

---

improving the businesses and the lives of their artisan suppliers. Fabindia regularly also provides working capital to their suppliers to ease cashflow difficulties. Suppliers are also educated by Fabindia to improve the quality and consistency of their production. Director Sunil Chainani makes the point that Fabindia is an important contributor to the empowerment of women in rural India, as women, especially those working part time in order to fit work around their family duties, are a substantial part of Fabindia's supplier base.

When a business transforms itself, grows very quickly, and moves from the entrepreneurial passion of a charismatic founder to a more corporatized approach, the drive for growth and profits can sometimes overwhelm the former centrality of the enterprise's social objectives. This has not happened to Fabindia. Fabindia works hard to bring into its business only those who understand and share its social objectives. It also works to ensure that its approximately 2,500 employees stay very close to its small artisan suppliers, including organizing and encouraging very regular visits to suppliers by head office personnel from all functions, not just buying and merchandising. But mostly the maintenance of its strong social mission is a consequence of the perspective of the leaders of the business. For Fabindia there is no contradiction between its commercial and social objectives. Rather, commercial success enables the fulfilment of Fabindia's social objectives. As William Bissell puts it: 'Don't get me wrong; I am not a bleeding-heart liberal, more a libertarian. I don't believe in charity or giving things out free. I believe that the only way to alleviate rural poverty is to generate sustainable employment, and the only way to do that is if we run our business in a profitable manner.'[50] Sunil Chainani has a pithy way of expressing the same thought: 'People thought we were an NGO [Non-Governmental Organization]. We never were. We've always wanted to make good profits.'

For Fabindia, the key to delivering on its social objectives is to align them as closely as possible to the commercial objectives. The business has sought to make this link still more explicit by recently introducing a Social Impact Balance Sheet, performance in which will be a key performance measure for all teams in the business. As Sunil Chainani says, 'We need to ensure our suppliers perform, else their non-performance will not just affect them, but impact thousands of other similar artisan suppliers.' Fabindia does not paternalistically support suppliers. While some suppliers have been with Fabindia throughout its entire history, others have been exited when they fail to meet Fabindia's needs. Nor does the business lead with or even particularly promote its social objectives to its customers. In India it is certainly well understood that Fabindia has a very strong social mission, but the product and the high-quality store environments are central to the proposition for the shopper. For William Bissell, 'Only fresh product will bring the customer in the store.'

When Sunil Chainani talks of the future for Fabindia he talks of 'exponential growth'. Such growth will be enabled by better technology, especially to gain more insights into their shoppers; of being 'solutions centric' for their customers and developing more customized garments; of rotating non-core range SKUs through the business quickly in order to minimize discounting; and of mobile commerce as offering 'huge growth'

---

[50] M. Khaire and P. Kothandaram, *Fabindia Overseas Pvt. Ltd.* Cambridge, MA: Harvard Business School, 2010.

possibilities. In all of these respects, Fabindia can sound like a very conventional, corporatized retailer with the same concerns and priorities of many others. But when asked whether John Bissell would recognize today the business that he founded and whether he would be proud of Fabindia, Sunil Chainani becomes quiet and thoughtful and then answers, 'Yes. Because if anything our values are even more important to us today.'

Fabindia is an impressive business for its combination of wonderful merchandise, strong commercial performance and a strong social mission. We have suggested already (Chapter 1) that many shoppers are more concerned about the social, environmental, and ethical practices of the businesses they support and, in particular, of their relationships with their supplier base. Fabindia is in no sense responding to this trend. Rather it has always been integral to the way the company operates. It is not promoted or made explicit, it is simply *done*.

For enterprises committed to a strong social mission as well as to commercial goals, Sunil Chainani has one piece of advice: 'The key is to make this part of the company's DNA and get everyone involved. Otherwise it will become a charity type donation or the mission of just a few people.' Fabindia also serves as a reminder that in spite of the tsunami of change enveloping the retail sector globally, great merchandise and a strong moral compass are at least as relevant and important today as they have ever been.

Conclusion

We have suggested that the new landscape of retail requires all retail enterprises to re-examine their capabilities, the extent to which traditional strengths continue to be relevant, and the extent to which greater focus needs to be given to capability areas that historically received much less attention. We have suggested also that retailers need now and in future, more than ever before, to be able to combine hard engineering capabilities with softer competencies. Retail businesses that have historically been process-orientated will need to develop softer skills around brand management and shopper engagement, while traditionally high touch businesses will need to strengthen their process enablers, especially around IT and logistics, if they are to execute effectively their omni-channel strategies.

Such a re-examination may well lead to fundamental reappraisals of enterprise requirements, organizational structures, and investment priorities. In some instances this may lead to giving reduced attention (and investment) or even outsourcing entirely functions that were historically regarded as core capabilities integral to business success. (What size and capability of property department is needed if you are closing down far more stores than you are opening?) Other capability areas will need to be given much more attention and investment. We have suggested three that require especial attention: logistics, IT, and branding.

Such is the new landscape of retailing. It is difficult to conceive that, for established retail enterprises, the capabilities and priorities which have supported the enterprise in the past are going to be similarly relevant for the present and, especially, the future. Because change in the retail landscape is so far-reaching and discontinuous in nature, it is not just legitimate but necessary to question the very fundamentals on which an enterprise has historically operated. This goes to the very heart of what a retail business even is any more. It is also appropriate to question whether historic organization and ownership structures remain 'fit for purpose'. Crucially, the extent to which an enterprise needs to change versus the extent to which it has the ability to change will challenge many leaders and their teams. This is one of the themes we discuss in Chapter 10.

10

The New Needs of Retail Enterprise Leaders

Changed Enterprises—Changed Leadership Needs

Historically, retailing has been particularly notable for the presence and impact of single-minded, often charismatic individuals as leaders. What such leaders—like Bernardo Trujillo (NCR), Jack Cohen (Tesco), Gottlieb Duttweiler (Migros), Ingvar Kamprad (IKEA), and Gordon Selfridge—had in common was that they were ambitious builders of enterprises. They were intensely competitive, creative, and driven. We cited in Chapter 5 the reaction of Amazon's Jeff Bezos when he took a group of Harvard Business School students to task over their dim view of his business prospects. Bernardo Trujillo, who in the 1950s inspired a whole generation of French retailers from Bernard Darty to Marcel Fournier at Carrefour, was no less spirited at meetings of his peers: 'let's observe a minute's silence', he would observe, 'for those amongst you who are going to disappear—but don't yet realize it'. The gradual professionalization of the retail sector; the growth of publicly listed companies and of sector regulation, has led to the development of much more structured and formally accountable organizations which have more in common with similarly large and complex organizations in other sectors and require similarly skilled leadership. Across the retail enterprise leaders were needed who had deep expertise in all of those areas that enable a large business to operate effectively—people management, financial management, enterprise resource planning, and so on. Investors during that time were not especially keen on charisma. Often such firms were run by individuals who could (and often did) turn their hands to running any large organization.

In the new landscape of retailing, what kind of leadership is needed? In practice, of course, many of the personal attributes required of retail enterprise leaders have not changed and neither are they retail-sector-specific. It hardly need be said that all enterprise leaders are expected to have personal integrity, leadership, communication, and organizational skills. But certain of the leadership skills and perspectives that are required of those individuals do look rather different now and in the future to those that were required of them in even the recent past. It is instructive to read the preamble to the annual 'Retail Power List' produced by the UK retail trade magazine *Retail Week*. For them in 2015, the best (or 'most powerful') retail leaders are 'the people whose actions and words are influencing the broader sector and redefining what excellence looks like'. Further, 'when they speak, others listen'. While this might not sound too far from the days of Trujillo and Selfridge, we are not advocating a return to the kinds of 'hero leaders' of the past. Indeed, broader work on the changing nature of leadership conducted by the University of Oxford's Saïd Business School confirms that 'being a charismatic leader is not enough and the idea of a "superhero" chief executive is no longer relevant'.[1] Rather, effective leaders need to manage uncertainty and ambiguity, whilst at the same time setting a vision for the business against a backdrop of different expectations of different stakeholders and social activism. These new, more complex, models of leadership may be considerably challenging at both a personal and an enterprise level. In Chapter 9 we looked at the capability requirements of retail enterprises and in this, related, chapter we consider the attributes that will be needed by the leaders of these enterprises.

The leadership requirements of retail enterprises naturally go beyond the single individual at the head of the organization. We suggested in Chapter 9 that it is certainly possible to envisage a future where retail enterprises are much 'thinner' organizations than they have been historically as many more functions are outsourced. But this should not be taken to suggest that leadership should not be distributed, nor that retail-sector-specific skills are no longer important in the new landscape of retailing. Far from it. Multiple leaders with deep expertise in merchandising, store operations (assuming there are any), property management, marketing, logistics, and technology will all continue to be important for many retail enterprises. But, here again, the *relative* importance attached to each may change considerably (as we discussed in the previous chapter). Indeed, as the scale and complexity of retail enterprises increases, it will be very usual for still deeper expertise to be required in many areas. Sir Charlie Mayfield, Chairman of the UK's John Lewis Partnership of department and grocery stores, talks of his businesses needing much 'deeper specialisms' than in the past and of the borders between different areas of the business being as a result 'much less porous' in the sense that it is far harder for people to move between different areas of the enterprise today because those areas are so much more specialized.[2]

---

[1] A. White, 'Image of "Superhero" Needs a Rethink', FT.com, 21 Aug. 2015. <http://video.ft.com/4412995642001/Being-a-charismatic-leader-is-not-enough/Business-School>.

[2] Personal conversation, Sir Charlie Mayfield, Chairman, John Lewis Partnership, 2015.

New Landscapes—New Capabilities and Perspectives Needed

Our focus in this chapter is on the personal capabilities and perspectives that we believe will be especially important for retail enterprise leaders in the new landscape of retail. We suggest that there are five:

(i)   Accept the certainty of uncertainty
(ii)   Be prepared to widen the risk envelope
(iii) Be constantly vigilant (the price of risk)
(iv)   Champion innovation
(v)   Prioritize

Accept the Certainty of Uncertainty

The new landscape of retail is defined by uncertainty, especially in relation to consumer and competitor environments. The ways in which shoppers might wish to be engaged, even in the near-term future, cannot be anticipated with total certainty by even the most far-sighted leaders, not least because the technologies and platforms which could come to the fore very possibly have not yet even been invented, let alone shoppers' reactions to them understood and addressed. For example, many people are getting excited about the possibilities of virtual reality headsets. Mark Zuckerberg believes that the Oculus Rift virtual reality headset device has the potential to 'change everything'.[3] This led Facebook to spend US$2 billion to buy Oculus at a time when the Rift device itself existed only in prototype form—but no one can know the eventual outcome with certainty.[4] After all, Google said that its Google Glass product was a step towards ubiquitous computing and *Time* magazine voted the technology one of the best inventions of the year in 2012. Yet it was withdrawn as a consumer product in 2015, with tentative plans for Glass 2 to be introduced as a wearable device for the workplace later in that year.[5]

Neither can the competitor set be understood or even identified with total clarity in environments where new business models and engagement platforms are being brought to market at great speed. It is no longer possible to achieve success by setting a direction for an enterprise to orientate towards and then relentlessly pursuing that single trajectory alone. Certainly, business leaders need to have a clear view of where they are seeking to take their enterprises, but the pathway of how to get there must be developed in a far

---

[3] P. Rubin, 'The Inside Story of Oculus Rift and How Virtual Reality Became Reality', *Wired*, 20 May 2014. <http://www.wired.com/2014/05/oculus-rift-4>.

[4] <http://www.wired.com/2014/05/oculus-rift-4>.

[5] <http://www.forbes.com/sites/mikemontgomery/2015/04/16/life-after-the-alleged-death-of-google-glass>.

less linear and one-dimensional way today than it has been—or at least has been portrayed to have been—in the past. In a 2015 survey of over 150 CEOs of some of the world's largest enterprises conducted by the University of Oxford's Saïd Business School, one (anonymous) CEO observed that 'The paths to the future are made, not found, and the process of making them changes both us and our final destination.'[6] Quite.

Case 10.1 GAP AND THE 'MESSY MOSH PIT OF CHANGE'

Art Peck became CEO of the iconic but challenged clothing retailer, Gap, in early 2015. He already knew the business very well, having spent the previous ten years as, first, adviser and then in a number of senior executive roles. The immediate challenge for Gap is the timeless and familiar one that many retailers have faced—'fixing the product'. Beyond that, Peck is determined to build enduring strength back into the business. He is firmly of the view that times of great change and uncertainty are the best of times to do this. Peck talks of the need 'to be out there in the messy mosh pit of change with unclear direction and unclear implications'.[7] As Peck sees it, this is the era of Retail 3.0 for Gap. Retail 1.0 was the era of the mall as the centre of the shoppers' world and that was when Gap thrived. Retail 2.0 was the era of fast fashion (Zara, Mango, H&M, Uniqlo, Topshop, etc.) when Gap has floundered, with time to market too long and product too safe. This new era of Retail 3.0 is, in Peck's view, defined by mobile commerce in which physical stores have a new role to play and where Gap can leapfrog over its competitors. Peck says: 'We've been doing business the same way for 40 years, and there are very few 40-year-old business models that are successful forever. Periods of disruption are periods of disproportionate opportunity. More money is made during disruptive times—but is also lost—than is made during times of stability.'[8]

For all business leaders, not just of retail enterprises, it can be very difficult to come to terms with the certainty of uncertainty. But it is only by accepting the reality of uncertain futures that business leaders can coherently prepare and effectively 'future-proof' their enterprises. For many, the nature and timeframe of enterprise strategic planning will need to change. Many enterprises have long since moved away from the notion of strategic planning as a one-off activity conducted every three to five years to planning as a rolling exercise. Karl Moore, the strategic management theorist, distinguishes between Michael Porter's 'world of deliberate strategy' and Henry Mintzberg's view that 'strategy emerges over time as intentions collide with and accommodate a changed reality'—so-called 'Emergent Strategy' which 'implies that an organization is learning what works in practice'. Moore is also of the view that, 'given today's world . . . , I think emergent strategy is on the upswing . . . It

---

[6] *The CEO Report*. Oxford: University of Oxford Saïd Business School for Heidrick & Struggles, 2015. <http://www.sbs.ox.ac.uk/sites/default/files/Press_Office/Docs/The-CEO-Report-Final.pdf>.
[7] <http://www.fastcompany.com/3042434/gapquest>.
[8] <http://www.fastcompany.com/3042434/gapquest>.

is precisely because we cannot, try as we may, control the variables that factor into business decisions that Mintzberg's emergent strategy is so useful.'[9]

The retail industry globally exhibits just this characteristic. Not only are retail enterprise leaders not able to control all of the variables relevant to their business decisions, they typically do not even have perfect clarity on what they all are, nor the importance that they may come to have. In this environment, the key is not to be paralysed into inaction. Writing in *Harvard Business Review*, organizational development consultant Patti Johnson gives the example in the USA of incoming Target CEO Brian Cornell. Cornell joined Target in August 2015 and inherited several major uncertainties, including the impact of a major data breach, a poor understanding of omni-channel, and a major problematic foray into Canada. Understanding that the Canadian business was unlikely to break even until 2021, Cornell sought to reduce one area of the business's uncertainty by closing down the operation. This experience points to a wider proposition: namely that, for retail enterprises, emergent strategy as a planning tool is likely to be more relevant than Porter-esque deliberate strategy. It should be emphasized too that strategy design is not framed solely around identifying and being equipped to deal with potential challenges or crises. It should be framed also around the identification of the full richness of opportunities that exist in uncertain environments.

Be Prepared to Widen the Risk Envelope

There is a risk paradox in the new landscape of retail: playing safe will very likely prove to be the riskiest plan of all. When one looks across the graveyard of failed retail enterprises, the common theme is not that they took too much risk, but that they took too little—usually by staying too wedded for too long to a customer proposition, retail format or way of working that had become obsolete and that was no longer valued by shoppers before management either realized or was able to act. Retail enterprises, more than most others, are defined by the momentum they have—either strongly upwards or strongly downwards; a middling steady-state that lasts for any length of time is very unusual.

In one of the great exchanges in one of Ernest Hemingway's great novels (*The Sun Also Rises*[10]), Bill asks Mike 'How did you go bankrupt?' to which Mike replies 'Two ways. Gradually and then suddenly'. Retail enterprises have much of this characteristic: when they slide, it starts gradually and then becomes very sudden. Lord Simon Wolfson, CEO of Next—one of the most

---

[9] <http://www.forbes.com/sites/karlmoore/2011/03/28/porter-or-mintzberg-whose-view-of-strategy-is-the-most-relevant-today>.

[10] Ernest Hemingway, *The Sun Also Rises*. London: Arrow Classic, 1994 edn.

successful UK fashion retailers—explained Next's corporate attitude to risk in the context of merchandising decisions in the following way:

> we will continue to push our design teams to adopt new trends in depth and with conviction. This approach of taking greater fashion risk may sound counter-intuitive but in today's fast moving fashion environment, to fall back on 'safe' historical ranges would merely guarantee failure. On the whole, our experience is that where we have been braver in buying into new trends we have been successful.[11]

This is, in our view, a proposition that has a wider relevance beyond merchandising.

In addressing themselves to the risk paradox that playing safe will likely prove to be the biggest risk of all, retail enterprise leaders will need to achieve three goals. They will need to re-evaluate their own perspective on risk (their personal risk propensity), gain a proper appreciation of the extent of risk in a particular situation (their risk perception), as well as educate stakeholders within and outside the enterprise of the risk profile that it is necessary to accept in the new landscape of retail. Embracing the notion of risk and widening the tolerance of risk within an enterprise and amongst its external stakeholders does not mean taking ill-considered leaps of faith into the unknown. Re-evaluating and perhaps changing their personal propensity to take risks will require leaders to reflect more carefully on their past experiences, decisions, and outcomes. Improving risk perception is a matter of framing a problem carefully and appropriately. When Sir Terry Leahy reflected on his very successful tenure as CEO of Tesco and the lessons he learned, he offered two important and related perspectives on the risks that he felt he needed to take, 'The greater the risk, the greater the precautions you must take. Yet doing nothing is often the greatest risk of all.'[12] In being prepared to tolerate more risk—for either defensive or offensive reasons—it is incumbent upon business leaders to undertake more, not less, due diligence in order to understand both the scale of the risk they are prepared to take and the consequences of failure.

Considerations of risk are a key concern for enterprise investors as well as for business leaders. Where there is a wide divergence between the risks that investors identify as suitable for pursuing a chosen path and the commitment that management has to that path, then it is also reasonable to question whether the ownership structure is appropriate and not just whether the proposed actions of management are appropriate. Governance structures in retailing are still enormously varied: from family-owned firms, to conglomerates; from public

---

[11] Lord Simon Wolfson, Next results presentation, Mar. 2014.
[12] T. Leahy, *Management in Ten Words*. London: Random House Business Books, 2013, 84.

to private ownership. For example, writing of the costs and benefits of private equity, managing director of retail consultancy Conlumino, Neil Saunders, sets out some of the advantages over public ownership that he sees: more flexible capital (able to respond more quickly to emergent opportunities), more effective governance (closer involvement in management ambitions and decision-making), sustainable management (taking a longer term view, albeit to a profitable exit, than institutional investors in public companies), and greater retail expertise (many private equity firms such as Bridgepoint Capital, KKR, and Sycamore have deep specialization in the sector).[13] To be sure, private equity models in retailing also have their critics: they are accused of being short-termist, loading down their acquisitions with debt, and asset-stripping.[14] This is not to suggest that one ownership model is better or worse than another. Rather it is to say that it is entirely rational to want to look at, and potentially change, an ownership model if the expectations of owners cease to be aligned with the plans of management and the needs of the enterprise.

Be Constantly Vigilant (the Price of Risk)

The need for constant vigilance is the consequence of operating in environments of high uncertainty and attendant risk. At an enterprise level, this means having the capability to both capture and interpret customer insights, competitor and enterprise performance information in order to extract meaning and to find the early evidence of both opportunities and challenges. We discussed in Chapter 3 the enterprise technology requirements to achieve this level of insight. For the business leader it means having both access to information as well as finely honed abilities—at both a personal and an enterprise level—to interpret and find the implications of the insights for the enterprise. But sometimes, the signals that leaders are required to interpret can be overwhelming and contradictory. The notion of an excess of information and an insufficiency of actionable insights is well understood and has been noted extensively in numerous academic and management consultancy studies.[15] (The fact that there exists an Information Overload Research Group, 'Reducing Information Pollution'—yes, really—perhaps bears testimony to

---

[13] N. Saunders, 'Is Private Equity Good for the High Street?', Conlumino blog, 19 Jan. 2013. <http://conlumino.com/?p=871>.

[14] R. Thomson, 'Analysis: Has Private Equity Been Good for Retail?', *Retail Week*, 28 Mar. 2013. <http://www.retail-week.com/topics/analysis-has-private-equity-been-good-for-retail/5047596. article>.

[15] For a review of the academic literature see e.g. Angela Edmunds and Anne Morris, 'The Problem of Information Overload in Business Organisations: A Review of the Literature', *International Journal of Information Management*, 20 (2000), 17–28.

just how institutionalized this challenge has become.[16]) One consequence of this is that, as prerequisites to action, retail leaders must search for plausible interpretations for circumstances based on merely sufficient evidence, rather than totally comprehensive ones based on all the evidence. Making sense of the world in these circumstances is 'not about truth and getting it right. Instead, it is about continued redrafting of an emerging story so that it becomes more comprehensive, incorporates more of the observed data, and is more resilient in the face of criticism.'[17] Working in this way reinforces an emergent strategy approach to change.

Champion Innovation

As we have suggested already, it is almost certainly the case that the strategies and attributes which have made a retail enterprise successful in the past—even the very recent past—are no guarantee of success in the future. Indeed, some may not even be relevant at all in the future. This is understandably uncomfortable territory for many business leaders who have grown up in environments where there was a received way of doing things and steering a steady course was the prime objective of the CEO. Indeed, there is evidence that the working practices that characterize large, established firms (including the development of routine ways of doing things and a primary focus on cost reduction and incremental innovation) are actively inimical to the prospects for radical innovation. But the retail world is very different today.

For leaders of retail enterprises there are two areas in particular where championing more radical innovation is a high order imperative—innovation in shopper engagement and innovation in go-to-market techniques. Clearly, these two territories are closely related. In both areas it is important for business leaders to be *thinking* radically. The question of whether they should also be *acting* radically may have a different answer, however.

An appetite for exploring innovation potential is made necessary by the radical nature of the change that is reframing shopper and competitive landscapes and which we explored in Part 1 of this book. Retail enterprise leaders have to be prepared to let go of at least some of the tenets of the past if they are to secure their future. For established retail enterprises, this should not be interpreted as a call to throw everything away, tear up the old rulebooks, and start afresh with a blank sheet of paper. On the contrary, the

[16] <http://iorgforum.org/about-iorg>.
[17] K. E. Weick et al., 'Organizing and the Process of Sensemaking', *Organization Science*, 16(4) (2005), 409–21.

challenge for business leaders is to be profoundly clear on what the essential raison d'être of their business is and to which the enterprise must always be true. For most retail enterprises—we are tempted to suggest for all—this will be much more to do with the values of the enterprise and its essential reason for being than it will be to do with the techniques of how those values are communicated, how offers are brought to market, and how corporate goals are achieved.

To illustrate the point, consider, for example, a price-led discount general merchandise retail business in which the reason for being has been codified as: 'We exist to make our customers' lives better through our compelling value'. The leaders of such a business have a licence—even an obligation—to explore all of the ways in which that essential proposition can best be defined and delivered to its shoppers. The notion of 'compelling value' could be interpreted as 'lowest price', but it might well be more useful to define 'value' in a variety of other ways—quality relative to price, range of assortment, ease of access across online and offline touchpoints, and so on. Moreover, dimensions of 'value' are different for different shopper groups so perhaps the essential proposition needs to be defined in different, and very granular, ways for different shoppers in their different purchase realms. Similarly, a shopping centre developer might define itself as being in the business of 'creating engaging environments where people want to meet, spend time, and, ultimately, make purchases'. This should not limit such a business to seeing itself as purely a developer of physical shopping centres, given that its potential audiences want increasingly to meet and spend time online. Nor does it imply that the physical centre space must be occupied by a conventional collection of tenants.

The mantra must surely be 'do what is best for the shopper, not what is easiest for the business'. True customer centricity means organizing an enterprise around the shopper rather than forcing a shopper to fit into the existing operations of the enterprise. If a shopper wants to engage with an enterprise through a smartphone app that cost perhaps US$20,000 to create in a few weeks rather than through a network of 500 stores developed for hundreds of millions of dollars over 100 years or more, then so be it. The role of the retailer in the new landscape should not be to force shoppers to engage with them in a prescriptive way. It must be to present an appropriate range of options to the shopper and then make it as easy as possible for the shopper to engage with the business howsoever they wish. If a shopper wants to order three dresses online, collect them at a store near their office, return the two they don't like at a secure kiosk in a train station, then so be it. Being able to deliver this flexibility in a properly seamless way is hugely challenging for the retailer (as we discussed in Chapters 7 and 9) but it is, quite rightly, of no concern at all to the shopper.

Case 10.2 FEDERICO MARCHETTI: A SOMEWHAT UNLIKELY FASHION
REVOLUTIONARY

In the early years of online retailing, the prevailing logic was that clothing—and especially expensive, premium clothing—could not be sold online. In 2000, Rick Greenbury,
then Chairman of M&S (at the time the second most profitable retailer in the world, after
Walmart), reflected the views of many when he said, 'most or all of our customers live
within an hour's travel of a Marks and Spencer store. The internet just hasn't had the
same impact on clothing and department store retailers here. Why switch when there's
nothing onerous about the current situation?'[18] In the same year in Italy, Federico
Marchetti founded Yoox, 'a pioneer in fashion e-commerce, introducing in the digital
world leading fashion and luxury brands'.[19] Fifteen years later, Yoox achieves sales well in
excess of US$560 million and is significantly profitable at a trading level.[20] In May 2015,
Yoox announced its plan to merge with Net-a-Porter which, in the words of the
Chairman of the Richemont luxury brands group and owner of Net-a-Porter, will create
'an independent, neutral platform for a sophisticated clientele looking for luxury brands',
and with combined sales of around US$1.5 billion.[21]

There are two parts to the Yoox business: its *multi-brand* and *mono-brand* platforms. The
multi-brand platform came first and is an online means for Yoox to sell a wide range of,
mostly, premium fashion clothing brands. Mono-brand platforms have been established
since 2006. There are now 38 websites 'powered by Yoox' for premium fashion brands,
including Armani, Valentino and Lanvin, Ermenegildo Zegna, and Dolce & Gabbana. The
multi-brand platform is around 70 per cent of revenues and the mono-brand platforms 30
per cent. Yoox's domestic Italian market accounted for around 16 per cent of revenues in
FY2014, with the remainder of Europe 47 per cent and the US 22 per cent.[22]

Rick Greenbury was described by Sir Simon Marks, part of the Marks side of the M&S
dynasty, as a 'retailer through and through'.[23] Federico Marchetti is anything but. He is a
technology entrepreneur with a background in merchant banking who saw an opportunity in 2000 to persuade luxury fashion brands to sell him end of season stock that he
could then sell online on Yoox. This, at a time when luxury products accounted for 'zero
per cent' of e-commerce.[24] Marchetti himself appears entirely sanguine about the big
risk that he took to leave merchant banking to pursue and sell the dream of Yoox.
Marchetti calls himself a 'geek to the chic'.[25]

---

[18] Quoted in R. Burke et al., 'Retailing: Confronting the Challenges that Face Bricks & Mortar
Stores', *Harvard Business Review* (July–Aug. 1999), 159–68.

[19] <http://www.yooxgroup.com/pages/what-we-do>.

[20] <http://cdn3.yoox.biz/cloud/yooxgroup/uploads/doc/2015/pr_yoox_spa_fy2014_preliminary-
net-revenues_final.pdf>.

[21] R. Mac, 'Net-a-Porter to Merge with Yoox Creating Online High Fashion Giant', *Forbes*, 15 Mar. 2015.
<http://www.forbes.com/sites/ryanmac/2015/03/31/net-a-porter-merges-with-yoox-creating-online-high-fashion-
giant>.

[22] <http://cdn3.yoox.biz/cloud/yooxgroup/uploads/doc/2015/pr_yoox_spa_fy2014_preliminary-
net-revenues_final.pdf>.

[23] Sir Simon Marks, quoted in J. Bevan, *The Rise and Fall of Marks and Spencer...and How it Rose
Again*. London: Profile Books, 2007.

[24] J. Ellison, 'Federico Marchetti', *Financial Times*, 29 May 2015. <http://www.ft.com/cms/s/2/
4d842f1a-0396-11e5-a70f-00144feabdc0.html>.

[25] R. Sanderson, 'Federico Marchetti: Geek to the Chic', *Financial Times*, 3 Apr. 2015. <http://
www.ft.com/cms/s/0/c9ab3892-d91e-11e4-b907-00144feab7de.html#axzz3dzM7vOUs>.

What Marchetti and Yoox are especially good at are what might be thought of as the new skills of retailing necessary for an online age: logistics and data analysis. Marchetti describes Yoox's Bologna distribution centre as 'an amazing operation. You wouldn't expect so much perfection from an Italian company—about 0.0001 per cent of mistakes. . . . You need it to be right [for the shopper] otherwise it's a loss of credibility.'[26] For Marchetti, sales data accumulated over fifteen years of operations is an important—but not an omnipotent—source of insight. Yoox launched a website just selling shoes (shoescribe.com) because their data told them that when two-thirds of women buy shoes from Yoox that is all they buy—no clothing is added to their online shopping cart. As Marchetti says, 'The power of information is huge.'[27] But Marchetti recognizes also the limits of what Yoox's data can reveal to him and the enduring importance of creativity and leaps of imagination in the merchandising process. Marchetti again: 'There's a very common risk with data that you can become lost in it. At Yoox we still use a good part of commercial instinct for the buy. It's a mix. Using data is a piece of information but that doesn't necessarily mean that we are led by it. It's the sociological point of view that I'm missing. Why do women buy only shoes when they buy online? I don't know. I just know that they do.'

Federico Marchetti is a very different type of leader of a premium fashion apparel retail business. He did not start on the shop floor and grow up in the business. He does not have an instinctive feel for the merchandise. Neither is he a quasi-mythical figure who inspires the adoration of his employees, ('I think they feel inspired. But they don't need to love me . . . I don't need love. I need results.'[28]) Rather, he is a leader who took a substantial personal risk because he was convinced of the opportunity that he saw being created by the internet to sell luxury products in a very different way. What Marchetti does have is a deep understanding of the power of logistics and data—two of the capabilities that we have identified as crucial to the new needs of retail enterprises and to the leaders of those enterprises. Equally importantly, he recognizes that the traditional skills in his category—a merchandise sensibility and a willingness to take creative leaps—are just as important in the new age of retailing as they were in the old.

The corollary of championing innovation is to also be tolerant of failure. If all innovation initiatives are successful then it is almost certain they were not, in fact, very innovative at all. The likelihood is that many will fail and business leaders need to be accepting of this. (Despite the rhetorical claim that '80% of new products and projects fail',[29] the empirical evidence over the long run is that the figure is somewhere between 30 and 50 per cent.[30] We have no reason to think that the experience of retail innovators is any different from this figure.) What becomes especially important, therefore, is the appetite for and management of risk. Different leaders and the enterprises they lead will have different thresholds and perspectives in this regard. The important point is to be clear where one wants to live on that spectrum between the risk of doing

[26] Ellison, 'Federico Marchetti'.   [27] Ellison, 'Federico Marchetti'.

[28] Ellison, 'Federico Marchetti'.

[29] e.g. <http://newmr.org/blog/is-it-a-bad-thing-that-80-of-new-products-fail>.

[30] Quora, 'Is the 80% Product Failure Rate Statistic Actually True?', 8 Aug. 2013. <http://www.quora.com/Is-the-80-product-failure-rate-statistic-actually-true>.

nothing and the risk of doing too much, too radically, and/or too quickly. Being too far toward either end of this spectrum has the potential to inflict great damage on a business.

While Sir Terry Leahy spoke of doing nothing as being 'often the greatest risk of all', Ron Johnson's experience with the JC Penney department store business in the US illustrates the opposite truth—the risk of doing too much, too quickly. Johnson can properly claim great credit for being one of the main architects of Target's reinvention as a discount department store with real product flair and then for Apple's brilliant retail store business. Yet he is the same business leader who sought to reinvigorate JC Penney by radical and rapid change, including to Penney's marketing and promotions programme. This involved stripping away overnight almost all of its promotions and turning the business from one dependent on a frankly bewildering array of sales promotions into a 'consistent prices you can trust' platform ('Sale is not in our vocabulary', said Johnson when the strategy was first announced).[31]

Making such a radical change so quickly disenfranchised a huge swathe of shoppers and cost Penney around US$5billion in sales, US$1 billion in earnings, and Johnson his job. Too much change that overwhelmed the enterprise and disengaged too many shoppers had disastrous consequences. Organizationally, Johnson had separated out the merchandise buying and planning teams for stores and online. Momentum as well as sales were lost and five years later in 2015 online sales were still around US$400 million below their $1.6 billion peak.[32] The obituaries of Ron Johnson's seventeen-month term as the leader of JC Penney were not kind. Mark Cohen, former CEO of Sears Canada and now Director of Retail Studies at Columbia Business School, said that, 'There is nothing good to say about what he's done. Penney had been run into a ditch when he took it over. But, rather than getting it back on the road, he's essentially set it on fire.'[33] As a wise leader once said, 'If you're half a step ahead of the shopper you've got a successful business. If you're ten steps ahead you're bankrupt.'

Prioritize

In a world and an industry defined by rapid and disruptive change, there can be an almost irresistible tendency to view everything as equally important and requiring urgent attention. Establishing priorities is crucial. Our discussion in this section owes much to the work conducted by Saïd Business School at the University of Oxford for executive search firm Heidrick & Struggles and

---

[31] S. Marchese, 'J C Penney CEO Ron Johnson sits down with CNBC's Courtney Reagan Today on CNBC', transcript, 31 July 2012. <http://www.cnbc.com/id/48249720>.
[32] <http://fortune.com/2015/02/26/j-c-penney-ron-johnson-era>.
[33] <http://business.time.com/2013/04/09/the-5-big-mistakes-that-led-to-ron-johnsons-ouster-at-jc-penney>.

presented at the Davos 2015 forum and in their paper, *The CEO Report*.[34] As the authors of this work say, 'The key ... is to focus not only on the speed of change, but on its scope and significance as well, offering an "S^3" understanding of change.' Figure 10.1 presents this S^3 matrix.

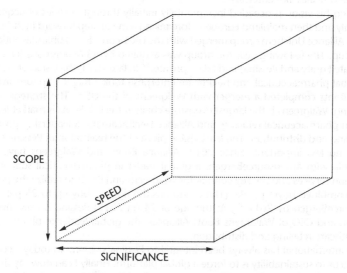

Figure 10.1 The S3 matrix and the three interacting dimensions of change
Source: Saïd Business School, University of Oxford, 2015.

Considering change in these three dimensions—Speed, Scope, and Significance—allows priorities to be set that align to more than just the speed with which change is occurring. But as the authors also acknowledge, 'The impact of scope can be difficult to predict: even systemic changes can have root-causes that were initially contained and local—for example, the seemingly localized US sub-prime credit crunch that became the global financial crisis.'[35] Hence, finely tuned antennae, constantly rolling planning, and effective risk identification and management, remain of the greatest importance.

Prioritizing is not only about identifying the challenges and the opportunities that an enterprise may face in the future. It is also about prioritizing which areas the enterprise should focus on and the amount of effort and resources to allocate. In this regard, as the Oxford research team has suggested, 'CEOs face perplexing choices between "what is right and right" ... rather than simply right and wrong. It is these dilemmas that make decisions so vexing and alignment so difficult.'[36] As we have suggested, it is incumbent now upon business leaders to think the unthinkable. The wisest ones plan somewhat before the unthinkable has become thinkable and act somewhat before the thinkable has become necessary.

---

[34] *The CEO Report.*   [35] *The CEO Report, 7.*   [36] *The CEO Report, 22.*

Case 10.3 STEFANO PESSINA: CREATING THE NEW RETAIL (AGED 70+)

Stefano Pessina has spent the last forty years buying, restructuring, and merging pharmaceutical businesses with the ultimate objective of creating a truly global pharmaceutical and healthcare enterprise.

Realizing his vision proceeded incrementally initially through a series of acquisitions across Italy and then mainland Europe before taking a major step forward in 2006 when Pessina's Alliance Unichem group merged with the UK's iconic Boots pharmaceutical and retail group. The following year the group was acquired by AB Acquisitions (created by KKR Private Equity and Pessina) and taken private.[37] In late 2014, the vision of creating a truly global pharmaceutical and healthcare enterprise took a major leap forward when Alliance Boots completed a merger with Walgreens of the US.[38] The strategic logic is compelling: Walgreens is the largest drugstore chain in the US, Boots is market leader in Europe in pharmaceutical retailing, and Alliance Healthcare has a leadership position in wholesaling and distribution. The least visible piece of the realization of Pessina's global vision is no less important. Since 2013, Alliance Boots and Walgreens have had a partnership with AmerisourceBergen, a global leader in pharmaceutical sourcing and distribution services and the key conduit for Walgreens and Boots to realize the potential of their combined buying scale. (The group has the right to buy up to 25 per cent of AmerisourceBergen by 2017.[39]) At the age of 74 (in 2015) Pessina is Executive Vice-Chairman and CEO of Walgreens Boots Alliance—the global leader in pharmaceutical and healthcare retailing and distribution.

Being international has always been integral to Pessina's vision: 'In today's economy the shortcut to sustainability is to forge a global platform. Finally I can now say that with the creation of Walgreens Boots Alliance we are truly global.'[40] Vision realized then? Well, actually, no. The vision is still a work in progress and the ambition is unabated. Shortly after announcing the Walgreens/Boots deal, Pessina outlined his plans for China—the world's third biggest pharmaceutical market: 'It's clear that we are number one in Europe, we are now number one in the US. We want to be either say number one, [or] at least number two or number three in China . . . Why not number one over time? We cannot create a global company without being in Europe and in the US and in Asia, particularly in China.'[41] The group owns 50 per cent of China's sixth largest pharmaceutical wholesaler and has a minority stake in that country's fifth largest pharmaceutical wholesaler. Nor does it end there. In early 2014, Alliance Boots (as the group was at the time) made its first acquisitions in Latin America (in Mexico and Chile). Pessina said at the time, 'This is the first step. Of course there are other big countries in Latin America we are still interested in.'[42]

As a business leader who is restructuring and transforming an entire retail (and distribution) category globally, Pessina's views on leadership are well worth listening to: 'I often say that I am an engineer by background [he graduated in nuclear

---

[37] <http://www.stefanopessina.com/about.html>.

[38] George MacDonald, 'The Engineer Who Built a Global Retail Powerhouse', *Retail Week*, 13 Mar. 2015, 43–4.

[39] <http://www.dailymail.co.uk/money/markets/article-2590203/Medicine-man-taking-Boots-world-At-72-Stefano-Pessina-says-deal-making-elixir-youth.hztml>.

[40] Stefano Pessina quoted in MacDonald, 'Engineer'.

[41] <http://www.ft.com/cms/s/0/0d96fc2a-b415-11e2-ace9-00144feabdc0.html#axzz2yCrLxnkM>.

[42] <http://www.ft.com/cms/s/0/124ba49c-d53d-11e3-adec-00144feabdc0.html#axzz3113tD3H2>.

engineering from Politechnico di Milano], so I like designing and building things that last. This has always been my strong motivation.'[43]

For Pessina, strong, coherent cultures are critical to success within the businesses in his group and if mergers are to be effective. 'Within the shared culture, there should be common values, goals and strong ethics. I always insist it's fundamental that people work in the interest of the company and not their own personal interest.'[44] Nevertheless, Pessina is not averse to internal differences provided they are channelled to create a stronger business if people 'refocus their energies on achieving what is right for the company and not on their disagreements'.[45] In regard to addressing the substantial risks that accompany major acquisitions, especially when they are cross-border, Pessina advocates discipline: 'My golden rule is that a good deal has to be with the right partner, at the right price and at the right time. It is important to be disciplined, have clear limits that you will not overstep, no matter how big or small the transaction is. Never let emotions get involved, being rational is crucial. . . . The [combined] management team is the first that has to demonstrate some key values: leadership, team spirit, merit and commitment to the company.'[46]

Stefano Pessina is a revolutionary in the new retail landscape. His vision, ambition, and drive are transforming an entire sector of retailing globally. It will not surprise if, in hindsight, the Boots–Walgreens merger looks like the start of the next phase of realizing the vision, not the end of the project. Revolutionaries in the new retail don't all come with crew cuts and black turtle neck sweaters.

Conclusion

This is a wonderful and simultaneously a terrifying time to be a retailer. The new landscape of retailing is one that is rich in possibilities. Rather more so, in our view, than it is defined by challenges. Disruptive change creates opportunities to engage with shoppers in entirely new ways; to create entirely new enterprises; to extend the reach of existing ones into new parts of shoppers' lives as well as into new geographies and product categories. But there can be no question either that such environments are also tremendously challenging for those tasked with delivering success for their enterprises. Challenging in the sense both of realizing new opportunities as well as of resisting more intense and diverse competitive pressures. We have noted already (Chapter 9) that the gap between successful and unsuccessful enterprises is likely to become much more sharply defined in such environments and the possibility of muddling along by delivering 'underwhelming underperformance' is no longer

---

[43] Stefano Pessina quoted in MacDonald, 'Engineer'.
[44] Stefano Pessina quoted in MacDonald, 'Engineer'.
[45] Stefano Pessina quoted in MacDonald, 'Engineer'.
[46] Stefano Pessina quoted in MacDonald, 'Engineer'.

an option—not when choice for the shopper is so broad and the competitor set so diverse.

In such landscapes, effective leadership of the enterprise becomes still more important and the appropriateness and quality of the skills and perspectives of enterprise leaders will become still more defining of the success—or not—of the enterprises they lead. We are not suggesting that all of the 'traditional' skills of retail enterprise leaders are no longer of any relevance in the new landscape of retailing. But we are certainly suggesting that some of them are not. As enterprises move still further away from their historic approaches and activities, it is inevitable that new skills are indeed needed and that different priorities have to be established. Effective enterprise leaders embrace, rather than resist, the need for such change.

We have concerned ourselves in this chapter not with the technical competencies of enterprise leaders, but rather with the leadership capabilities and perspectives which we believe will need greater emphasis and be more defining of success in the new landscape of retail. We have suggested that there are five:

1. Accept the certainty of uncertainty
2. Be prepared to widen the risk envelope
3. Be constantly vigilant
4. Promote innovation
5. Prioritize

Just as at an enterprise level (as we discussed in Chapter 9), so too at a personal leadership level it is the essentially uncertain and far less predictable nature of the new landscape of retailing that is central to defining the set of leadership capabilities and perspectives which will be most important to delivering success. Indeed, if readers are inclined to view points 2 to 5 as subsets of point 1, we would not disagree.

Conclusions

Challenges and Opportunities

> *The best way to predict the future is to invent it.*
> (Alan Kay, Computer Scientist, 1971[1])

A central defining thesis has framed the content of this book; namely that the retail industry globally is in the early stages of a transformation which will be more profound and far-reaching than any which has gone before. What makes the current era of change unique is that it is being driven by both the strength *and* the interaction of forces of fundamental change—the transformational impacts of technology on shoppers, enterprises, economies, and countries; transformation in shopping behaviours and, especially, the impact of Millennials; and the accelerating modernization of the so-called emerging markets. Any one of these drivers of change would have important impacts on the retail industry. The fact that they are all happening simultaneously is what makes the current era of change so transformative, so challenging, and also so rich in possibilities. This era of change challenges and dismantles many of the fundamental tenets on which retailing has been conducted and on which retail enterprises have operated for at least the last 100 years:

- Stores are no longer a prerequisite for being in the business of retailing.

- Traditional retailers are not the only enterprises able to be in the business of retailing. Neither, for many shoppers, will they be the most preferred.

- Geography does not define and constrain the choice set for the shopper or the competitor set for the retailer.

- Shoppers are at least as well informed as the enterprises from which they buy.

---

[1] 1971 meeting at PARC (Palo Alto Research Center).

Disruptive new-to-retail enterprises are able to build tremendous scale, reach, shopper equity, and influence at a considerable pace. Such enterprises have a starting point, a culture, and an ethos which, if not rejecting entirely the usefulness of traditional retail enterprise attributes in the new landscape, are certainly more likely to see them as disadvantageous rather than as a source of strength. 'We're a bunch of tech guys who saw an opportunity in retail' is the mantra for many. These enterprises see themselves as being in the vanguard of the new retail. They are not trying to transition an enterprise to be fit for purpose in the new world; rather they are leading the invention of that new world. But what has become evident in these early years in the new landscape of retailing is that these self-confident, new to retail enterprises face their own challenges. Prominent in particular is the issue of 'profitless growth': the more sales volume they add and the more customers they secure, the further away consistent and acceptable profits can seem to be. Moreover, this 'profitless growth' serves to dilute the profitability of their more traditional competitors. Many of the enterprises in the vanguard of the new retail are facing their own transition in moving from an era of high growth and elusive profits and into an era of consistent, sustainable returns in which they are judged according to normal commercial criteria. In this respect, the question that will be asked of them is no different to that being asked of traditional retailers in the new landscape, 'Is there really a sustainable business model here?'

'Is There Really a Sustainable Business Model Here?'

The dimensions of change in the new landscape of retailing tend most often to be framed around the challenges that they represent for traditional retailers. That these are considerable is undeniable. Crossing the Rubicon from old world retailing and into the new will challenge many enterprises and their leaders. Many will not survive—both enterprises and leaders—as the line between success and failure becomes still more sharply defined and the comfortable middle ground of 'reliable underperformance' disappears. Many shopping centres will close (but new ones, perhaps with different features and objectives, will open also); some traditional town and city centres will, alas, be decimated (but others will reinvent); and some investors will be disappointed and poorer (but others will be enriched).

The counterpoint needs to be emphasized also: the new landscape of retailing is rich in possibilities for established retail enterprises. This is the nature of eras of disruptive change—there is a fluidity of opportunities, which are not present in static eras of little change. Shoppers want to shop in different ways; they want to be engaged in different ways; geography is, in principle if not always in actuality, no longer an inhibitor of opportunity; huge new market opportunities exist in the so-called emerging markets; trends move around the world at speeds unfathomable in an earlier, pre-internet, era. Moreover the investment needed to realize the opportunities in the new retail landscape can be multiples lower than in previous eras when stores had to be built if shoppers were to be engaged.

Are there more opportunities than challenges for established retail enterprises in the new landscape of retail? In principle, we believe so. We could—perhaps should—apply innumerable caveats to our assertion: on the one hand, and then again and so on. But the central point is this: in the new landscape of retailing, the old conventions no longer apply and this creates entirely new possibilities. We have referenced in this book many retailers who are finding new ways of engaging shoppers, developing new business propositions, and finding impressively innovative ways to harness the opportunities of the new technology landscape. There are many, many more that we might have chosen to profile also. It is this proliferation of innovation and opportunity that is so uplifting.

Whether established retailers are able to realize the opportunities available to them is a rather different matter. We have argued that they may well, in fact, be much better placed to be successful in the new retail landscape than some commentators and analysts have assumed. It may not be a matter of substitution, but of agile evolution. Many of the capabilities and competencies that have been nurtured and developed—often over many years—are at least as relevant in the new landscape as they were in the old. Merchandise still needs to be bought and—in most cases—delivered somewhere, vendor relationships still matter, and customer service is still paramount. And many established retailers have scale, capabilities, and customer relationships that new-to-retail enterprises do not. There is an important caveat, however. All of these attributes and competencies may need to be radically reframed and redefined if they are to continue to be relevant to the shopper and useful to the enterprise in the new landscape of retail.

Being Successful in the New Retail Landscape: There is No Roadmap . . .

In essence, for established retail enterprises addressing the challenges and, moreover, realizing the opportunities in the new retail landscape is a question of transitioning the enterprise from where it is today to where it needs to be for the present and the future. It might seem beguilingly appealing to be able to present a 'roadmap for delivering success' in the new retail landscape. But to do so would be the worst kind of deceit because this would be to imply not only that is there a roadmap, but also that there is a single route to discern and to follow. There is not. We choose to speak of *navigating* the new retail landscape, not marking out and following a single, specific course through it.

The futility of the notion of a roadmap to follow in order to achieve success is a consequence, in particular, of the reality that retail and consumer landscapes are transforming so quickly, often in such unanticipated ways, and being impacted by disruptive technologies to such a degree that it becomes difficult to forecast what is around the next corner, let alone over the far horizon. We discussed in Chapter 10 how business leaders might go about the task of prioritizing in a world of disruptive and uncertain change. There are some markers that can usefully be put down.

- Change in the retail landscape is accelerating. The last decade has been extraordinary in the amount of change the sector has undergone and to which retail enterprises have had to address themselves. The next ten years will be far more dramatic still.

- It is not difficult to foresee a future where, in the developed markets of Western Europe and North America, retailers are radically changing their physical store portfolios. This may very well include having to reimagine the whole notion of what a retail store even is any more, as well as transforming their portfolios out of some types of formats and into others and exiting a lot of property in consequence. As well as being painful for enterprises, this will have very important implications for the communities in which that real estate is located.

- Trend identification, especially in respect of shopper engagement as well as retail fulfilment, will look ever more to the East and the Far East in particular. Engagement with shoppers using digital technologies and platforms is accelerating globally but nowhere more so than in the Far East where technology is allowing shoppers and enterprises to 'skip' many of the phases in shopper engagement and retail advancement that the European and North American markets have gone through.

. . . There may be Alternative Futures . . .

That there is no single roadmap to achieve success carries with it the implication that there may be several viable alternative strategies to consider and, therefore, significant choices for business leaders to make in the new landscape of retailing. For so (too) long, enterprises have relied upon five-year timeframes, deliberate strategy, and linear forecasting methods to set their future plans. The present degree of uncertainty and volatility that is so defining of the retail landscape and which rules out a 'roadmap to success' view of the future suggests that traditional tools and approaches may be useless—or worse. A different way of thinking about the challenge of extreme uncertainty is to acknowledge the possibility of alternative futures and to think and plan accordingly.

While we cannot predict with certainty what *will* happen in the future in times of extreme uncertainty, it is nevertheless possible to develop useful guidance about the future by both reducing complexity and identifying those elements which are certain in an uncertain world. Scenario planning is a useful tool to employ in such circumstances. It accommodates the kind of structural uncertainty that the new retail landscape presents, by addressing how each of the (many) possible interpretations would create change in the future business environment. Whilst scenario planning cannot eliminate uncertainty, it can reduce it and help business leaders to come to a reasonable judgement on the degree of robustness of a specific decision across a range of uncertainty.

The process of creating scenarios of a range of possible futures also enables more informed sense to be made of the current environment. Finer insights into current realities are achieved in two ways. First, previously implicit assumptions are made explicit and, secondly, scenarios are used to both challenge current group thinking and encourage more futuristic thinking. For example, in a recent analysis of the future of Indian retailing, scenario planning results transcended 'common-sense' perspectives and provided insights that were less expected and obvious. The conventional narrative that retail modernization would destroy traditional retailing in that country was, through scenario planning, reframed into an alternative future perspective that the nuances of Indian culture and the complexities of consumer behaviour made it more likely that traditional and modern retailing would, in fact, continue to coexist in India.

... And there are Building Blocks

There are attributes that retail enterprises and their leaders will, in our opinion, need to have if they are to remain relevant, resist competitive challenges, and realize the opportunities that present themselves in the new landscape of retail:

(i)   Be truly customer centric
(ii) Be digitally skilled
(iii) Innovate
(iv) (Re)turn to strong, clear values
(v)   Lead.

Be Truly Customer Centric

There is a somewhat uncomfortable sense in which, in a more forgiving era, some retail enterprises were rather 'getting away with it' in the sense of preaching a commitment to customer centricity but without *truly* delivering on those words or aspirations. A (largely) borderless world of (almost) fully informed shoppers with (almost) limitless choices is a very unforgiving environment. Being truly customer centric is not a slogan to be rolled out annually at a company conference. It has to be a mantra around which the enterprise and everyone in it is organized and lives by all of the time.

Because the landscape of customer engagement is changing so quickly and in often unanticipated ways—largely because of the impacts of technology in the hands of shoppers—any enterprise needs constantly to revisit how it is performing on its customer-centricity aspirations; and then be prepared to make what may very well be radical changes that go to the heart of the enterprise. This includes being willing to move away—often very far away—from the conventional tenets of 'the way we do things here'. Being truly customer centric in the new landscape of retail may mean exiting 50 per cent or more of an expensively assembled store network; reconfiguring stores as mini-warehouses; investing in entirely new capability areas while exiting others. As well as new go-to-market approaches, skills, and organizational structures, it might also mean revisiting the suitability of current ownership structures when the reasonable expectations of stakeholders no longer align with the needs of the enterprise and the expectations of its shoppers.

Be Digitally Skilled

Retail and consumer engagement landscapes are being transformed above all else by technology, in the hands of the shopper, within the enterprise, across value chains, societies, and entire economies. In the near-term future, change will accelerate still more sharply as the Young Millennials enter their high spending years with a mindset of retailing as a 'digital first, store maybe' activity. One thing that the last decade has taught us is that the appetite for shoppers to embrace new technologies to fulfil their shopping needs has consistently exceeded many people's expectations.

In the new landscape of retailing it is difficult to imagine that any retailer can be effective without having a digital perspective and capability. After all, how many retailers would feel able to operate without electricity? Sir Ian Cheshire, the highly regarded former CEO of the Kingfisher home improvement retail group, has said that, 'businesses are much more complex now, and the way the internet is changing consumer shopping patterns—it's becoming so much more profound and the rate of change is accelerating not declining. The intuitive merchant prince is great but I don't think it's enough now. If that intuition isn't complemented by really good data, you're going to die.'[2]

---

[2] Sir Ian Cheshire, quoted in 'Sir Ian Cheshire on the Art of Retail', *Retail Week*, 13 Mar. 2015, 32–6.

Being digitally skilled at both an enterprise and a personal leadership level is a multi-faceted proposition but divides into four main parts:

1. Capture and interpret customer insights
2. Organize and execute across multiple touchpoints—physical and/or digital
3. Engage customers with digital communication
4. Apply digital technologies to deliver enhanced shopper experiences.

Innovate

In the new landscape of retailing, enterprises and their leaders must be willing to explore innovation possibilities. It is difficult to imagine that a customer-facing enterprise that was 'fit for purpose' even ten years ago still will be today let alone in ten years' time. This does not, and for many should not, mean being on the 'bleeding edge' let alone the leading edge of innovation: fast follower and/or enhanced imitator are perfectly legitimate and appropriate positions to want to occupy in respect of innovation activity. But all enterprises and their business leaders must, we feel, have an appetite to explore innovation possibilities. This means being willing to break with the past and to accept that attributes, capabilities, and investments which have made the enterprise successful in the past may not be relevant or valued now and in the future. It also means that enterprises will likely need new skills, capabilities, and people in order to be able to identify, create, and deliver innovative approaches that engage shoppers.

A key question, then, is whether shoppers are more difficult to reach today and looking forward than they have been in the past. The conventional narrative holds that they are. But is this really true? As we move quickly towards close-to-ubiquitous internet access—at least for populations with some level of disposable income in organized economies—*reaching* billions of potential shoppers all of the time becomes remarkably affordable relative to the cost of traditional means of engagement in a pre-internet world. Achieving reach is, relatively speaking, perhaps not so difficult. It is meaningful engagement with shoppers that is the real challenge. Here again, our glass is rather more than half full. So-called big data holds out the promise of being able to understand at a very granular and actionable level the subtleties of how shoppers might be persuaded to purchase. Moreover, technology in both the hands of the shopper and the retail enterprise (traditional or new) creates fascinating opportunities both to enrich the engagement experience and to move the points of greatest influence closer to the point of purchase.

(Re)turn to Strong, Clear Values

Much of the transformation in retail landscapes globally is a transformation in techniques—in the *how* of retailing: how shoppers are engaged; how merchandise is presented and delivered to shoppers; how new market opportunities are realized and competitive challenges addressed. In environments where all of the techniques of retailing are fluid and able to be radically changed, it becomes still more important for enterprises and their leaders to be very clear and to communicate clearly both across their enterprises and to their shoppers the values that the business stands for and stands behind. Retail enterprises are no longer the automatic, default custodian of the relationship with the shopper. Many other enterprise types are seeking to occupy this ground—FMCG, logistics, and payment companies as well as 'new to retail enterprises', perhaps most notably the internet-enabled platform providers. As such, retailers are no longer competing for the customer against other retail enterprises alone—that was the old retail. In the new landscape of retailing, they are competing for the customer against a plethora of different enterprise types—many of which they may not know especially well, if at all. It is also the case that in the fluid world of the new retail, enterprises may find themselves collaborating with an enterprise that, in another part of the market or in another geography they are competing against.

Moreover, shoppers will, we believe, become still more concerned to know of and be influenced by the attitudes and values of the enterprises with which they engage. While this is by no means a universal concern of shoppers today, the direction of travel is clear: shoppers are becoming more concerned about the values of the enterprises with which they engage *and* they have the motivation and the means to find out whether or not they are living up to those values.

As retail enterprises transform into very different types of organizations and move further away from their traditional practices, so it becomes still more important to be clear on what the core values are that define the enterprise, to be true to them, and to articulate them with clarity and purpose to the shopper. While the *how* of what an enterprise does is being radically transformed, the *why* of what an enterprise stands for needs to be communicated clearly and adhered to strongly, especially as the complexity of an enterprise and its points of engagement with the shopper increase.

Lead

Competitive advantage in the digitalised world demands a commitment from the very top, not only to invest in the right infrastructure but to acquire the new skills of retail.[3]
(Laura Wade-Gery, Executive Director, Multi-Channel, M&S UK)

In times of disruptive change, rich in possibilities but also full of challenges, effective leadership matters more than ever. For most leaders of retail enterprises—new or established—this will surely be the most exciting,

---

[3] Laura Wade-Gery, quoted in 'What Next for E-tail?', *Retail Week*, 15 Aug. 2014, 5.

challenging, opportunity-rich time of their professional lives. Anything seems possible. But the stakes are uniquely high too. Momentum shifts happen very quickly. It is now possible to build enterprises of enormous reach and influence and at almost bewildering speed. But equally some of the icons of the retail industry globally are discovering in the harshest possible terms that modern shoppers are no respecters of great deeds of the past—it is great deeds of the present that they crave and engage with.

In the new landscape of retailing, success can happen quickly but failure can happen more quickly still. Great leadership cannot be a 'steady as she goes' mantra, a 'five more years of the same' perspective. Leading effectively in the new retail landscape demands a lot of enterprise leaders—the ability to reframe how an enterprise delivers its core purpose; to be willing to break away from the past and yet keep those skills and values which remain important and relevant; the ability to prioritize and distinguish the important from the urgent; and to manage the complexity that comes with operating across multiple touchpoints with fast-changing shoppers. But above all effective leadership in the modern era of retailing is about the ability to manage effectively in environments defined by uncertainty, where there is no true north to aim for and no route map of how to get there.

Periods of disruption are periods of disproportionate opportunity.
(Art Peck, CEO, Gap Inc, 2015[4])

In Part 1 of our book we discussed the nature of change in the retail sector globally. We unambiguously took the view that we are in the early stages of a reframing of the landscape of retailing. It may well feel challenging but, far more than this, it seems truly exciting, epoch making, and rich in possibilities. In Part 2 we shifted focus to discussing how enterprises and their leaders may need to reinvent in order to remain relevant and desired by shoppers—by reimagining the role of stores and reinventing the store experience even to the point of addressing the question 'what is a store anymore'; by mastering and executing their omni-channel ambitions; by creating enterprises equipped with the skills, structures, and capabilities to be successful and led by leaders equipped to be successful in the new landscape of retailing. We spoke of the necessity for enterprise leaders to be able to operate effectively in environments of uncertainty and to be comfortable with the reality that there is no single path to success and often no clear vision of even what the end goal is.

Christopher Columbus (1451–1506) appears to have been a man not without considerable flaws and his legacy has been subject to much debate, controversy, and revision. But what is not in doubt is that he was one of the

[4] <http://www.fastcompany.com/3042434/gapquest>.

greatest explorers and navigators of his or any age. While reliable attribution is frustratingly elusive, Columbus is thought to have said of one of his four voyages of discovery: 'Following the light of the sun, we left the Old World.' This seems a rather apt summation both of where we are heading in the new landscape of retailing and of how in this book we have tried to navigate our readers from the Old World to the New.

Index

Figures, tables, and footnotes are indicated by an italic *f*, *t*, and *n* following the page number.